God's Ploughman

Hugh Latimer: a "Preaching Life" (1485–1555)

God's Ploughman

Hugh Latimer: a "Preaching Life" (1485–1555)

Michael Pasquarello III

Copyright © Paternoster 2014

First published 2014 by Paternoster

Paternoster is an imprint of Authentic Media
52 Presley Way, Crownhill, Milton Keynes, Bucks, MK8 0ES

www.authenticmedia.co.uk
Authentic Media is a division of Koorong UK, a company limited by guarantee

09 08 07 06 05 04 03   8 7 6 5 4 3 2 1

The right of Michael Pasquarello to be identified as the Author of this Work
has been asserted by him in accordance with the Copyright, Designs
and Patents Act 1988.

British Library Cataloguing in Publication Data A catalogue record for this
book is available from the British Library

ISBN 978–1–84227–797–3

Printed and bound in Great Britain for Paternoster
by Lightning Source, Milton Keynes

To Dan and Nicole
with much love

STUDIES IN CHRISTIAN HISTORY AND THOUGHT

Series Preface

This series complements the specialist series of Studies in Evangelical History and Thought and Studies in Baptist History and Thought for which Paternoster is becoming increasingly well known by offering works that cover the wider field of Christian history and thought. It encompasses accounts of Christian witness at various periods, studies of individual Christians and movements, and works which concern the relations of church and society through history, and the history of Christian thought.

The series includes monographs, revised dissertations and theses, and collections of papers by individuals and groups. As well as 'free standing' volumes, works on particular running themes are being commissioned; authors will be engaged for these from around the world and from a variety of Christian traditions.

A high academic standard combined with lively writing will commend the volumes in this series both to scholars and to a wider readership

Series Editors

Alan P.F. Sell	Visiting Professor at Acadia University Divinity College, Nova Scotia
D.W. Bebbington	University of Stirling, Stirling, Scotland
Clyde Binfield	Professor Associate in History, University of Sheffield, UK
Gerald Bray	Anglican Professor of Divinity, Beeson Divinity School, Samford University, Birmingham, Alabama, USA
Grayson Carter	Associate Professor of Church History, Fuller Theological Seminary SW, Phoenix, Arizona, USA
Dennis Ngien	Professor of Theology, Tyndale University College and Seminary, Founder of the Centre for Mentorship and Theological Reflection, Toronto, Canada

CONTENTS

CONTENTS

ACKNOWLEDGEMENTS

I am grateful to Paternoster for accepting this revised dissertation for publication in monograph form. Its preparation was made possible by the able assistance of Mr. Jay Endicott of Asbury Theological Seminary, whose technical expertise has been indispensable for the task of formatting the manuscript.

I want to thank my dissertation mentor, Dr. Peter Iver Kaufman, for suggesting that I write on the English Reformation and Hugh Latimer. Without Peter's constant challenges, enthusiasm, and encouragement as well as his expertise in the religion of Tudor England, this project would not have been possible. I also want to express my deep appreciation for the members of my dissertation committee, Professors Lance Lazar, David Steinmetz, John Wall, and Richard Lischer for their contributions as teachers, scholars, and friends. Each played an important role without which this project could not have been brought to completion.

Finally, I owe my children, Dan and Nicole, a debt of thanks for watching their dad return to life as a graduate student during their middle school and high school years. They patiently endured many dinner time conversations during which the topic of discussion would inevitably turn to my "friends" such as Latimer, Augustine, Erasmus, Cranmer, Fisher, and Luther. Their strong desire to learn, which has not diminished, continues to inspire me in my work. This book is dedicated to them with much love.

Michael Pasquarello III
Wilmore, KY 2013

Introduction

God's Ploughman, Hugh Latimer:
A "Preaching Life"

> But happy is the man whom death takes as he meditates upon this literature [of Christ]. Let us all, therefore, with our whole heart covet this literature, let us embrace it, let us continually occupy ourselves with it, let us fondly kiss it, at length let us die in its embrace, let us be transformed in it, since indeed studies are transmuted into morals (Erasmus, the *Paraclesis*).

The purpose of this book is to illumine vital aspects of Hugh Latimer's identity and activity as a preacher within the context of late medieval England. Laboring as God's ploughman from the 1520s until his death in 1555, Latimer was arguably England's most significant preacher and advocate for preaching as the primary instrument of personal regeneration and social reform. This identity, or character, of the ploughman, the humble preacher of God's word, was modeled after the figure of Christ. The activity of the plough, a familiar figure of the cross, depicted the power of the gospel which works through preaching to root up sin in the soul and plant seeds of godliness for salvation. Latimer's vision of "reformation through practice" was grounded in the conviction that the future of the commonwealth depended upon the renovation of the church on a foundation built by priests committed to speaking God's word by means of vernacular scripture. As Richard Rex concludes, "Latimer was a towering figure among the early Reformers, exercising a preaching ministry whose contributions to the English Reformation are incalculable."

This construction of a "preaching life" situates Latimer within the larger religious, political, and intellectual world of late medieval England. This approach differs from previous works about Latimer, since it is neither a biography, work of intellectual or confessional history, nor a literary analysis of discrete sermon texts. Rather, as a work in homiletic history, it draws from the details of Latimer's milieu to construct an interpretive framework for his sermons, but without allowing these details to overshadow the preaching performances that formed the core of his identity as a religious reformer who successfully mediated between the crown, church, and common people. Its goal, therefore, is to illumine the practical wisdom embodied in the content, form, and style of Latimer's sermons and to recapture a sense of their over-arching purpose, movement, and transforming force in the reform of early modern England.

Situated within recent scholarly conversation regarding the role of pastoral ministry in the English Reformation, this project discusses Latimer's sermons as pastoral discourse spoken for particular times and places and to accomplish particular purposes and effects. Sermons are thus treated as both text and context to illumine their respective themes, forms, and rhetorical strategies in relation to their final shape and physical, ceremonial, and liturgical circumstances. Latimer's preaching, therefore, is construed as a series of improvisations that enact a central theme which predominates throughout his career: the urgent need for religious and practical reform of church and society by means of the spoken word.

By integrating both historical and homiletic interpretation, this "preaching life" provides an appropriate medium through which to demonstrate the significance of Latimer's accomplishments by means of "reformation through practice." It shows that Latimer made an immense contribution to the elevation of preaching from its late medieval status to become a primary instrument of reform, enabling listeners to overcome past sins and habits, and taking up new forms of faith and obedience. According to Latimer, a preaching clergy was equivalent to a sacerdotal priesthood, ". . . we cannot be saved without hearing the word, it is a necessary way of salvation . . . there must be preachers, if we look to be saved." The preaching office, therefore, was of necessity the office of salvation, and the only means that God had appointed to salvation. Latimer articulated and embodied a radical redefinition of priestly status and function, predicated not upon a sacerdotal character conferred at ordination, but on standards of personal godliness, and above all on the willingness and ability to preach the word of God.

In addition, Latimer's contribution to "reformation through practice" was instrumental in promoting a process of change that led to the official adoption of a new vision of preaching in the Church of England. From 1534 clergy were required to preach regularly in support of the royal supremacy and against the papal authority. The royal injunctions of 1536 obliged priests to declare the *Ten Articles*, to announce the abrogation of superfluous holidays, and to teach congregations the *Pater Noster*, the Ten Commandments, and the *Articles of Faith*. In 1538 priests were to ensure that at least once a quarter they would "purely and sincerely declare the Gospel of Christ." In 1547 the Edwardian *Injunctions* stipulated the reading of homilies every Sunday, while the 1550 *Ordinal* declared the clergy to be primarily a Ministry of the Word, set apart for the tasks of common prayer and preaching. A theology of the Word became the defining characteristic of the Church of England and its primary instrument of salvation.

At the heart of the struggle for reform in England was the definition and control of public discourse, the dissemination of knowledge, and the verbal articulation of faith. Accordingly, this study begins by exploring the religious and intellectual setting in which Latimer was trained for pastoral ministry. It argues that educational improvements and innovations at Cambridge, most notable those introduced by John Fisher and Erasmus, stimulated a quantum leap in the importance of preaching for the renovation of English religious life. Intellectual foundations laid by evangelical humanism, especially the biblical scholarship of Erasmus, provided Latimer with the necessary tools for constructing a reformist vision of preaching that emphasized the power of scripture to render the living image of Christ, the defeat of superstition, the removal of religious abuses, the regeneration of faith, and the inspiration of devotion to God and charity toward neighbor. Informed by the wisdom of humanist rhetoric, Latimer's practice of *decorum* enabled him to identify with changing audiences and to accommodate his speech for a variety of conditions. His preaching discourse, therefore, was simple, concrete, and enlivened by personal appropriation; it called for the revival and conversion of listeners by means of a "vernacular" theology that cut across the barriers of society.

Chapter 2 traces Latimer's move from academic evangelist to parish priest and describes his emergence as a leading evangelical voice in support of the "King's Great Matter" and royal supremacy. It argues that Latimer was one of a generation of university-trained clergy and scholars that hoped to turn England towards a national church. Many of these viewed the realm as fallow ground for spiritual revitalization and moral reform, sharing a common desire to unite England around the word of God, to defeat superstition, to educate the laity, to improve priestly performance, and for a godly commonwealth free from papal authority. However, a key factor in Latimer's promotion and rise to national prominence was the Crown's recognition of the communicative power of speech as an instrument of reform.

During the 1530s Latimer capitalized on opportunities provided by his new role in local parishes, at Paul's Cross, before the Convocation of clergy, and from the cathedral of Worcester. His reformist speech and activity contributed to an explosion of preaching that utilized existing structures and provisions for new religious and political purposes. Due to the ambiguous nature of Henrician reform, Latimer's sermons were about neither doctrine nor structures in the church, but rather aimed to stir the imagination to promote elemental changes in worship, devotional practices, and personal piety. Latimer's protest, therefore, was aimed primarily against the church and its clergy for losing much of the fire, zeal, and passion for evangelism and pastoral work that would have guarded it from misapplied affections and abuses, failures that hindered an emphasis on inner grace, personal knowledge of God, salvation by faith, and growth in holiness.

Chapter 3 discusses the major role played by Latimer in the early years of the Edwardian period. From 1548-1550 he was appointed to preach at strategic locations in London, most notably Paul's Cross and the royal court, where he vehemently attacked traditional religion and aggressively promoted a Protestant vision of a Christian commonwealth that radically redefined the role of church, priesthood, and people. An exposition of Latimer's *Sermon of the Plough* highlights his use of biblical farming metaphors such as plowing, sowing, and harvesting to introduce an interpretation of the gospel prescribed by Edward's *Injunctions* and the official *Book of Homilies*. This timely performance, moreover, introduced Latimer as England's model ploughman; it established him as a prophet who spoke by means of scripture to inspire action towards the future, for the renewal of the church and Christianizing of the social order.

The fourth chapter discusses the content and purpose of Latimer's dramatic Lenten performances at the court of Edward VI in 1549-50. To provide a fresh hearing of Latimer's authoritative use of biblical rhetoric, the court sermons were treated as prophetic and pastoral discourse within the context of royal pageantry. Conspicuous throughout Latimer's court preaching was a fear of God's wrath should England not heed the call to repentance, and a conviction that the resolution of the nation's troubles must be accomplished throughout the preaching of God's word and the obedience of God's people. This message inevitably lent a polemical edge to Latimer's sermons since, on the one hand, his speech was directed against idolatry, and on the other, against social injustice. Latimer therefore viewed his primary task as bringing the Bible to life to overcome sin and create social righteousness; from first to last, his goal was to promote a Christian commonwealth through the power of the spoken word.

Chapters 5 and 6 follow Latimer to the diocese of Lincolnshire where he preached among the commons from 1550-53. These chapters show how his plain, vernacular sermons embodied the homiletic wisdom required to implement the commonwealth vision articulated in the *Sermon of the Plough*. To shed new light on Latimer's popular preaching, his ministry in Lincolnshire is interpreted against the background created by Cranmer's more "gradualist" pastoral and liturgical program to convert England from traditional religion to evangelical faith and devotion. A discussion of Latimer's Lincolnshire sermons displays the manner in which he adopted a strategy of "evangelism through persuasion" for that contested region. Bridging the gap between "high and low," Latimer accommodated his discourse to listeners' capacities through the use of plain, biblical speech, thus opening lines of communication that cultivated new habits of faith and devotion embodied in the *Homilies* and *Book of Common Prayer*. This rhetorical strategy thus increased the potential for receptivity and softened the impact of the Edwardian reforms. Finally, Latimer utilized the popular sermons as a form of polemic to defend the new church and its faith against critics and opponents. On the one hand, he attacked traditionalists who remained loyal to the Church of Rome; on the other, he attacked the perceived threat of radicals, particularly Anabaptists, who desired faster and more far-reaching changes. Thus the purpose of Latimer's moderate discourse among the commons was to break ground for a "middle way" that planted new habits of faith and life for the creation of a Protestant nation.

Because the English Reformation began as an argument among Catholic insiders, its early period was a time when what eventually became Protestantism developed alongside reformist Catholicism. Despite contrasting claims, the common roots of both sides within humanist soil meant that in

4

practice there was more similarity in approach than either side was willing to admit. This study shows that while Latimer attacked the failures of the pre-Reformation church, his discourse displayed continuity with important patterns of late medieval reformist thought and practice that were derived from his Cambridge years. It also demonstrates that during both the Henrician and Edwardian periods Latimer's polemical discourse intentionally highlighted differences between himself and his more traditionalist opponents as a way of accommodating his listeners to England's changing religious and political situation. This dialectic of continuity and change enabled Latimer to justify and, at times, realign Christian discourse and practice with the authority of scripture and the support of the royal supremacy. As a major contributor to England's reformation *through* preaching, Latimer ploughed new ground and sowed new seed for a reformation *of* preaching.

Chapter 1

Latimer's Cambridge:
Cultivating the "Preaching Life" (1506-1530)

> Studies such that from them they may proceed forth well versed in true learning
> and in sober discussion, men who can preach the Word of God in a serious and
> evangelical spirit (Erasmus – on the training of preachers at Cambridge).

Intellectual changes in early Tudor England stirred an increasing desire for
biblically inspired personal regeneration and social reform.[1] This chapter
discusses educational improvements and innovations at Cambridge during
Hugh Latimer's years at University. It shows that humanist learning, most
notably a return to the New Testament, the Fathers, and classical learning,
stimulated a quantum leap in the importance of scripture and its use in
preaching for the renovation of the late medieval church.

Latimer matriculated to Cambridge in 1506, proceeded to B.A. in 1510, was
elected a fellow of Clare Hall in 1511, earned an M.A. in 1514, received
deacon's orders at Lincoln in April of 1515, with ordination as a priest coming
one year later. During this time Latimer was bound to lecture and to participate
in disputations and convocations while retaining his fellowship at Clare and
beginning the more advanced program in divinity—the B.D.—which required a
minimum five years of study. In 1522 Latimer was appointed one of twelve
University preachers, a position of some prominence at Cambridge. He
completed his education by proceeding to B.D. in 1524, offering a refutation of
the doctrines of Philip Melanchthon in his disputation for the divinity degree.[2]

---

[1] Horton Davies, *Worship and Theology in England: From Cranmer to Hooker, 1534-
     1603* (Princeton, 1970), II.227-54; Richard Rex, *Henry VIII and the English
     Reformation* (New York, 1993), 76-78, 124-26; Lucy E.C. Wooding, *Rethinking
     Catholicism in Reformation England* (Oxford, 2000), 16-48; Susan R. Wabuda, "The
     Provision of Preaching during the Early English Reformation: with Special Reference
     to Itineration, c.1530-1547" (Cambridge PhD, 1992), 1-28; idem, *Preaching During
     the English Reformation*, 117-19; Alec Ryrie, *The Gospel and Henry VIII in the
     Early English Reformation* (Cambridge, 2003), 157-93. See the extensive argument
     in G.W. Bernard, *The King's Reformation: Henry VIII and the Remaking of the
     English Church* (New Haven/London, 2005), 1-224.
[2] Allan G. Chester, *Hugh Latimer: Apostle to the English* (Philadelphia, 1954), 1-10;
     Robert Demaus, *Hugh Latimer: A Biography* (Nashville, 1903), 11-42. For an
     interpretation of Latimer's thought that argues for the formative role of his

Historians have tended to emphasize Latimer's role as a leader of the "Cambridge Reformers" during the 1520s, focusing on informal theological gatherings at the White Horse Inn, also known as "Little Germany," where conversation presumably revolved around the latest Protestant doctrines imported from the continent.[3] When viewed from this perspective, Latimer is typically identified with Thomas Bilney and others who are considered to be England's "earliest Protestants."[4] Indeed, the insights of scholars who have studied this period of Cambridge history have contributed to our understanding of the historical context from which the English Reformation emerged.[5]

This chapter reconsiders the impact of John Fisher and Erasmus at Cambridge that was instrumental in shaping a generation of preachers, prelates, and scholars who shared a common faith that would eventually divide them.[6] It shows that prior to the existence of two distinct churches in England—Protestant and Catholic—Fisher and Erasmus worked to cultivate an intellectual and spiritual environment that created common ground for thinkers of diverse persuasions, cultivating the rich soil in which Hugh Latimer began to flourish as a preacher. Thomas Becon, a student at that time, would later remember Latimer's Cambridge sermons.

> I was sometime a poor scholar at Cambridge, very desirous to have the knowledge of good letters; and in the time of being there; this godly man [Latimer] preached many learned and Christian sermons both in the Latin and in the English tongue, at which all I for the most part was present; and, although at that time I was but a child of sixteen years, yet I noted his doctrine so well as I could, partly reposing it in my memory, partly commending it to letters, as most faithful treasures unto memory.[7]

relationship with Bilney and Lollardy see, Dunnan, "Hugh Latimer: A Reappraisal of His Preaching," ch.2.

[3] H.C. Porter, *Reformation and Reaction in Tudor Cambridge* (Cambridge, 1958), 41-49; William A. Clebsch, *England's Earliest Protestants: 1520-1535* (New Haven, 1964), 26-46; Dickens, *The English Reformation*, 91-105.

[4] D.S.F. Thomson and H.C. Porter (eds), *Erasmus and Cambridge: The Cambridge Letters of Erasmus* (Toronto, 1963), 98; Wooding, *Rethinking Catholicism in Reformation England*, 1-48.

[5] E.G. Rupp, *Studies in the Making of the English Protestant Tradition: Mainly in the Reign of Henry VIII* (Cambridge, 1949), 15-47; Clebsch, *England's Earliest Protestants*, 270-303.

[6] Dickens and Jones suggest that during the later 1510s the *Novum Instrumentum* of Erasmus rather than Luther would have commanded attention at the White Horse Inn. Dickens and Jones, *Erasmus the Reformer*, 206; McConica, *English Humanists and Reformation Politics*, 13-43, 76-105. For comments on notable graduates of late medieval Cambridge see H.C. Porter, *Reformation and Reaction in Tudor Cambridge* (Cambridge, 1991), 3-20, 41-73; Rex, *The Theology of John Fisher*, 12-30.

[7] Thomas Becon, *The Cathechism of Thomas Becon, S.T.P., Chaplain to Archbishop Cranmer, Prebendary of Canterbury* ed. Rev. John Ayre, M.A. Parker Society

Continuing a trend that began in the fifteenth century, John Fisher, Chancellor of Cambridge from 1504-34, made an immense contribution to the development of the University into a center for traditional Christian scholarship and humanist learning, and especially devoted to cultivating a strong preaching ministry for the reform of the church. Fisher, moreover, exemplified great personal zeal for this objective during a time when the Episcopal office was primarily conceived in juridical and institutional terms, thereby distinguishing himself as arguably the foremost preacher in early Tudor England.[8] Fisher's Elizabethan biography alludes to his pastoral activity within his own diocese of Rochester.

> We have hitherto declared unto you his great and painful diligence in preaching the word of God: which custom he used not only in his younger days when health served, but also even to his extreme age, when many times his weary and feeble legs were not able to sustain his weak body standing, but forced him to have a chair and so to teach sitting.[9]

Fisher's steadfast commitment to preaching was also characterized by its versatility. For example, he delivered a notable and popular cycle of ten sermons on the penitential psalms before the Queen Mother, Margaret Beaufort, and her household. In addition, he was the preacher for the funeral sermon of her son, King Henry VII, and the "month-mind" or memorial sermon, for Lady Margaret, after her death in 1509. He also preached a celebrated but yet undated sermon on the Passion for Good Friday, most likely in his diocese of Rochester.

Moreover, Fisher also played a leading role in the fight against heresy. In 1521 he was the preacher at the solemn ceremony in St. Paul's churchyard when the papal sentence of excommunication against Luther was read and the works of the reformer burned. In 1526 Henry VIII chose him to preach at the formal abjuration of Robert Barnes and other heretics, when more books were burned.[10] As his biographer notes,

> Many other sermons and homilies to the same effect he made besides at London . . . taking thereby great occasion to tax as well the negligence of curates as the rashness and levity of the people, exhorting all sorts of vocations to play the

---

(Cambridge, 1844), 424-25.

[8] Richard Rex, *The Theology of John Fisher*, 30-50; Brendan Bradshaw, "Bishop John Fisher 1469-1535: the man and his work" in ed. Brendan Bradshaw and Eamon Duffy, *Humanism, Reform and the Reformation: the Career of Bishop John Fisher* (Cambridge, 1989), 1-24; Wabuda, "The Provision of Preaching during the Early English Reformation" 82-86; idem, *Preaching During the English Reformation*, 64-106.

[9] Early Life, I, ed. F. Van Ortroy, *Analecta Bollandiana* (1891), X.219, 221—cited in Maria Dowling, *Fishers of Men: A Biography of John Fisher* (London, 1999), 76.

[10] Dowling, *Fishers of Men*, 78.

valiant soldiers in stoutly resisting these devilish assaults of heresy.[11]

Fisher also demonstrated a capacity for preaching with good effect in situations that required pastoral discernment for the care of souls. For his sermon one month after the death of Lady Margaret in 1509, Fisher drew from the conversation between Christ and Martha during the episode of the raising of Lazarus in John 11:23-27.[12] His use of this narrative was vivid and personal, praising Lady Margaret's way of life and piety, presenting her as a model of Catholic faith and obedience. Fisher drew parallels between Lady Margaret and Martha to highlight the simple truth of her virtue and achievement, depicting the two women as noble, self-disciplined, and devout. He compared Martha's service to Christ with Lady Margaret's service to the poor, treating her acts of mercy to the lowly as to Christ himself.

The final consolation of the sermon was built around the exchange between Christ and Martha on the resurrection and Martha's confession of faith in him. Fisher again compared Lady Margaret with Martha, remembering her profession of Christ's presence when served the Blessed Sacrament. The sermon concludes with a pastoral exhortation for a grieving audience, calling listeners to believe that whomever has faith in Christ will never die, offering assurance that the teaching, piety, and practices of the Church will be sufficient for salvation: "Therefore put we aside all weeping and tears, and be not sad nor heavy as men without hope, but rather be glad and joyous, and each of us herein comfort. Always praising and magnifying the name of our Lord, to whom, be laud and honor endlessly. Amen."[13]

In 1526 Cardinal Wolsey appointed Fisher to preach against the threat of heresies, for which Fisher utilized the power of biblical imagery to address a large crowd of listeners at Paul's Cross, London. Fisher drew from the Gospel of the day, Luke 18:31-43, to tell the story of a blind man who signified spiritually blind heretics in need of restoration to sight—or restoration to the faith. Fisher claimed that heretics must hear from the multitude surrounding Jesus to receive the truth of the Church; that heretics must cry for mercy, being reduced to the ways of the Church; that heretics must desire sight with their whole will, assenting to the doctrine of the Church.[14] Continuing his use of figurative language, Fisher turned to the Parable of the Sower, Luke 8:4-15, in support of Catholic doctrine. The sower is Christ, the seed is the word, and faithful preachers are, "but as coffins and the hoppers wherein the seed is couched." Asserting that pastoral eloquence is empty unless a preacher is moved by the Spirit of God, Fisher articulated the primary requirement for homiletic effectiveness: "The preacher may well rehearse the words of

---

[11] Early Life, I.252; cited in Dowling, *Fishers of Men*, 77.
[12] *The English Works of John Fisher: Bishop of Rochester*, Part I. ed. John Mayor (London, 1876), 308-10.
[13] *English Works of John Fisher*, I.310-11.
[14] *English Works of John Fisher*, I.436-42.

scripture; but they be not his words, they be the words of Christ. And if our savior Christ speak not within the preacher the seed shall be cast in vain." On the other hand, Fisher declared, "heresy is a perilous seed; it is the seed of the devil; the inspiration of wicked spirits; the corruption of our hearts; the blinding of our sight; the quenching of our faith; the destruction of all good fruit; and finally murder of our souls."[15]

An assiduous preacher, Fisher believed his primary purpose was to call listeners to repentance and to bring them to Christ, a message he personally embodied in the content and pastoral style of his sermons.[16] This commitment was permanently fixed in the chapel he founded at St. John's College, Cambridge, where above his tomb is engraved this sentence, *Faciam vos piscatores hominum* (I will make you fishers of men).[17] Fisher fulfilled this calling with exemplary devotion to Christ, which was evinced by his sincerity, humility, and repentant attitude, his trust in divine mercy and grateful love of God. His sermons, which were typically exegetical and Christocentric in focus, did not often discuss the intercession of the saints but rather he usually expounded a psalm or the liturgical text of the day.

In all his preaching, Fisher attempted to elevate listeners' minds towards God, leading them to the act of repentance: contrition, confession and satisfaction for sins, and thereby amendment of life. For Fisher the real sickness of the church was not the corruption of its piety, but its lack of piety. His preaching did not seek to strip or simplify the Christian life, but rather sought an increase in piety by presentations of scripture and the symbolic and sacramental world of medieval Catholicism, a style of interior devotion that was already meeting many of the needs to which Reformed religion would later appeal.[18] As Dowling concludes, "It would be hard to exaggerate the value Fisher placed on the preaching ministry of the church."[19]

In addition to his exemplary sermons, Fisher's work for the transformation of Cambridge into a preacher-friendly environment was assisted by changes that were occurring in the role of university chancellor during the fifteenth-century. The office was to be filled by a chancellor-patron, well placed to advance the interests of the university, most specifically in the corridors of government and court. Fisher was well suited for this post since he had served as personal confessor to the Lady Margaret Beaufort, Queen Mother of Henry VII, for a short time prior to his election as Vice-Chancellor of Cambridge in 1501. His contact with the Lady Margaret enabled him to direct her pious

---

[15] *English Works of John Fisher*, I.447-54.
[16] Wabuda, "The Provision of Preaching," 65-66; Rex, *The Theology of John Fisher*, 31-34.
[17] Dowling, *Fishers of Men*, 20.
[18] Eamon Duffy, "The spirituality of John Fisher" in ed. Brendan Bradshaw and Eamon Duffy, *Humanism, Reform and the Reformation* (Cambridge, 1989), 216; Rex, *The Theology of John Fisher*, 48-49.
[19] Dowling, *Fishers of Men*, 73-89.

charity into the practical forum of university endowment, precipitating a major expansion of the University's facilities, a readership (to become a chair) in theology, and two new colleges, Christ's and St. John's. Significantly, the endowment also funded a University preacher-ship in 1504, specifying where the sermons were to be given: six each year at St. Paul's Cross, St. Margaret's or Westminster, and in parishes in the London, Ely, and Lincoln dioceses.

Beyond the preacher-ships endowed by Lady Margaret Cambridge was granted a papal bull by Alexander VI in 1503 through the efforts of Thomas Cabold of Gonville Hall, papal penitentiary in 1499-1500. This papal bull empowered the Chancellor to appoint annually twelve doctors, masters, or graduates in priestly orders to preach throughout England, Scotland, and Ireland to the people and clergy. These papal licenses for preaching were for life as long as a candidate preached in the University within two years. Between 1504 and 1522, 175 such licenses were granted at Cambridge—with Latimer being one of the recipients—a sign of Fisher's commitment to the significance of preaching.[20]

Under Fisher's direction, St. John's College, a conservative academic institution, but predisposed towards reform, epitomized the unity of preaching, lecturing, and theological study. Fisher sought a balance of the old and the new in learning, viewing traditional scholastic training in the arts as indispensable to the study of theology. He also acknowledged the benefits of the "New Learning," the study of classical literature, languages, speech, and style recovered by humanists for effective written and spoken communication. Preaching of the word of God, however, was the primary objective towards which all other intellectual and educational concerns were subordinated. In the statutes of 1516-18 for St. John's, a quarter of the fellows were given the duty of preaching to the people in English, thus giving preaching a higher priority than before by creating a class of preaching fellows.[21]

Fisher was not content to rely solely upon traditional resources and methods for training preachers: medieval treatises in the art of preaching (*De arte predicaendi*) collections of sermons, and exempla, illustrative stories for particular points of doctrine.[22] With an eye towards the future he continued to expand the University's academic resources through the attraction of foreign scholars. The most important of these was Erasmus, who, during his longest visit at Cambridge, from 1511 to 1514, resided at Queen's College, teaching Greek and theology.[23] As Richard Schoeck asserts, "In studying the thought and letters of Tudor England one cannot ignore the presence of Erasmus and

---

[20] Damien Riehl Leader, *A History of the University of Cambridge* (Cambridge, 1988), I.264-319.

[21] Malcolm Underwood, "John Fisher and the promotion of learning" in ed. Bradshaw and Duffy, *Humanism, Reform and the Reformation* (Cambridge, 1989), 25-46; Rex, *Theology of John Fisher*, 50-64.

[22] Leader, *A History of the University of Cambridge*, I.108-91.

[23] Porter and Thomson, *Erasmus and Cambridge*, 25-92.

the centrality of Erasmian Humanism, and it would be difficult to overstate the importance of that influence."[24]

Soon after his arrival at Cambridge, Erasmus wrote to Fisher to report of his work on the translation of St. Basil's commentary on Isaiah and to express his gratitude for the bishop's gifts to him. Erasmus' praise for Fisher reveals a desire to minister to both the intellectual and spiritual condition of Christians.

> Best and most learned prelate, your acts of great kindness and generosity to me have been a challenge to me to show that I am not blatantly ungrateful, so I am beginning to consider whether at least I might offer you some literary gift that should be worthy of your Eminence—should be, that is to say, both scholarly and edifying.[25]

During the past thirty years there has been a shift away form certain traditional interpretations of Erasmus, a bias shared by both Protestants and Catholics that has viewed him has a skeptic, indifferent or hostile to doctrine, a rationalist, and a precursor of enlightenment. Some interpreters have contended that his humanism, his love for philology and pagan letters and wisdom threatened Christian theology, while his dogmatism led to a moralist view in which Christianity was confined to a life of ethical purity. Eschewing creed, cult, and ceremony, the religion Erasmus promoted was a spiritualized one, a form of deception and modernism.[26]

Hilmar Pabil argues that we must not overlook the main purpose of Erasmus' religious work; namely, the practice of piety (*pietas*). While Erasmus had no interest for writing theological books in the mode of scholastic discourse, his desire was to arouse his contemporaries from their spiritual slumbers, and to awaken them to a revitalized Christian way of life, to a spirit devoted to loving God and neighbor through loving obedience to Christ and his *philosophia*.[27] John O'Malley has persuasively argued that Erasmus' piety was pastoral, that nothing is more characteristic of Erasmus in this regard than his striving to integrate piety, theology, and the practice of ministry in service to

---

[24]   Richard J. Schoeck, "Humanism Beyond Italy" in *Renaissance Humanism: Foundations, Forms, and Legacy* ed. Albert Rabil, Jr. (Philadelphia, 1988), II.12. I am indebted to Wabuda's excellent discussion of Erasmus' work and influence in England, *Preaching During the English Reformation*, 65-99.

[25]   *CWE* 2.172-73.

[26]   For discussion of shifts in interpretations of Erasmus, see Hilmar M. Pabel, *Conversing With God: Prayer in Erasmus' Pastoral Writings* (Toronto, 1997), 1-10; idem, "Promoting the Business of the Gospel: Erasmus' Contribution to Pastoral Ministry" in ERSY 15 (1995), 53-70; Manfred Hoffman, *Rhetoric and Theology: The Hermeneutic of Erasmus* (Toronto, 1994), 15-26; idem, "Erasmus on Church and Ministry" in *ERSY* 6 (1986), 1-30; John O'Malley, "Introduction" in *CWE* 66 (Toronto, 1988), ix-xxx; Cornelius Augustijn, *Erasmus: His Life, Works, and Influence*, trans. J.C. Grayson (Toronto, 1986), 185-200; Leon-E. Halkin, *Erasmus: A Critical Biography*, trans. John Tonkin (Oxford, 1987), 289-96.

[27]   Pabel, *Conversing With God*, 4-5.

the church: "Piety, theology and ministry were for him but different aspects of the one reality." Moreover, Erasmus' piety was corrective, reforming, in large part, an alternative in comparison with much that was around him. His goal was to use the past as an instrument to correct, not confirm, the present.[28] As Erasmus communicated to Pope Leo X, "To restore great things is sometimes not only harder but a nobler task than to have introduced them."[29] Erasmus occupied a moderate position that cultivated both a Catholic sense for the traditional development of doctrine and a Protestant critique of tradition on the basis of the once-and-for all evangelical standard. He could neither support radical reformers, nor would he join Catholic theologians who tended to use the Gospel to justify the status quo of ecclesiastical tradition and practice.[30]

Although Erasmus was not a preacher, his teaching and writings articulated the intellectual and evangelical virtues Fisher desired to impart in forming devout and learned pastors. His evangelical humanism aimed to reunite the activities of theology, ministry, and piety within the philosophy of Christ: sacred rhetoric derived from the holy page of scripture. Because Erasmus hoped to provide both laity and clergy with a model of clear, simple, scriptural faith, he viewed patristic piety and wisdom as better and more fruitful than the arid, complex, and proud disputations of medieval schoolmen which had led to malpractice in preaching and pastoral ministry.[31]

O'Malley notes that in the piety of Erasmus, Christ stands out as a teacher and exemplar for the life one must live in order to imitate him. Yet Erasmus' philosophy of Christ does not forget that Christ is also Redeemer and Savior. Writing to Jan Schlecta in November 1519, Erasmus offers a clear précis of this vision for his fellow priest,

> Besides which the whole of Christian philosophy lies in this, our understanding that all our hope is placed in God, who freely gives us all things through Jesus his Son, that we were redeemed by his death and engrafted through baptism with his body, that we might be dead to the desires of this world and live by his teaching and example, not merely harbouring no evil by deserving well of all men; so that, if adversity befall, we may bear it bravely in hope of the future reward which beyond question awaits all good men at Christ's coming, and that we may ever advance from one virtue to another, yet in such a way that we claim nothing for

[28] O'Malley, "Introduction" *CWE* 66: xvii.
[29] *CWE* 3: 221-22; Allen, II.184.
[30] Hoffman, *Rhetoric and Theology*, 268. See the excellent discussion in Wabuda, *Preaching During the English Reformation*, 64-80; John O'Malley, "Form, Content and Influence of Works about Preaching Before Trent: the Franciscan Contribution," chapter IV of *Religious Culture in the Sixteenth Century: Preaching, Rhetoric, Spirituality and Reform* (Aldershot, 1993); Gregory D. Dodds, *Exploiting Erasmus: The Erasmian Legacy and Religious Change in Early Modern England* (Toronto, 2009), 4-29.
[31] Eugene F. Rice Jr., *Saint Jerome and the Renaissance* (Baltimore,1985), 93-94.

ourselves, but ascribe any good we do to God.[32]

Erasmus viewed himself as a steward of the philosophy of Christ who continued the cure of souls by speaking through priests to minister to Christians, applying to their lives and for their benefit the teaching and wisdom of scripture.[33] Marjorie O'Rourke Boyle comments, "If Erasmus had wished, he could have mounted the pulpits of Europe. He was no preacher, however, but a teacher of teachers. The printing press could straddle the Continent more effectively than any sermon, and it served him well."[34] In spreading *docta pietas* through the written word, Erasmus committed himself to the business of the Gospel, which he hoped would bear fruit in godly wisdom and virtue. Thus, the aim or conversion and transformation were constitutive of all he wrote, ". . . the seamless robe of his pietas."[35]

Erasmus considered Fisher to be a salutary exemplar of the excellence of preaching he hoped to cultivate through his scholarship. In 1535 the dedicatory preface of his manual on sacred rhetoric, the *Ecclesiastes sive de Ratione concionandi*, remembered Fisher for being "a man of unexampled piety and learning," whose patronage at Cambridge was directed towards,

> the formation of theologians not so much fitted for the battles of words as equipped for the sober preaching of the Word of God. He himself was endowed with considerable charm in his discourse . . . this Bishop who is the supreme pattern of true piety, did judge and decide that there is nothing of more moment in improving public morals than the sowing of the seed of instruction in the Gospels through fit and proper preachers.[36]

While in residence at Cambridge from 1511-14, Erasmus completed *De Copia* and *Parabolae,* educational works that made important contributions towards the goal of employing humanism in the service of theology and learning in the formation of sound character and speech.[37] *De duplici copia merborum ac rerum* was Erasmus' handbook on rhetorical abundance, "Foundations of the

[32] Eugene Rice Jr., *Saint Jerome and the Renaissance* (Baltimore, 1985), 93-94. See the excellent discussion of Erasmus' use of biblical scholarship for training clergy and laity to distinguish faithful and unfaithful pastoral practice in Jane E. Philips, "The Gospel, the Clergy, and the Laity in Erasmus 'Paraphrase on the Gospel of John' in *ERSY* 10 (1990), 85-100.

[33] Pabel, *Conversing with God*, 9.

[34] Marjorie O'Rourke Boyle, *Erasmus, On Language and Method in Theology* (Toronto, 1997), 69.

[35] O'Malley, "Introduction," *CWE* 66.xxx.

[36] Trans. in Porter and Thomson, *Erasmus and Cambridge*, 188; Wooding argues for continuities between late medieval piety and the *devotia moderna*, which may account for the mutual interests of Fisher and Erasmus in the spiritual life, despite differences in theological styles. Wooding, *Rethinking English Catholicism*, 24-27.

[37] R.J. Schoeck, *Erasmus Grandescens: The Growth of a Humanist's Mind and Spirituality* (Nieuwkoop, 1988), 113-16.

Abundant Style."[38] It was written for use in John Colet's school at St. Paul's, and for the purpose of contributing to the education of youth who would later serve the church, the state, and the learned professions in and for a society professedly Christian. *De Copia*, which drew its inspiration from the writings of Cicero and Quintillian, means abundance as rich flow, as well as ability, power, resources, or a means of doing things with words. Through a vast number of examples, Erasmus taught an abundant and varied style of expression by thickening and enriching verbal texture and increasing subject matter, copia of words and copia of ideas.[39] In addition, Erasmus advised on decorum, a concept that pervades all of his writings on rhetoric, since it is intrinsic to the abundant style and is only efficacious if discriminately applied. Erasmus taught that decorum is the ability to adapt speech to circumstance, speaking forcefully, clearly, richly, and appropriately: "the fundamental requirement for eloquence is to speak as the occasion demands, and no utterance is well spoken which is lacking in this quality of appropriateness."[40]

While *De Copia* showed the aspiring writer how to express himself fluently, it also stressed propriety and precision, aiming at that harmonious marriage of meaning and language to enlighten and move the reader. Erasmus described this aim: "Such considerations have induced me to put forward some ideas on copia, the abundant style myself, treating its two aspects of content and expression, and giving some examples and patterns."[41] Moreover, since *De Copia* drew many of its examples from non-academic oral activity it was useful for enhancing everyday speech and offering valuable assistance for preparing and delivering sermons. Erasmus offered his assessment on its homiletic value: "It is a useful handbook for future preachers, but such things are scorned by the scorners of all good literature."[42]

Fisher shared Erasmus' desire for the promotion of good literature in teaching the art of faithful persuasion. For example, during Erasmus' visit at Cambridge, Fisher wrote expressing effusive praise for the *De Inventione dialectica* of Rudolph Agricola, stating that he had "never read anything, as far as that art is concerned, more enjoyable or better informed; he [Agricola] seems

---

[38] *CWE* 24.295-659; *Opera omnia*, ed. J. Le Clerc: 11 vols. (Leiden, 1703-6, rpr.1962) I.3A-110C. Hereafter cited as LB. The prefatory letter is addressed to Matthias Schurer, *CWE* 24.288-9, Allen II.32. See the introductory essay in *CWE* 23.xxxii-xli.

[39] Walter J. Ong, S.J. *Rhetoric, Romance, and Technology* (Ithaca, 1971), 48-80; McConica, *English Humanists*, 31-43.

[40] *CWE* 24.559, LB, I.72D. The principle of accommodation—decorum—is at the heart of Erasmus' understanding of ministry: Pabil, 63-68; Manfred Hoffman "Erasmus on Church and Ministry" in *ERSY* 6 (1986), 25-26; Kathy Eden, *Hermeneutics and the Rhetorical Tradition: Chapters in the Ancient Legacy and Its Humanist Reception* (New Haven, 1997), 64-78; Victoria Kahn, *Rhetoric, Prudence and Skepticism in the Renaissance* (Ithaca, 1985), 34.

[41] *CWE* 24.295, LB, I.3A.

[42] Thomson, *Erasmus and Cambridge*, 186.

to have put every point so clearly. How I wish I had him for a teacher! I would rather that—and I am speaking the truth—than be made an archbishop!"[43]

The training of preachers for the art of faithful persuasion also was enhanced by Erasmus' *Parabolae,* which had close ties with *De Copia* and other educational writings he published between 1512 and 1515, the period when Latimer was at Cambridge preparing for ordination to the priesthood. Erasmus considered the *Parabolae* or 'Parallels" to be a kind of supplement to *De Copia,* since it too was meant to contribute to abundance of style. The "Parallels" are similitudes elicited from observations of nature, humanity, history, and customs. They are written with the assumption that such study is useful since it furnishes countless phenomena from which the interested observer may draw instructive comparisons, analogies, images, and metaphors. These abiding commonplaces of moral experience, when elegantly expressed in images and metaphors that call imagination to assist reason, become persuasive enthymemes.[44] For example, "Good seed, if it fall on good ground, comes up true to its kind, while a barren and marshy soil kills it; and it is the same with the principles of philosophy, when they happen on a good spirit or a bad."[45] Another states, "A brilliant artist displays his art in more than one material, and a wise man bears himself well whatever may befall."[46]

The rich variety of uses offered to preachers by this collection of "jewels" is highlighted by comments in Erasmus' dedicatory letter to Pieter Gillis, Secretary of Antwerp.

> For the Greek parabolae, which Cicero latinizes as collatio, a sort of comparison is nothing more than a metaphor writ large . . . Do you wish to entertain? Nothing adds more sparkle. Are you concerned to convey information? Nothing makes your point more convincingly, so clearly. Do you intend to persuade? Nothing gives you greater penetration. Have you a mind to expatiate? Nowhere is plenty readier to your hand. Or to be brief? Nothing leaves more to the understanding. Have you a fancy to be grand? Metaphor can exalt anything, and to any height you please . . . Would you be vivid and picturesque? Metaphor brings it before one's eyes better than anything else . . . Take metaphor and parable, parabolae, away from the Prophets and the Gospels, and you will find that a great part of their charm is gone.[47]

The *Parabolae* emphasized an important characteristic of Renaissance writers: the use of metaphor and the role of imagination, the utilization of pictures formed in the mind for moral deliberation and for thinking and feeling in images. This was of critical importance for preachers since biblical language

[43] *CWE* 3.110, Allen, II.90.
[44] *CWE* 23.l-li.
[45] *CWE* 23.212, LB, I.593D.
[46] *CWE* 23.214, LB, I.594E.
[47] *CWE* 23.130-31, Allen II.33-34.

uses an abundance of word pictures, whether metaphors, examples, descriptions, allegories, or dramatizations: expressions that are capable of making the invisible accessible to engage both the mind and the emotions. Erasmus provided reform-minded preachers such as Latimer with a theological rhetoric of conversion. When inspired by the Holy Spirit and passionately communicated, it would be capable of participating in the action of God so as to elicit love and enable the mind to move via analogy from the seen to the unseen, from human words to the sacred word, and, ultimately, to foster faith in Christ.[48]

In March 1516, Erasmus published the long-awaited *Novum Testamentum*, directing considerable attention to the subject of scripture and its importance for the church.[49] It consisted of a dedication, followed by preliminary matters, the *Paraclesis, Methodus,* and *Apologia,* respectively, a persuasive appeal to read the New Testament, guides for its use, and a defense of the undertaking. The Greek text was provided with a Latin translation by Erasmus himself. Finally were the *Annotations*, notes on the text, which take up almost as much space as the Latin and Greek texts put together. The introductory material pleads for a theology that would start from the words and concepts appearing in scripture to promote the normalization of biblical language as an instrument for bridging the gap between theology and pastoral practice. Erasmus notes how he often felt while listening to a sermon: "I see how simple people, who hang open-mouthed on the lips of the preacher, yearn for food for the soul, eager to learn how they can go home better people."[50]

In the introductory letter to the general reader Erasmus explains how he produced the work, describing it as "the humblest service in pious devotion," and "a work of piety, a Christian work." Its purpose is to render scripture more eloquent, lucid, and faithful to the apostolic discourse, thereby showing forth Christ and finding more followers for his sacred philosophy. This is repeated in the dedicatory letter to Pope Leo X, whom Erasmus addressed as, "a second Esdras, a re-builder of the Christian religion" to whom he offered the *Novum Instrumentum* as a gift for the daily advancement of the Christian life.[51]

Erasmus chose the title *Instrumentum,* which may mean organ, instrument, or means of teaching and writing.[52] His purified text of the New Testament is an instrument for the philosophy of Christ, the living Word spoken by the Father and revealed in scripture. A striking and controversial expression of its rhetorical purpose appeared in the 1519 edition, the *Novum Testamentum,* which rendered the translation of John 1:1, "In the beginning was the Word," as

---

[48] Shuger, *Sacred Rhetoric*, 203-11; Wabuda, *Preaching During the English Reformation*, 67-70.

[49] For a good discussion see Erika Rummel, *The Humanist-Scholastic Debate: In the Renaissance and Reformation* (Cambridge, 1998), 96-125.

[50] Cited in Augustijn, *Erasmus*, 103.

[51] *CWE* 3.204, Allen, II.166-67; *CWE* 3.222, Allen, II.185.

[52] R.J. Schoeck, *Erasmus of Europe* (Edinburgh, 1992), 190.

sermo rather than *verbum,* meaning not simply words uttered singly, but discourse that is copious, eloquent, and meaningful. Christ is the sermon of God, divine wisdom and eloquence incarnate, who in the writings of the evangelists and apostles, "still lives and breathes for us and acts and speaks with more immediate efficacy than any other way." The written word of scripture is the incarnation of divinity, and the spirit of this word possesses the power of revelation. Replete with the authority of God, the sacred text is alive with the presence of Christ as the transcendent and transforming Word who speaks through human speech.[53]

Erasmus, therefore, viewed his biblical scholarship as an instrument for communicating to readers the enlivening power of Christ. This purpose is embodied in the *Paraclesis,* arguably the classic statement of his biblical humanism.[54] Written in the form of a doxological hymn that praises the philosophy of Christ, the *Paraclesis,* or word of exhortation, appeals to Christians to read with a desire to be translated into the message of the New Testament.[55] Although Erasmus wrote his short "trumpet blast" to address a general readership, its startling force was felt particularly by preachers, generating an immediate response that anticipated its eventual popularity among Protestants who were drawn to its strong focus on the speech of Christ through the medium of scripture.[56]

Erasmus' striking claim is that scripture, if used appropriately, speaks with sufficient persuasiveness to accomplish its spiritual purpose: to render the living mind and image of Christ and to draw listeners into the transforming power of divine love. This requires rhetoric appropriate to its sacred subject, even if less ornate than sophistry which aims only to stimulate pleasure and delight. In contrast to the fleeting futility of classical oratory the eloquence of scripture renders the wisdom of Christ which, "not only captivates the ear, but which leaves a lasting sting in the minds of its hearers, which grips, which transforms, which sends away a far different listener than it received" (. . . *quae non aures tantum mox peritura voluptate transformet, quae multo alium dimittat auditorem quam acceperit.* LB, V.138E). When the word of scripture is unhindered by human syllogisms or exclamations the Spirit is free to inflame

---

[53] Boyle, *Erasmus on Language and Method in Theology,* 1-57; Hoffman, *Rhetoric and Theology,* 81-93.

[54] *Paraclesis, id est, Adhortatio ad Christianae Philosphiae Studium,* LB, V.138-44, ed. and trans. John Olin, *Christian Humanism and the Reformation: Selected Writings of Erasmus* (New York, 1987), 97-108. Hereafter page numbers are given in the text.

[55] Augustijn, *Erasmus,* 78-79. O'Malley, *CWE,* 66.xxvi.

[56] Dickens and Jones, *Erasmus the Reformer,* 198. See the assessment of Margaret Mann Phillips, *Erasmus and the Northern Renaissance* (Woodbridge, 1981), "Almost all the ideas expressed in the *Paraclesis* were in accordance with those expressed by Luther," 85. See the excellent essay by Mark Vessey, "Introduction" in eds. Hilmar Pabel and Mark Vessey, *Holy Scripture Speaks: The Production and Reception of Erasmus' Paraphrases on the New Testament* (Toronto, 2002).

and incite hearts that sing Christ's praises (98). Erasmus saw Christian people everywhere for whom the word of Christ had been muted and even silenced by uninspiring performances, pastoral malpractice, and lukewarm piety. The *Paraclesis* extended a compelling invitation to acquire new capacities and possibilities for reading and speaking scripture in a life-changing manner.

To introduce his subject—the philosophy of Christ—Erasmus cited examples drawn from human philosophy. There are Platonists, Pythagoreans, Academics, Stoics, Cynics, Peripatetics, and Epicureans, communities whose members possessed not only a deep understanding of their teachings but also committed them to memory, fought on their behalf, and even died in their defense (98). Teachers of ancient philosophic schools addressed the most painful problems of human life, working as compassionate physicians of the soul whose arts could heal many types of human suffering. Their practice of philosophy, the love of wisdom, was neither for the purpose of intellectual technique nor the display of their own cleverness, but rather was an activity of grappling with human misery, distorted passions and disordered loves; a "therapy of desire." Philosophers made therapeutic use of speech, utilizing their words as instruments of pastoral care—psychagogy—to promote human happiness through the art of living well.[57]

While Erasmus believed pagan philosophy was capable of promoting the human good, he considered it sheer foolishness that Christians would ascribe to Aristotle or any other teacher authority equal to Christ. Only the new and wonderful philosophy of Christ is to be wholeheartedly pursued, since it presents a simpler and more satisfying form of life than all human philosophies. Moreover, its wisdom may be only acquired through intimate attachment to its Author and Prince.

> He who was a teacher who came forth from heaven, He alone can teach certain doctrine, since it is eternal wisdom, He alone, the sole author of human salvation, taught what pertains to salvation, He alone vouches for whatever he taught, He alone is able to grant whatsoever he has promised (99) (*Certe solus hic e coelo profectus est Doctor, solus certa docere potuit, cum sit aeterna sapientia: solus salutaria docuit unicus humanae salutis auctor: solus absolute praestitit, quidquid umquam docuit: solus exhibere potest, quidquid promissit.* LB, V.139D).

From the time of the Greek Apologists, adherents of Christianity absorbed the practice of philosophy as a way of life: the love of Christian wisdom was practiced as an exercise of thought, will, and one's whole being, demanding radical conversion within a particular community. Christianity therefore

---

[57] Martha C. Nussbaum, *The Therapy of Desire: Theory and Practice in Hellenistic Ethics* (Princeton, 1994), 3-7; Piere Hadot, *Philosophy as a Way of Life: Spiritual Exercises from Socrates to Foucault*, ed. Arnold I. Davidson, trans. Michael Chase (Oxford, 1995), 47-144; John T. McNeill, *A History of the Cure of Souls* (New York, 1951), 17-41.

presented itself as *philosophia*, love of wisdom, and as a method of forming a people to live in and look at the world in a new way. For ancient Christianity, learning how to read scripture facilitated the acquisition of habits of the soul that focused the attention of readers to both method and content, thereby extending their spiritual and moral progress. Christian philosophy was a way of life conducted according to the mind of Christ—philosophy himself.[58]

Why is Christ's philosophy unique? Erasmus acclaims, "To teach this wisdom God became man; He who was in the heart of the Father descended to earth, rendering foolish the entire wisdom of the world." Formal training in a philosophical school cannot lead to knowledge of Christ, only a pious, open mind and simple faith will do, "The journey is simple, and is ready for anyone." (*Simplix & cuivis paratum est viaticum, tantum fac adferas pium ac promptum animum, & inprimis simplici puraque praeditum fide.* LB, V.140A). Advancement is granted to the docile and humble, those whom Christ inspires and draws like a good teacher, communicating the grammar of piety to eager young minds (100).

Presumably, many in Latimer's Cambridge would have heard the *Paraclesis* as a trumpet blast to awaken England from its spiritual slumbers. Erasmus asserted that if Christ accommodates his wisdom to all who love him, his embrace must include the highest to the lowest, regardless of one's position in life. Since Christ and his wisdom are more common than the sun, only the proud are excluded from his reach. Even the humble and lowly may share in Christ's riches, the Gospels and Epistles, so that "the farmer sing some portion of them at his plow, the weaver hum some parts of them to the movement of his shuttle, the traveler lighten the weariness of the journey with stories of this kind (101).[59] The language of scripture is the medium by which Christian conversation and life are renewed (101) (*Ex his sint omnia Christianorum omnnium colloquia.* LB, V.140C).

Moreover, this new possibility exists since the divine *sermo* has come into the world through the word of Christ, the ultimate expression of the divine nature and power. Thus, if Christ's word is received and translated into life, a person will speak a living language simply and from the heart. The spirit of Christ will inspire human speech to become a theological instrument that exhorts, incites, and encourages (102). (*Haec, inquam, & hujusmodi, si quis afflatus spiritu Christi praedicet, inculcet, ad haec horteur, invitet, animet, is dimum vere Theologus est ...* LB, V.140F). As Hoffman notes: "Language plays a pivotal role in Erasmus' thinking . . . The truth of both the sensible and intelligible world is so deeply embedded in the word that there is no other way

---

[58] Jaroslav Pelikan, *Christianity and Classical Culture: The Metamorphosis of Natural Theology in the Christian Encounter with Hellenism* (New Haven, 1993), 178-80.
[59] "So the humanist effort was not restricted to scholarly pursuits and the world of intellectual elites. Its clear objective was the education and salvation of simple folk, and this aim was to unleash a flood of vernacular literature," Wooding, *Rethinking Catholicism*, 22.

to comprehend it than by reading and hearing, and no other way to communicate it than by writing and speaking."[60]

As a divinity student in Cambridge, Latimer presumably would have been among a growing number who heard the message of the *Paraclesis* as a persuasive call to the practice of reading scripture as a means of conversion and a holy life. Erasmus exults in the generative power of Christ's wisdom, the rebirth of humanity and its restoration by God to its original goodness. (*Quid autem aliud est Christi Philosophia, quam ipse renascentiam vocat, quam instauratio bene conditae naturae?* LB, V.141F). Because this wisdom has been perfectly proclaimed in the Gospels and Epistles, it is inscribed with power to effect what its Author has spoken. Everything that is required has been provided: a teacher and model to imitate, divine happiness and satisfaction for the mind, healing for troubled souls, passion and strength for the journey as learners of Christ. (*Nimirum, hic unicus est Doctor, hujus unius discipuli sitis.* LB, V.143C). Erasmus summons his readers to this journey: "Let us, therefore, with our whole heart covet this literature, let us embrace it, at length let us die in its embrace, let us be transformed in it, since indeed studies are transmuted into morals (102) (*Has igitur toto pectore sitiamus omnes, has amplectamur, in his jugitur versemur, has exosulemur, his demum immoriamur, in has transformemur, quandoquidem abeunt studia in mores.* LB, V.144C).

The *Paraclesis* concludes with a critical glance at traditional devotional practices that utilized religious relics, remains, and images of saints. Erasmus urged Christians to redirect their vision toward the words and images of scripture since they render, "the living image of his [Christ's] holy mind and the speaking, healing, dying, rising Christ Himself ... so fully present that you would see less if you gazed upon him with your very eyes" (102-103)[61] (. . . *at hae tibi sacrosanctae mentis illius vivam referunt imaginem, ipsumque Christum loquentem, sanantem, morientem, resurgentem, denique, totum ita prasentem reddunt, ut minus visurus sis, si coram oculis conspicias.* LB, V.144D).

Although the *Paraclesis* was written for a general audience, it produced significant implications for preachers, since it demonstrated a lively faith in the real presence of Christ rendered by the scriptural text, the divine *sermo* of the

---

[60] Hoffman, *Rhetoric and Theology*, 61; Schoeck, Erasmus Grandescens, 83-84; Rex, *The Theology of John Fisher*, 60-61; O' Rourke Boyle, *Erasmus on Language and Method in Theology*, 100-101.

[61] For a discussion of Erasmus' critique of late medieval piety and its reliance on images, see Carlos M.N. Eire, *War Against the Idols: The Reformation of Worship from Erasmus to Calvin* (Cambridge, 1996), 36-45. "Erasmus, in the first place, considered religious images as powerless . . . the Christian ought to revere the portrait of God's mind that the skill of the Holy Spirit has portrayed in the writing of the Gospels," 39. On Erasmus' view of history and human responsibility for the past, see Istvan Bejczy, *Erasmus and the Middle Ages: The Historical Consciousness of a Christian Humanist* (Leiden, 2001), 182-90.

Father spoken in the persuasive power of the Spirit. As Hoffman concludes, for Erasmus, "Christ is the living word of God, the image of God's mind, and as such he is the supreme preacher endowed with the utmost power of persuasion." Since preaching is learned by conforming to the life and practice of those who know how one should not presume to do so without first being taught by God. Reading the Bible in this manner is an act of desire to know and to obey, a sacramental act in which God answers the reader's prayer. In Christ's school of preaching, reading and listening precedes speaking, wisdom comes before style, and truth before expression. The better and clearer the theology, especially when taught by Christ, the more persuasively the human heart may bring sacred rhetoric to human speech.[62] Wabuda observes that for Erasmus, "The person of the preacher was the pivot, in the sacredness of the moment, the mouthpiece of the wisdom of God, infused with the spirit of Christ, who dwelt in his heart."[63]

Although Erasmus declared that Christ is more vividly present in scripture than he was during his earthly ministry, he asserted Christ cannot be apprehended without the volitional assent of sincere faith.[64] Thus, a preacher cannot shine without burning; a preacher cannot inflame others without the mind being fired, without the transport of thought. Only when preaching and life, study and prayer, are one, does proclamation pass over into hearers' lives with persuasive power. One who presumes to speak God's word must be so consumed and transformed by whom and what one knows, that one becomes a living sermon, an instrument of the word of Christ who, ". . . preaches, teaches, inculcates, exhorts, incites, and encourages . . . " (102).[65]

In 1518, a new edition of the *Enchridion militis Christiane* "Handbook of the Christian Soldier" was published. This work extended the message of the *Paraclesis*, articulating a vision of scriptural wisdom embodied by Christian people.[66] In the prefatory letter to Paul Volz, Erasmus described the *Enchridion* as an expression of piety that would contribute to the making of "theological lives" (*vitam theologicam*) rather than theological arguments. He reiterated his desire that Christ be made accessible to even the untrained multitudes, that

---

[62] See Shuger's discussion of the emphasis placed by Renaissance rhetorics on the passion of the preacher's heart and speech being enflamed by divine charity; Shuger, *Sacred Rhetoric*, 221-40.

[63] Wabuda, *Preaching During the English Reformation*, 69, 65-69. See the discussion in John O'Malley, "Erasmus and the History of Sacred Rhetoric" which forms chapter VII of *Religious Culture*.

[64] Boyle, *Erasmus on Language and Method in Theology*, 80-83.

[65] Manfred Hoffman, "Erasmus on Church and Ministry" in *ERSY* 6 (1986), 23-25. I am indebted to Hoffman's essay in formulating this section.

[66] *CWE* 6.72-90; Allen, III.362-70; *Letter to Paul Volz*, ed. Olin, *Selected Essays of Erasmus*, 109-29. Hereafter page numbers will appear in the text. Volz was Abbot of the monastery at Hugshofen, in Alsace. See Wabuda, *Preaching During the English Reformation*, for a discussion of Erasmus' influence on the political nature of preaching, 65-90.

pastors teach the path of sincere faith, unfeigned love, and confident hope, kindling desire for it by their passion and example.

Erasmus envisioned a Christian society reconstituted by preaching that renders the living image of Christ as its *scopus*, or its goal.[67] Radiating outward from Christ are a series of concentric circles, the nearest comprised of priests, bishops, cardinals, and popes whose duty is to follow and adhere to the Lamb. Christ draws the orders of priests to himself, inflaming them with divine charity and purifying them from earthly stain. In succession of Christ, clergy must embrace what is pure, transfusing his teaching to rulers whose vocation is to defend the public peace and restrain evildoers. By mirroring Christ with sharpness, clarity, and purity, clergy accommodate the special needs of princes who have been called to exercise power without benefit of the fullness of divine justice (117).[68]

The third and most solid circle around Christ is the common people, the grossest part of this world, but who still belong to the body of Christ. Erasmus considers their greatest need to be pastoral forbearance and mercy. Thus in their dealings with common folk, clergy should imitate the decorum of Christ, who endued his disciples with gentleness and accommodated his teaching to their capacities. Clergy must support the weak with fatherly indulgence until they grow strong in Christ, since to strive after Christ is the vocation common to all citizens of a Christian realm (120).

The philosophy of Christ is his simple eloquence proclaimed for the cultivation of pure Christianity, "in the dispositions of the soul, not in the mode of life; in the soul, not what a person eats or wears." Christian vocation is not the exclusive possession of those who live according to a religious rule; rather it is granted to all in baptism for a common life under the rule of Christ. Erasmus exclaims, "What else is a city but a great monastery?" (. . . *quid aliud est civitas quam magnum monasterium?* Allen, III.376). All Christians are monks, *monachi*, called to purity of heart and singleness of mind in devotion to Christ (122). The task of clergy is to render Christ's lively presence intelligible through the proper use of scripture, thus promoting charity and concord throughout the commonwealth (123-27).[69]

In 1522, William Tyndale translated the *Enchiridion* into English. It enjoyed great popularity in England, sounding its central themes of returning to scripture, simplicity of faith in Christ, and whole-hearted devotion to his

---

[67] Here I am following the excellent discussion of Boyle, *Erasmus on Language and Method in Theology*, 84-97. "Christ is the center of theological attention."

[68] Boyle, *Erasmus on Language and Method in Theology*, 84-87. See Wabuda's discussion of Erasmus' influence on the political nature of preaching, *Preaching During the English Reformation*, 89-99.

[69] "Erasmus perceived the grave mistake of separating Christian faith from the theological life." Romanus Cessario, O.P., *Christian Faith and the Theological Life* (Washington, DC, 1996), 132.

word.[70] Its First Rule of True Christianity states:

> Since faith is the only avenue to Christ, it is fitting that the first rule should be to understand what the Scriptures tell us about Christ and his Spirit, and to believe this not only by lip service, not coldly nor listlessly or hesitantly, as does the common lot of Christians, but with your whole heart, with the deep and unshaken conviction that here is not one tiniest detail contained therein that does not pertain to your salvation.[71]

Interest in Erasmus' works in England continued rise after his return to the continent in 1514, with his piety being acclaimed by many.[72] In 1517 Fisher wrote to praise Erasmus for his biblical scholarship and its impact in England.

> The New Testament, as translated by you for the common benefit of us all, can offend no one of any sense; for you have not only shed light on countless places in it by your scholarship; you have provided an absolutely fresh commentary on the whole work, so that it can now be read and enjoyed by anybody with much more pleasure and satisfaction than before.[73]

The wisdom offered by the *Novum Testamentum* and *Enchridion* was supplemented by the publication of the *Paraphrases on the New Testament* (1517-24) for providing preachers with a continuous exposition of scripture that rendered the philosophy of Christ in homiletic style.[74] As Cardinal Campeggi wrote to Erasmus in 1519, "I seized every opportunity to acquire your image, which I found reflected . . . most recently in your sermon-paraphrase on the Pauline Epistles."[75] The sermon-paraphrase, which was an instrument for Erasmus to preach with pen and printing press, "says things differently without saying different things, especially in a subject which is not only difficult, but sacred, and very near the majesty of the Gospel."[76]

The goal of Erasmus' sermon-paraphrases was to render the genuine meaning of the biblical text, offering more than translation but less than commentary, writing by means of the language of scripture rather than writing about the language of scripture. Erasmus hoped the reader would not be offended by the fact that he had changed the words of Holy Scripture in order to enable the voice of Paul or even Christ to be heard. Thus the rhetorical object of the *Paraphrases*, therefore, was to get the mind of Christ off the pages of

---

[70] *CWE* 66.6-7; Wooding, *Rethinking Catholicism in Reformation England*, 20-23; McConica, *English Humanists and Reformation Politics*, 135-36.
[71] *CWE* 66.56, LB, V.22A.
[72] *CWE* 66.xxv; McConica, *English Humanists*, 88-105; Brigden, *London and the Reformation*, 68-81; Wooding, *Rethinking English Catholicism*, 28-38.
[73] *CWE* 4.397; Allen II.598.
[74] Augustijn, *Erasmus*, 99-102; Albert Rabil Jr., *Erasmus and the New Testament: The Mind of A Christian Humanist* (San Antonio, 1972), 115-41.
[75] *CWE* 7.5, Allen, IV.4.
[76] *CWE* 5.196, Allen, III.138.

scripture and into the minds of readers, since in spiritual regeneration Christ is the content, goal, and final efficient cause.[77] When used in this manner, the words of scripture and the words of the *Paraphrases* would serve a mediating function, respectively, between Christ and the church, Erasmus and his readers, preachers and their people.[78] By accommodating himself to both the biblical text and the contemporary context, Erasmus presented himself as a model of pastoral discourse.[79] Selected passages from the *Paraphrases* will help to illumine this pastoral pedagogy.

In preaching the gospel, as in writing homiletic paraphrase on it, the spirit of Christ proceeds through the soul (or mind) of the preacher into the soul of the hearer or reader.[80] In the paraphrase of I Peter 4, Erasmus describes how this spiritual transformation enables the word of Christ to be spoken and heard.

> If it falls to a person's lot to receive sacred doctrine or the gift of a learned tongue, he is not to use it for personal gain or pride or empty glory but for the salvation of his neighbor and the glory of Christ, and his audience should perceive that the words they hear are from God, not from men, and that the one who speaks to them is but an instrument of the divine voice.[81]

Erasmus also used the *Paraphrases* to increase the confidence of preachers, offering assurance that in times of adversity the Spirit provides strength. He renders 2 Timothy 2,

> God has given us who have become his sons through evangelical faith a far different Spirit, this Spirit does not make us timid and downcast from fear and diffidence, but brave with heads held high because we have confidence in our innocence and we hope for the immortality promised us. This Spirit makes us free and courageous because of our love which both trusts totally in God's help and is not afraid to undergo danger for a neighbor's sake. Lastly, this Spirit does not allow our minds to be thrown into turmoil but enables us to persevere with hearts resolute and unbroken always. Therefore, since you have received this Spirit display power and courageously manifest what you possess . . . Through it you proclaim the cross and death of our Lord Jesus Christ. Do not be ashamed to be the disciple of this apostle, burdened though I am with these chains . . . The cross of Christ is our glory.[82]

Erasmus admonished preachers to remain faithful to the simplicity of the

---

[77] J.J. Bateman, "From Soul to Soul: Persuasion in Erasmus' 'Paraphrases on the New Testament'" in *Erasmus in English* 15 (1987-88), 8.

[78] *CWE* 42.xiv-xviii; Albert Rabil Jr. "Erasmus's Paraphrases on the New Testament," Richard DeMolen, ed. *Essays on the Works of Erasmus* (New Haven, 1978), 145-62.

[79] *CWE*, 41.x-xii; Bateman, "From Soul to Soul: Persuasion in Erasmus' Paraphrases on the New Testament," 7-16.

[80] Bateman, "From Soul to Soul," 13-14.

[81] *CWE* 44.103, LB, VII.1097.

[82] *CWE* 44.45, LB, VII.1060.

Gospel, guarding the purity of their life and language so that evangelical teaching might achieve its intended effect. As the paraphrase of 2 Timothy directs,

> Do your best to show yourself a evangelical workman and not a debater, and a workman not approved by men but by God . . . You will do this if you cut away all superfluous disputations and keep the teaching of the Gospel on the direct road of faith and if, once you have cleared away the thicket of perplexing questions, you divide and handle the word of God with right judgment, presenting to the people only those matters which are properly relevant to the work of godliness and salvation.

Elsewhere in the paraphrase of 2 Timothy, Erasmus instructs preachers on the moral qualities required for their ministry, exhorting them to fulfill its evangelical duties.

> The need to strengthen in advance the hearts and minds of our people is all the greater because hereafter there will be, as I said, a grave and dangerous time when some will abandon their evangelical confession and will not tolerate the true and healthy teaching of Christ . . . Be watchful, enduring everything for the gospel's sake. Make yourself truly a herald of the gospel . . . be sure to conduct yourself in a way that is completely persuasive and deeply implanted in people's minds, so that they are not easily shaken by those who will endeavor to teach a contrary doctrine.[83]

The *Paraphrase on Acts* was a model for the renewal of the sixteenth-century church. Erasmus' portrait depicts the Spirit as the ever-present source of action, and its leading figures as exemplars for clergy in his own day. The description of Peter's sermon on the day of Pentecost is highly rhetorical, reflecting Erasmus' commitment for training preachers to become worthy instruments of sacred eloquence.

> Sounds are not uttered without breath, without a tongue. Accordingly, the breath from heaven puts forth a heavenly sound; a tongue of fire carries off and sets aflame the hearts of hearers. The tongue of the Pharisees is cold, the tongue of the philosophers, however erudite, or of the orators, however fluent, moves no one. This gift comes from heaven; the disciples are only the instruments through which the Holy Spirit puts forth his voice. A man cannot give this gift to another man, nor does anyone impart it to himself, but God bestows it upon each person as he sees fit . . . The spirit is a thing of force; fire is something lively and always in motion.[84]

Erasmus' *Paraphrases on the New Testament* was an instrument for the education and formation of preachers. Through his sermon-paraphrases,

---

[83] *CWE* 44.52, LB, VII.1059.
[84] *CWE* 50.15, LB, VII.667.

Erasmus identified himself with pastors, instructing and encouraging them for the highest calling and function: to spread the teaching of the gospel. His biblical scholarship was received by many in England, and especially at Cambridge, where it rendered the word of God both attractive and accessible for readers to cultivate habits of faith and speech.[85]

Among those indebted to the scholarship of Erasmus were Thomas Bilney and Latimer at Cambridge, following events that were remembered by many Protestants as effectively marking the beginnings of the English Reformation. According to Foxe, around 1524, Erasmus' elegant translation of the New Testament caught the eye of Bilney, who stated that he, "heard speak of Jesus, even then when the New Testament was first set forth by Erasmus: which . . . I understood to be eloquently done by him, being allured rather by the Latin than the word of God." Bilney read a passage in the Pastoral Epistles from which he claimed to apprehend, "God's instruction and inward working." Moreover, according to Latimer, soon after this experience Bilney was "the instrument whereby God called me to knowledge . . . that I have of the word of God . . . So from that time forward I began to smell the word of God, and forsook the school-doctors and such fooleries."[86]

The evangelical humanism of Erasmus became a moving force for spiritual and moral change in England.[87] It paved the way for others to prove what scripture could actually achieve in pastoral ministry through the cultivation of intellectual habits and dispositions shaped by learned piety and embodied in the practice of pastoral ministry.[88] Soon after leaving Cambridge, Erasmus wrote to Thomas Bullock regarding changes that had occurred, giving special attention to the impact on preaching.

> Now tell me, what has been the effect of all this upon your university. Why, it has blossomed forth so as to rival the leading modern schools, and now contains men of such quality that in comparison, those of the old time appear near shadows of

---

[85] A good summary of Erasmus' work in England is provided in Thomson and Porter, *Erasmus and Cambridge*, 1-109; McConica, *English Humanists and Reformation Politics*, 76-106; Wooding, *Rethinking English Catholicism in Reformation England*, 16-30; O'Malley points out that Erasmus emphasized sermons more than other parts of the liturgy, *CWE*, 66.xxv. On Erasmus and Henry VIII, see G.W. Bernard, *The King's Reformation*, 234-43.

[86] H.C. Porter, *Reformation and Reaction in Tudor Cambridge*, 37-44. Chester, *Hugh Latimer*, 11-12, defines 'new learning' and 'new scholarship' as being contiguous in the case of Erasmus, which demonstrates Erasmus' aim of using learning to serve the renewal of theology. See R. Rex, "The New Learning" JEH 44 (1993), 28; Wabuda, *Preaching During the English Reformation*, 84-85; Dodds, *Exploiting Erasmus*, 27-59.

[87] Jones and Dickens conclude that England was the nation most receptive to Erasmus' philosophy of Christ. See "The English Erasmians," 192-216.

[88] On Erasmus' rhetorical reading of scripture and the relation of human and divine discourse see Debora Shuger, *The Renaissance Bible: Scholarship, Sacrifice, and Subjectivity* (Berkeley, 1998), 25-26; idem, *Sacred Rhetoric*, 243-49.

theologians rather than the reality . . . As to your preaching, I applaud your course of action in doing this and offer my congratulations on your success: especially since you teach Christ in purity and make no boast of merely human subtleties.[89]

More than any other writer, Erasmus took the biblically derived imperatives uncovered by the New Learning and applied them to the reform of the church to re-appropriate the power of sacred rhetoric for the life-changing communication of sacred teaching.[90] Although the spirit of Christian humanism was essentially orthodox, it created a new context for interpreting reform, which prepared the way for a more radical vision to impact the polity at large. The intellectual foundations for this vision were deeply influenced by Erasmian biblicism and its catalogue of "things indifferent," which for many provided a purer, simpler, and more appealing way of construing and practicing the faith.[91] As Hoffman notes, "Erasmus wished for the church's external means of grace to operate according to their spiritual purpose. This pertains particularly to the ministry of proclaiming God's word incarnate in Christ and the Scripture."[92]

In trumpeting the power of scripture over external forms of religion, and by promoting the inward apprehension of faith for salvation, Erasmus sought to stir his readers to action for the revival of the church and reform of the commonwealth. In its fundamental form, this program was neither a reform of ideas nor of social structures; rather it represented a deeper, more radical shift in religious imagination for the practical renovation of Christian people. Erasmus stated this quite eloquently in *The Praise of Folly*,

> Finally, no fools seem more senseless than those people who have been completely taken up, once and for all, with a burning devotion to Christian piety: they throw away their possessions, ignore injuries, allow themselves to be deceived, make no distinctions between friend and foe, shudder at the thought of pleasure, find satisfaction in fasts, vigils, tears, labors, shrink from life, desire death above all else—in short, they seem completely devoid of normal human responses, just as if their minds were living somewhere else, but not their bodies. Can such a condition be called anything but insanity? In this light, it is not at all surprising that the apostles seemed to be intoxicated with new wine, and that Paul seemed mad to the judge Festus.[93]

---

[89] Cited in Thomson and Porter, *Erasmus and Cambridge*, 195; *CWE* 4.47, Allen, II.322.

[90] Wooding, *Rethinking English Catholicism*, 30.

[91] Margaret Aston, *England's Iconoclasts*: Vol. I., Laws Against Images (Oxford, 1988), 196-200; Carlos Eire, *War Against the Idols: The Reformation of Worship from Erasmus to Calvin* (Cambridge, 1986), 28-46; Paul O'Grady, *Henry VIII and the Conforming Catholics* (Collegeville, 1990), 64-82; Bernard J. Verkamp, *The Indifferent Mean: Adiaphorism in the English Reformation to 1554* (Athens, 1981), 1-14, 24-41.

[92] Hoffman, "Erasmus on Church and Ministry," 27.

[93] Erasmus, *The Praise of Folly*, Clarence H. Miller, trans. (New Haven, 1979), 132.

Preaching persuasively with his pen, Erasmus issued an enthusiastic call for preachers to take up the evangelistic task of making Christians through the message and spirit of Christ as communicated by scripture. Uncovering what had been overlaid by neglectful practices and obscured from inattentive or ignorant readers and listeners, his writings cleared the way for a biblically-derived spirituality. In this he shifted the focus from traditional visual images to verbal images as the primary medium of imagination, vivid means God uses to evoke faith through direct contact with his Word.[94] Just as Christ is the image and embodiment of God's Son, the Bible is the embook-ment of Christ's image and Spirit. It is capable of regenerating faith, spiritual vitality, and moral commitment by means of human words.[95] In emphasizing the need for pastors to learn, absorb, and rely upon the wisdom and persuasiveness of scripture—a *theologica rhetorica*—Erasmus called for a return to the model of the preaching life depicted by Augustine in *De doctrina christiana*. The serious business of preaching is simply Christ, the eloquent "sermon" of God who communicates himself through the speech of pastors who are his "living sermons."[96] Wabuda concludes,

> Erasmus unleashed now vision of what the preacher should be: dedicated and humble yet imposing; the vessel of God, yet unafraid to wield the authority of the deity too, no matter what the personal cost, even if it led to martyrdom. The connection between priest and preacher was inseparable . . . The simple spirituality and rigor that had been traditionally associated with the episcopate and mendicant orders Erasmus now extended throughout the entire priesthood. The ability and erudition of the bishop should now be the goal of the humble curate.[97]

The impact of Erasmus' biblical humanism played a significant role in stimulating desire for practical reform at Cambridge.[98] The scope of Latimer's

---

[94] Shuger, *Sacred Rhetoric*, 200-11; Peter Matheson, *The Imaginative World of the Reformation* (Edinburgh, 2000), 1-24, 119-40; John O' Malley, 'Introduction' in *CWE* 66.xxv-xxx.

[95] Eire, *War Against the Idols*, 38-41; Boyle, *Erasmus on Language and Method in Theology*, 83; Matheson, *The Imaginative World of the Imagination*, 125-26.

[96] On the importance of Augustine for sacred rhetoric in the sixteenth-century see, Shuger, *Sacred Rhetoric*, 47-65. For a discussion of Erasmus and his use of Augustine see Peter Iver Kaufman, *Augustinian Piety and Catholic Reform: Augustine, Colet, and Erasmus* (Macon, 1982), 111-28; James McConica, *Erasmus* (Oxford, 1991), 14-15; On the rhetorical theology of Erasmus see, O' Malley, "Introduction" in *CWE* 66.xxviii-ix; Charles Trinkaus, *In Our Image and Likeness* (Chicago, 1970), I.126-28; John D'Amico, "Humanism and Pre-Reformation Theology" in ed. Albert Rabil, Jr., *Renaissance Humanism: Foundations, Forms, and Legacy.* (Philadelphia, 1988), III.369-73.

[97] Wabuda, *Preaching During the English Reformation*, 70.

[98] Porter, *Reformation and Reaction in Tudor Cambridge*, "The 1520s saw the effective beginnings of the Reformation in Cambridge," 44; Wooding, *Rethinking Catholicism in Reformation England*, 38-39.

preaching in the late 1520's reflects this influence, as Thomas Becon later wrote,

> I was present when, with manifest authorities of God's word and arguments invincible, besides the allegations of doctors, he proved in his sermons, that the holy scriptures ought to be read in the English tongue of all Christian people . . . neither was I absent when he inveighed against temple-works, good intents, blind zeal, superstitious devotion, etc.; as the painting of tabernacles, gilding of images, setting up of candles, running on pilgrimage, and such other idle inventions of men, whereby the glory of God was obscured, and the works of mercy the less regarded.[99]

As hopes for reform intensified, Erasmus' comments on religious renewal, a *restoratio*, were radicalized and endowed with controversial meaning exceeding that of their author's original historical context.[100] In 1529 an English translation of the *Paraclesis,* "an exhortation to the diligent studye of scripture," was published in a volume with Martin Luther's, "an exposition to the seventh chapter of the Epistle to the Corinthians." The work was attributed to William Roye, a radical reformer who one year earlier had co-authored a scurrilous and irreverent verse satire, *Rede Me and Be Nott Wrothe*, a running commentary on clerical immortality brought about by misguided and unscriptural vows of chastity, and the demeaning of marriage by the Roman Church.[101] The *Paraclesis* presumably appeared to reformers as a tract which gave clear and unequivocal expression to many of their beliefs and criticisms of the Roman Church: it was a work that came close to denying the efficacy of anything except scripture in inculcating Christian virtue—a clear reformist position.

Moreover, reading the *Paraclesis* in a climate created by the distribution of Tyndale's New Testament invited access to Protestant positions presumably endorsed by Erasmus' pen.[102] He called for a vernacular Bible and for universal accessibility, perhaps unconsciously subverting the Roman Church's view of its own singular teaching authority; he questioned the value of scholastic disputation and by so doing undermined the church's support of that method in seeking truth; he subtly attacked monasticism, he criticized worldly divines, seemed to call for a priesthood of the laity, and put forms of traditional devotion well behind the Gospels and Epistles. The issues raised in the

---

[99] *The Cathechism of Thomas Becon*, 425.

[100] Erika Rummel, "Monacthus non est pietas" in ed. Hilmar Pabel, *Erasmus' Vision of the Church*, 44.

[101] *An exhortation to the diligent studye of scripture and an exposition into the seventh chapter of the Epistle to the Corinthians*, ed. Douglas H. Parker (Toronto, 2000), 3-8. See "Introduction" to *Rede Me and Be Nott Wrothe*, ed. Douglas H. Parker (Toronto, 1992).

[102] David Daniell, *William Tyndale: A Biography* (New Haven, 1994), 63-79, 181-85; Brigden, *London and the Reformation*, 106-28.

Paraclesis are clear how Erasmus might have been interpreted by England's most reform-minded, a view that was strengthened by his textual proximity to Luther.[103]

In 1529 Latimer rose to prominence as a reformist preacher in Cambridge while Parliament was convening to address the political fate of Cardinal Wolsey. The seven-year assembly, called the "Reformation Parliament," saw no widespread changes in doctrine or practice at its start when the "King's Great Matter" was simply his desire to divorce Catherine, a wish with international implications. When Wolsey failed to obtain Rome's approval for the divorce, he proved that he was of limited use to the king, who called Parliament to Westminster.[104]

Latimer's initial contact with Wolsey was in 1527 when the powerful Cardinal initiated a crackdown on Lutheran opinions at the universities. Unfortunately, none of Latimer's earliest Cambridge sermons survived, but Ralph Morice, who was later to become Cranmer's secretary: "Preaching daily in the University of Cambridge, both in English and *ad clerum*, to the great admiration of all men that aforetime had known him of a contrary severe opinion." According to Morice, Nicholas West (Bishop of Ely) once came to hear Latimer preach. Morice reports that when the prelate entered the church, Latimer changed the theme of his sermon to address the honorable estate of a bishop. Morice states that West challenged Latimer on the content of his sermon and requested that he preach against Martin Luther. Latimer pleaded ignorance (to the bishop's great displeasure), leading West to monitor his preaching further. West charged Latimer with preaching seditious doctrine and eventually placed him before Cardinal Wolsey. Apparently, Latimer satisfied the Cardinal with his answers, so that Wolsey dismissed him with a gentle admonition and a license to preach throughout England. Latimer continued his reformist preaching at Cambridge while Parliament was humiliating Wolsey. Morice ends his account with a comment by Latimer: "For he [Wolsey] being, I trust, reconciled to God from his pomp and vanities, I now set more by his lisence than I ever did before, when he was in his most felicity."[105]

Wolsey's dismissal proved to be a pivotal event for English politics and religion, since his inability to deliver in the matter of the King's divorce provided an opportunity for his enemies to act.[106] On the first day of the legal

---

[103] See Parker's discussion of the religious context in is introduction and commentary, *An exhortation to the diligent studye of scripture*, 11-12, 31-6, 55-67.

[104] Susan Doran and Christopher Durston, *Princes, Pastors and People: The Church and Religion in England 1529-1689* (London, 1991), 124-44; Christopher Haigh, "Anticlericalism and the English Reformation" in *The English Reformation* revised ed. Christopher Haigh (Cambridge, 1990); James K. McConica, *English Humanists and Reformation Politics: Under Henry VIII and Edward VI* (Oxford, 1965), 106-50; Rosemary O'Day, *The Debate on The English Reformation* (London, 1986), 122-32.

[105] Hugh Latimer, *Works*, Vol. II.xxvii-xxxi.

[106] John Guy, "Thomas Wolsey, Thomas Cromwell and the Reform of Henrician

term, they indicted Wolsey in King's Bench for *praemunire,* claiming that he infringed jurisdictions in England by exercising his legatine authority. For the next month Henry and Wolsey's enemies debated over the cardinal, his authority and his future. At last, on November 3, the final day of Parliament, Wolsey's enemies distributed throughout London copies of Simon Fish's "A Supplication for the Beggars" which denounced clerical wealth. With Wolsey's enemies united against him, Henry replaced him with a layman, Thomas More.[107] These proceedings were watched closely in Cambridge, which was quickly divided by the controversy.[108] Shortly before Christmas of that same year, Latimer preached a reformist sermon that gave great offense to conservatives. John Foxe records that a certain Benedictine, Dr. John Venutus, attacked Latimer's preaching in response, and that the first of Latimer's *Sermons on The Cards* could be his rejoinder.[109] Because these are the only extant sermons by Latimer from this period, they are important for understanding the influence of biblical humanism in Cambridge and on Latimer's rise to national prominence as a reformist preacher. The only surviving accounts of the *Sermons on the Cards* are included in successive editions of Foxe, *Acts and Monuments of the latter and perilous days, touching matters of the Church, wherein are comprehended and described the great persecutions and horrible troubles, that have bene wrought and practiced by the Romish Prelates, Speciallye in this realme of England and Scotlande, from the yeare of our Lorde a thousand, unto the tyme nowe presente.*[110]

Government" in ed. Dairmaid MacCulloch, *The Reign of Henry VIII: Politics, Policy, and Piety* (New York, 1995), 35-58; G.R. Elton, *Reform and Reformation: England, 1509-58* (Cambridge, 1977), 42-103; Doran and Durston, *Princes, Pastors and People,* 54-63; Haigh, *English Reformations,* 88-120; McConica, *English Humanists and Reformation Politics,* 106-30.

[107] Christopher Haigh, *English Reformations,* 88-102; Susan Brigden, *London and the Reformation,* (Oxford, 1989), 172-215; David Loades, "Anticlericalism in the Church of England before 1558: an 'Eating Canker'?" in ed. Nigel Aston and Matthew Cragoe, *Anticlericalism in Britain,* c. 1500-1914 (Thrupp, 2000), 44-73.

[108] Chester, *Hugh Latimer,* 16-40; Porter, *Reformation and Reaction,* 44-73.

[109] Foxe's account of Latimer's preaching and the response it provoked is given in the *Actes and Monuments,* ed. Stephen R. Catley (London, 1838), vii.437-451. On Foxe's polemical purposes see, Patrick Collinson, "Truth, lies, and fiction in Sixteenth-Century Protestant historiography" in Donald R. Kelley and David H. Sacks ed., *The Historical Imagination in Early Modern Britain: History, Rhetoric, and Fiction* (Cambridge, 1998), 37-69. On the Cambridge reformers see Porter, *Reformation and Reaction,* 46-48.

[110] Foxe's account of Latimer's sermons, "The Tenor and Effect of Certain Sermons Made by Master Latimer in Cambridge, About the Year of Our Lord, 1529" and the controversy they provoked appear in the 1563 edition under the heading, "The lyfe, actes, and doynges of master Hugh Latimer, the famous preacher and bishop, servant of Christ and his Gospell" (1298-1308). The 1563 edition was imprinted by John Day at London. Day also printed the early editions of Latimer's sermons. See Hugh Latimer, *Works,* Vol. I.xiv-xvi. I. "These Sermons on the Card are reprinted from the

The research of Thomas Freeman and other scholars has shown that, despite the universally acknowledged importance of Foxe's *Acts and Monuments*, the actual text of any of the original editions of it remains largely unknown to most scholars.[111] Yet many scholars continue to rely upon the more accessible unabridged Victorian editions of Foxe's book. As Freeman's textual criticism demonstrates, these popular nineteenth-century editions seriously distort Foxe's texts by concealing the differences between the various editions and through bowderlizations, omissions, and even extensive rewriting of them.

Freeman's findings serve to alert historians to pay careful attention to possible textual corruptions and their effects on subsequent scholarship. All of the later editions, which have become standard in most academic libraries, reprint with significant amendments, abridgements, and alterations the text of the 1583 edition of the *Acts and Monuments* (the last edition published during Foxe's life-time), with material from the 1563 edition (the first) being frequently added to it. Material printed in the second and third editions of the *Acts and Monuments* (published in 1570 and 1576), which was omitted from the 1583 edition, was also omitted from all of the nineteenth-century editions.[112]

The Victorian editions were published in the context of the rise of Tractarianism and were intended as straightforward descriptions of the persecutions of the "true" (i.e., Evangelical) church by the Church of Rome, and not as scholarly editions of Foxe's writings. As Freeman notes, this meant that the editors were more interested in presenting Foxe's work as an accurate history than presenting accurately what Foxe wrote. As a result, alterations were made in the original texts, which suited the apologetic purposes of the editors. Freeman concludes that Foxe's latter editors have not only placed great barriers between the modern reader and the original texts of the *Acts and*

---

first edition of the Acts and Monuments of John Foxe, pp. 1298 & c." An identical account is provided in Catley's edition. Cf. the previous footnote.

[111] Thomas Freeman, "Texts, Lies, and Microfilm: Reading and Misreading Foxe's 'Book of Marytrs'" in *Sixteen Century Journal* XXX.1 (1999), 23-46; Patrick Collinson, "Truth, lies, and fiction in Sixteenth-Century Protestant historiography" in ed. Donald R. Kelley and David H. Sacks, *The Historical Imagination in Early Modern Britain: History, Rhetoric, and Fiction* (Cambridge, 1998), 37-69; John King, "Fiction and Fact in Foxe's Book of Martyrs" in ed. David Loades, *John Foxe and the English Reformaton* (Aldershot, 1997), 12-35; David Loades, "The New Edition of the Acts and Monuments: A Progress Report" in ed. Loades, *John Foxe: A Historical Perspective* (Aldershot, 1999), 1-14; John King, "The World of John Foxe" in eds Christopher Highley and John N. King, *John Foxe and his World* (Aldershot, 2002), 1-9. The afterword by David Loades provides an update on the John Foxe project, a CD-Rom facsimile of Acts and Monuments established in 1993 by the British Academy. Loades, "Afterword: John Foxe in the Twenty First Century," 277-90.

[112] Freeman, "Text, Lies, and Microfilm," 23-24; King, "Fiction and Fact in Foxe's Book of Martyrs," 13-14.

Monuments; they have also placed a barrier between the modern reader and Foxe's sources.[113]

> In a text, to an extent, that deconstructs itself, how can an analysis of Foxe's authorship be made until Foxe's actual composition of the relevant passages is established? . . . Like artifacts in an archaeological site, the texts of the different editions are informative not only through their intrinsic qualities, but also in their contexts and relationships to each other. Foxe's Victorian editors, in effect, plundered the site and even where they did not damage the artifacts (i.e., emend or rewrite the text), they removed them from their locations and rearranged them.[114]

Latimer's *Sermons on the Cards* were spoken by following the Gospel narrative to call attention to the living word of Christ, to engender faith, to evoke humility, and to inspire neighbor love. Set against the background of Wolsey's fall and the Commons' challenge of clerical authority, Latimer painted a verbal portrait of prelates who abused pastoral authority and corrupted popular piety, thus appealing for acceptance of an alternative vision of Christian faith and devotion.[115]

Latimer began by announcing his theme, "Who art thou?" the question posed to John the Baptist by Pharisees who suspected he might be the promised Messiah (John 1:19). Latimer raised this question to define Christian identity, linking the Gospel narrative with the story of the creation and fall of Adam. He illumined the theme by means of a tale of the King of England and his captain, the defender of the town of Calais, who was negligent in his duties, thereby allowing the city to fall to the French. The king angrily relieved him of his office and relieved his heirs of their inheritance. Latimer drew the following conclusion: "So, likewise it was of our first father Adam. And so now this example proveth, that by our father Adam we had once in him the very inheritance of everlasting joy; and by him, and in him, again we lost the same" (Works, I.5-6). Returning to the sermon theme, "Who art thou?" Latimer announced the disastrous consequences of Adam's fall, "We be of ourselves the very children of the indignation and vengeance of God, the true inheritors of hell, and working all towards hell" (Works, I.7).

Returning to his opening question, "Who art thou?" Latimer announced the good news offered in the sacrament of Baptism, the possibility of a renewed identity in Christ: "I must say that I am a Christian man, a Christian woman, the child of everlasting joy, through the merits of the bitter passion of Christ. This is a joyful answer" (Works, I.7).[116] Two additional questions complete the

---

[113] Freeman, "Texts, Lies and Microfilm," 32-33.

[114] Freeman, "Texts, Lies and Microfilm," 34. Foxe's work is used sparingly for this dissertation. The following exposition of Latimer's *Sermons on the Cards* was written after a comparison was made between the 1563 and 1838 editions of the *Acts and Monuments and Latimer's Works*.

[115] Davies, *Worship and Theology in England*, I.17-25.

[116] On the use of exempla, historical or fictitious anecdotes and illustrations by medieval

setting of the theme: "What doth Christ require of a Christian man, a Christian woman? Now then what is Christ's rule?" Latimer's answer moved the sermon forward to its central claim: "Christ's rule consists of many things and in commandments and works of mercy" (Works, I.8).

Since the students of Cambridge were accustomed to playing card games during their celebrations of Christmas, it was quite fitting that Latimer introduce a game called Triumph to teach of Christ's rule and its requirements: "which if it be played well, he that dealeth shall win; the players shall like wise win; and the standers and lookers shall also do the same; in as much as their is no man that is willing to play at this triumph with these cards, but they shall be all winners, and no losers" (Works, I.8).[117] Latimer dealt one card at a time, presenting Christ's words from the Sermon on the Mount in answer to an important question, "What requireth Christ of a Christian man?" and to encourage his listeners' response, "Now turn up your trump, your heart (hearts is trump as I said before), and cast your trump, your heart on this card; and upon this card, you shall learn what Christ requireth of a Christian man; not to be angry, be moved to ire against his neighbor, in mind, countenance, nor other ways, by word or deed" (Works, I.13). His final call to repentance followed,

> Let us play therefore in this fashion with this card. This trump is the means by which faith triumphs over all that is contrary to the rule of Christ: evil dispositions, affections and sensualities, foul passions and Turks . . . considering we be so prone and ready to continue in sin let us cast down ourselves with Mary Magdelene; and the more we bow down with her toward Christ's feet, the more we shall be afraid to rise again to sin (Works, I.13-14).

Turning to the narrative of Mary Magdelene and Simon the Pharisee, Latimer's visually depicted the stark contrast between two forms of piety: one based on Christian humility and the other on human arrogance. His conclusion was a compelling invitation to choose a way of life focused on the love of Christ.

> And think you not, but that there be amongst us a great number of Pharisees, which think themselves worthy to bid Christ to dinner; which will perk; and presume to sit by Christ in the church, and have a disdain for the poor neighbor, with a high disdainous and solemn countenance? And being always desirous to climb highest in the church; reckoning themselves more worthy to sit there than another. I fear me poor Magdelene under the board and in the belfry, hath more

---

preachers, see G.R. Owst, *Literature and Pulpit in Medieval England* (New York, 1961), 149-53.

[117] Owst says of Latimer, "It is only a complete ignorance of medieval preaching in England that has prevented the editors and critics of his sermons from realizing that they follow directly the style of homely vernacular discoursing employed by the pulpits of the fourteenth and fifteenth centuries." Owst attributes the Game of Cards to the Dominican John of Reinfelden in 1377. Owst, *Literature and Pulpit in Medieval England*, 98-99.

forgiven of Christ than they have; for it is like that those Pharisees do less know themselves and their offences, whereby they less love God and so they be less forgiven"(Works, I.16).

The first *Sermon on the Cards* dealt a vision of Christian piety derived from the Sermon on the Mount and the Gospel narrative of Simon and Mary. Playing his final trump against proud prelates who were epitomized by Wolsey, Latimer rendered the wisdom and eloquence of Christ which, according to Erasmus, "Not only captivates the ear, but which leaves a lasting sting in the minds of its hearers, which grips, which transforms, which sends away a far different listener than it received."

The second *Sermon on the Cards* continued Latimer's call for a renewal of piety based on the rule of Christ. Beginning with two interrogatives, "Who art thou?" and "What doth Christ require of a Christian man?" he reminded his listeners of the cards each had been dealt in baptism: "By and by cast down your trump, your heart, and look first of one card, and then of another; thou shalt not kill, thou shalt not be angry . . ." (Works, I.21).

Asserting that faith in Christ requires obedience to the commandments, Latimer attacked excessive reliance upon voluntary works, claiming their demands had kept many from fulfilling their proper Christian duty. While acknowledging that voluntary works may accomplish much good, he declared them to be unnecessary for salvation.[118] He called instead for the revival of a scriptural way of life that had been obscured by ceremonies and exhibitions, and for the renewal of piety constituted by inward devotion to Christ, neighbor love, and works of mercy.

> Again, if you list to gild and paint Christ in your Churches, and honour him in vestments, see that before your eyes the poor people die not for lack of meat, drink, and clothing. Then do you deck the very true temple of God, and honour him in rich vestures that will never be worn, and so forth us yourselves according unto the commandments; and then, finally, set up your candles, and they will report what a glorious light remaineth in your hearts; for it is not fitting to see a dead man light candles. Then, I say, go your pilgrimages, build your material churches, do all your voluntary works; and they will then represent you unto God, and testify with you, that you have provided him a glorious place in your hearts" (Works, I.23-24).[119]

---

[118] For a discussion of the controversy over voluntary works see Davies, *Worship and Theology in England*, I.17-29; Alister McGrath, *Reformation Thought: An Introduction* (Oxford, 1993), 102-105; Doran and Durston, *Princes, Pastors, and People*, 13-17.

[119] Duffy provides a detailed description of late medieval Catholic practice in England. Duffy, *Stripping of the Altars*, 9-368; Christopher Haigh, *English Reformations*, 1-55; John A.F. Thomson, *The Early Tudor Church and Society: 1485-1529* (London, 1993), 187-212.

The *Sermons on the Cards* embodied the Erasmian conviction that scripture's message, when spiritually apprehended, is capable of rendering the word of Christ to instruct and convert eager, receptive listeners. Latimer articulated this view of scriptural authority in a letter to John Redman, conservative Master of Trinity College Cambridge, who, upon hearing the *Sermons on the Cards,* accused him of excessive certainty, arrogance, and conceit.[120]

> Reverend master Redman, it is even enough for me, that Christ's sheep hear no man's voice but Christ's; and as for you, you have no voice of Christ against me, whereas, for my part, I have a heart that is ready to hearken any voice of Christ that you can bring me. Thus fare you well, and trouble me no more from the talking with the Lord my God (Works, II.297.)

The *Sermons on the Cards* provoked a storm of protest, inciting "preachings and counter-preachings" within the Cambridge community, where many viewed Latimer as attacking the authority of the clergy and the unity of the church. Interestingly, the strongest opposition came from members of St. John's College, which was headed by John Fisher, Cambridge's most important patron of the "preaching life."[121] As the controversy continued to escalate, William Buckmaster, Vice-Chancellor of Cambridge, received a letter of reprimand from Edward Foxe, provost of King's, and a scholar as deeply involved in asserting the king's cause as Fisher was in defending the queen's. Desiring to communicate the king's interests more than declaring a halt to contentious preaching and divisive opinion, the provost hinted at the role Latimer would play in the Henrician drama of religious and political reform.

> It is not unlikely but that they of St. John's proceedeth of some private malice towards Master Latimer, and that also they be animated so to do so by their master, Master Watson, and such other of my Lord of Rochester's friends. Which malice peradventure cometh partly for that Master Latimer favoureth the king's cause; and I assure you it is so reported to the king.[122]

---

[120] For Redman's letter see, *Foxe, Actes and Monuments*, VII.435.

[121] Chester, *Hugh Latimer: Apostle to the English*, 46-54; Demaus, *Hugh Latimer: A Biography*, 86-90; Foxe, *Actes and Monuments*, vii.449-455. On Fisher's opposition to Henry's Divorce and the actions of Parliament, see J.J. Scarisbrick, "Fisher, Henry VIII, and the Reformation crisis," *Humanism, Reform and the Reformation*, 155-69.

[122] Lamb's Original Documents, etc. from Corpus Christi College, Cambridge, 14— cited in *Demaus, Hugh Latimer*, 88-89. See Wabuda's discussion of Erasmus' influence among evangelical preachers who became avid supporters of the Royal Supremacy, *Preaching During the English Reformation*, 91-99.

Chapter 2

The Henrician Reformation:
Making Room for the Word

> I would be ruled by God's book, and rather than I would dissent one jot from it, I
> would be torn with wild horses (Latimer, to Stephen Gardiner in 1539).

Latimer's controversial preaching at Cambridge quickly attracted attention
from the Royal Court.[1] In late 1530, after serving briefly as a court chaplain
and preacher around London, he was awarded the living of the West Kington
parish, just a short distance from Bristol. This appointment, made at Latimer's
request and with the patronage of Cromwell and Anne Boleyn, was bestowed in
recognition of his evangelical preaching and rigorous support of the "King's
Great Matter." In leaving his role as an academic evangelist, Latimer belonged
to a generation of university-trained clergy and scholars who moved out into
the realm of practical possibilities by the series of steps that turned England
towards a national church. Richard Rex observes: "It is arguable that the ideal
of a Christian community united in belief and worship before God, an ideal
pursued with such zeal by Protestant and Catholic Reformers alike, has never
been so closely approximated as in late medieval parish life."[2] Many viewed
England as fallow ground for spiritual revitalization and moral reform; they
shared a common desire to unite English society around the word of God, to
defeat superstition, to educate people, to improve priestly performance, and to
re-form a godly commonwealth under Henry VIII.[3] Wabuda writes, "Erasmus

---

[1] Chester, *Hugh Latimer*, 49-161; Demaus, *Latimer*, 80-352; Darby, *Hugh Latimer*, 42-166; Foxe, *Acts and Monuments*, vii.437-99.

[2] Richard Rex, *Henry VIII and the English Reformation*, 101. On the culture of conversion in early Tudor England see Peter Marshall, "English Conversion in the Reign of Henry VIII" in eds. Peter Marshall and Alec Ryrie, *The Beginnings of English Protestantism* (Cambridge, 2002), 84-110.

[3] Wooding, *Rethinking Catholicism in Reformation England*, 49-113; Peter Marshall and Alec Ryrie, "Introduction" in *The Beginnings of English Protestantism*. On pre-1530s activity of evangelicals see Dickens, *The English Reformation*, chapter 5; Clebsch, *England's Earliest Protestants*, 470-77; Hudson, *The Premature Reformation*, 409-17; Rupp, *The Making of the English Protestant Tradition*, 15-71. Here I follow the discussion by MacCulloch, *Thomas Cranmer*, 2-3, in using the word "evangelical" to describe the religious reformism that developed in England during the 1520s and 1530s, a religious outlook which makes the primary Christian point of reference the Good News, *evangelion*, or the text of scripture generally. The

new understanding of the homily and sermon was exploited most effectively by the evangelical reformers in promoting the royal supremacy, through establishing the king as the fixed arbiter of doctrine."[4] Moreover, as David Steinmetz comments,

> It is important to remember that the Reformation began as an intra-Catholic debate. All of the first generation of Protestant reformers and most of the second had been baptized and educated as Catholics. Their criticisms of the Catholic Church and its theology were based . . . on what they had experienced as children raised in traditionally Catholic homes and educated in traditionally Catholic schools.[5]

What eventually became two distinct churches in England—Catholic and Protestant—shared common roots in late medieval religion that were established by ecclesiastical and royal patronage. Both owed a great deal to the renewal of learning, especially in its Erasmian forms, and to its emphasis on returning to scripture and the early church for ecclesial authority and examples. While both parties desired similar pastoral ends driven by a single impulse—purification and reform within the Christian community—they were fired by different ways of imagining the shape of reformed Catholicity in Henrician England. On the one hand, conservatives who supported the royal supremacy expected that the king would use his authority to defend traditional faith. On the other, evangelicals expected Henry to continue to advance religious reform.[6]

The actions that moved the realm towards a more scripturally-based common life were potentially as much instruments of conformity and

---

terms "traditionalist" or "conservative" will not be used pejoratively, but rather to refer to mainstream English Catholicism. See the similar discussion in Davies, *A Religion of the Word*, 1-13. Here I have also benefitted from G.W. Bernard, *The King's Reformation: Henry VIII and the Remaking of the English Church* (New Haven and London, 2005), 236-91; Alec Ryrie, *The Gospel and Henry VIII: evangelicals in the early English Reformation* (Cambridge, 2003), 213-31.

4   Wabuda, *Preaching During the English Reformation*, 90.

5   David C. Steinmetz, "The Intellectual Appeal of the Reformation," *Theology Today*, 57.4 (January, 2001), 459.

6   Wooding, *Rethinking Catholicism in Reformation England*, 88-89. MacCulloch notes: "Humanist learning certainly led people to question the varied assumptions of medieval thought and to propose schemes of social, political, and religious reform, but this did not prevent English people interested in the humanist agenda from finding themselves on opposite sides in the struggles of the Reformation. Bishop Stephen Gardiner and Cardinal Pole can be seen as humanist scholars just as much their Protestant opponents like Cranmer, William Cecil or Sir John Cheke, the dominant academic at Cambridge University in the 1540s; the greatest English humanists of all had been the defenders of the old Church, Bishop John Fisher and Sir Thomas Moore." MacCulloch, *England's Later Reformation*, 56. See the discussion in Ryrie, "Counting sheep, counting shepherds: the problem of allegiance in the English Reformation."

uniformity as of dissent and diversity.[7] Ironically, this unsettling situation was in large part a consequence of Henry's desire to strike a balanced religious settlement that would provide stability within the realm. According to Cromwell, "the king leaned neither to right nor to the left hand." And as Henry lamented before Parliament in 1545, "that some be too stiff in their old Mumpsimus, and others too busy and curious in their new Sumpsimus."[8] The king's conservative inclinations led him to pour reforming motives and intentions into a mold, which still retained large amounts of traditional catholic structure, a strategy reflecting the humanist aim of cultivating new life within old forms and institutions.[9]

Increasing desire for biblically-inspired renewal quickly merged with political reform, making key the primacy of scripture in Henry's fight against papal authority. As Wooding concludes, "*Verbum Dei* was at the root of all his religious formulations."[10] Moreover, Henry's desire for a biblically justified vision of England freed from papal authority let loose a wave of preaching surrounding a single topic perhaps unparalleled in the history of the realm. In England, as on the continent, preaching to create a reformed Christian commonwealth proved central. It is true that England saw great deal of preaching on the eve of the Reformation by parish priests, cathedral preachers, monastic preachers, preaching friars, licensed preachers, preachers sent out from the universities, and preachers in collegiate churches and chantries. While much of this preaching may have been distasteful to the Reformers, there is good indication that in early Tudor England provision for preaching was plentiful and growing, providing readily available structures for mass communication.[11]

Wabuda's important study of preaching during the early English Reformation shows that homiletic practices during this period were characterized by both continuity and change. Prior to the sweeping reforms of the 1530s sermons at the parochial level were often regarded as an extension of the bidding prayer and prayers for the dead, which were supposed to help souls through their ordeal of purgatory. To protect orthodoxy, especially from the threat posed by Lollardy, sermons were heavily didactic and limited in scope, typically providing instruction in pastoralia: the Seven Deadly Sins, the Seven

---

[7] Rex, *Henry VIII and the English Reformation*, 105; Bernard, *The King's Reformation*, 277-82.

[8] Rex, *Henry VIII and the English Reformation*; MacCulloch, "Henry VIII and the Reform of the Church" in ed. MacCulloch, *The Reign of Henry VIII: Politics, Polity, and Piety* (New York, 1995), 175.

[9] Aidan Nichols, O.P., *The Panther and the Hind: A Theological History of Anglicanism* (Edinburgh, 1993), 8-10.

[10] Wooding, *Rethinking Catholicism in Reformation England*, 86-90.

[11] Rex, *Henry VIII and the English Reformation*, 29-30, 77-78; G.R. Elton, *Policy and Police: The Enforcement of the Reformation in the Age of Thomas Cromwell* (Cambridge, 1972), 171-216.

Virtues, basic doctrine, and the achievements of the saints. Even preaching by educated clergy was calculated to lead listeners to repentance and amendment of life within the established liturgical and devotional world prescribed by late medieval Catholicism.[12] Wabuda calls attention to the renewed importance Henrician reformers assigned to the role of preaching as a central means of purifying and rebuilding the church and disseminating official propaganda for obedience to the royal supremacy.[13]

Shedding light on these developments, this chapter discusses Latimer's role in the Henrician Reformation. It shows that while Latimer claimed to stand in continuity with classic Catholic orthodoxy, he was engaged in a prophetic protest for the evangelical renovation of deeply rooted convictions concerning the priesthood, preaching, and traditional Christian practices. Latimer's rhetoric was an expression of biblical humanism, rhetorical acts of pastoral imagination derived from scripture that aimed to challenge, and when necessary, to convert basic paradigms through which listeners perceived God, the church, and the clergy, and to rekindle zeal for evangelism and pastoral work.

When viewed from this perspective, the most important characteristic that emerges from Latimer's discourse is the manner in which his biblically shaped rhetoric probed deeply into the closed, presumed world of the late medieval church to challenge the authority and function of its clerical leaders. Such open language was pastoral in scope, since it aimed to purify and reform corrupt clergy and practices that had become obstacles to the word of Christ, thus making room for the cultivation of a scripturally inspired vision of the church and its salvation. This challenge required that Latimer present himself as possessing more credibility than his numerically superior conservative opponents; that his call to embrace religious innovation be sufficiently compelling to overturn familiar notions and loosen binding attachments. Yet to challenge the established church, its authority, and its leadership was no mean task, as Brigden notes, "For every Catholic the path to salvation was found only by following the teachings of the Church, and by receiving diving grace through the seven sacraments. None of the faithful could challenge the Church nor abandon its practices with consigning his immortal soul to eternal perdition."[14]

Latimer was particularly qualified for this challenge. Although he served as Bishop of Worcester from 1535-39, he saw himself primarily as prophet and

[12] Wabuda, "The Provision of Preaching During the Early English Reformation," 3-4.
[13] Wabuda, "The Provision of Preaching During the Early English Reformation," 99-107; idem, *Preaching During the English Reformation*, 99-105.
[14] Brigden, *London and the Reformation*, 12. See the discussion of doctrinal anticlericalism in David Loades, "Anticlericalism in the Church of England before 1558: an 'Eating Canker'" in ed. Nigel Aston and Matthew Cragoe, *Anticlerialism in Britain: c.1500-1914* (Thrupp, 2000), 8-11; Peter Marshall, "Evangelical conversion in the reign of Henry VIII" in ed. Peter Marshall and Alec Ryrie, *The Beginnings of English Protestantism* (Cambridge, 2002), 14-37.

evangelist, a practical visionary whose essential duty was to win souls and to contribute to the conversion of the whole nation to God. During the 1530s he emerged as the evangelicals' most prominent voice in pursuit of a primary aim, "to reconstruct religion out of the scriptural text of the Good News, the *euangelion*, and to return to the true spirit of Christ's Gospel, to the proposed Gospel shape of the church in its earliest generations."[15] The significance of preaching for the evangelicals' vision of personal and social reform cannot be overestimated, since they believed the future of the commonwealth depended upon the renovation of the church on a foundation laid by priests committed to speaking God's word in the "mother tongue." This conviction inevitably established as a leading priority the revival of the priesthood for the performance of preaching of which Latimer was the evangelicals' chief exemplar and advocate: "The towering figure among the early Reformers, exercising a preaching ministry whose contribution to the English Reformation is incalculable."[16]

Latimer's zeal for the practical realization of a biblically derived vision of church, its priesthood and people helps to account for his heavy reliance upon polemical discourse at a time when traditional religion continued to command loyalty from the realm's majority. Latimer's language reveals a bold presumption, although representing a minority position, that the dominant and habitual world of traditional religion could give way to the prophetic power of the preached word, thereby renewing religious and political arrangements in England. In attacking traditional religion, Latimer and his fellow evangelical preachers were not reluctant to use, amend, or capitalize on familiar medieval traditions of complaint and criticism, nor did they hesitate to radicalize the satire, ridicule, and irony of humanist literature.[17] In undermining papal authority, evangelicals focused on commonplaces of clergy corruption, ignorance, privilege, and greed, attacking priestly abuses of penance, confession, purgatory, relics, and images.[18]

Eamon Duffy describes this aspect of the English Reformation as the "stripping of the altars," a violent disruption in the late medieval symbolic and devotional world which enjoyed a diverse and vigorous hold over the imagination and loyalty of the English people.[19] Latimer sought to uproot this

---

[15] MacCulloch, "Henry VIII and the Reform of the Church," 168-69.

[16] Rex, *Henry VIII and the English Reformation*, 29-30,167; Wabuda, *Preaching During the English Reformation*, 99-105.

[17] Erik Rummel, "Monachatus Non Est Pietas" in ed. Hilmar Pabel, *Erasmus' Vision of the Church*, Sixteenth Century Journal Publishers Vol. xxxiii (Kirksville, 1995), 44.

[18] Owst, *Literature and Pulpit in Medieval England*, 210-86; Seymour Baker House "Literature, Drama and Politics" in ed. D. MacCulloch, *The Reign of Henry VIII*, 196-200; Loades, "Anticlericalism in the Church of England before 1558: an 'Eating Canker'?" 10; Ryrie, "Counting sheep, counting shepherds: the problem of allegiance in the English Reformation," 90-110.

[19] Duffy, *The Stripping of the Altars*, 4.

settled world with startling pronouncements of a prophetic God whose intrusive speech shatters false arrangements and demands new decisions, actions, and loyalties. Matheson comments on the rhetoric of reform: "it was no small thing to challenge the power of centuries-long ideas and values."[20]

Moreover, during the 1530s the Crown protected Latimer and other radical preachers in hope of mobilizing their evangelical rhetoric on behalf of the divorce and supremacy while official actions moved the realm towards the break with Rome.[21] The inspiration behind many of the changes was clearly evangelical and yet the changes themselves were not. As Block concludes, "Spiritual reformation rode in the shadow of political revolution."[22] In 1531 Henry VIII accused the entire English clergy of crimes against *Praemunire* by acquiescing in Wolsey's legatine authority, a move that prompted the Convocations to pass a motion recognizing the king's headship of the Church of England, "so far as the law of Christ allows." In 1532 Henry pressured the papacy by pushing through Parliament the "act in Restraint of Annates" which cut off the financial subsidy of the English Church to the Roman see. Its successor act, "in Restraint of Appeals," with its ideology of empire, offered in advance full theoretical justification of the eventual break from Rome, which would mark the dawning of a new era in England. Of particular importance for the protection and eventual promotion of evangelicals were key changes that occurred at the highest levels of leadership: Thomas More resigned his chancellorship, Thomas Cranmer was nominated to the see of Canterbury, Thomas Cromwell was promoted to succeed More, and Anne Boleyn used her influence at court to assist the evangelicals' cause.[23]

The following discussion of Latimer's correspondence from 1530-34 illumines his reformist activity during a time when evangelical preaching and literature were opposed by an anti-heretical campaign led by Thomas More and Stokesley, Bishop of London.[24] While Latimer's letters criticize traditional religion and its leadership, they may also be read as persuasive arguments that admonish readers to embrace a scripturally shaped renovation of the church, its priesthood, and its devotional life. Latimer wrote as a pastoral theologian, believing he was consciously engaged in the struggle against the powers of sin, evil, and the devil. His letters were means by which he sought to challenge, change, and form consciences, and to foster new faith and obedience to God's word. In depicting the ecclesiastical system as deviating from the teaching of scripture, deceiving the people, and distorting the practice of faith, Latimer sowed seeds of doubt to undermine the world of the late medieval church and

---

[20] Matheson, *The Rhetoric of the Reformation*, 3-6.

[21] Rex, *Henry VIII and the English Reformation*, 141-42.

[22] P.M. Block, *Factional Politics and the English Reformation: 1520-1540* (London, 1993), 4.

[23] John Guy, *Tudor England* (Oxford, 1988), 118-41; Block, *Factional Politics*, 50-58.

[24] Susan Brigden, *London and the Reformation* (Oxford, 1989), 179-89. Latimer's correspondence can be found in Hugh Latimer, *Works*, II.295-444.

to loosen the symbolic grip of its priestly guardians. The strangeness of this discourse was bound to disrupt both clergy and laity, since presumably they were bothered little by disenchantment, discontent, or the expectation for change. As recent scholarship convincingly demonstrates, the vulnerability of traditional religion owed less to its declining condition and more to a complacency born of success, to its habitual acceptance of old ways, and an unthinking presumption that its settled arrangements could continue indefinitely.[25]

The aim of Latimer's discourse was to expose the perceived vulnerability of late medieval religion to the prophetic insight of scripture, and to awaken his readers from complacency, challenging them to think and live in different ways. Deploying this tactic in a letter to Henry, Latimer urged for "restoring the free liberty of reading the holy scriptures" after Henry was advised that the provision of vernacular scripture would promote dissension in the realm, "to their [the people] further confusion and destruction than the edification of their souls."[26] As a participant in these discussions, Latimer joined Cranmer and Cromwell in upholding the minority point of view. In a letter that circulated freely among evangelicals, Latimer reiterated his commitment to an English Bible and reminded Henry of his promise to reconsider the project in the future: "But as concerning this matter, other men have shewed your grace their minds, how necessary it is to have the scripture in English" (Works, II.304). Writing with a strong conviction that the teaching of scripture, authorized by Christ and advanced by a godly prince, is the primary instrument for creating a Christian commonwealth, Latimer's letter demonstrates not only the weight evangelicals attached to the translation of scripture into the "mother tongue" but also displays Latimer's commitment to a biblical model of preaching based upon the example of Christ and the Apostles. In addition to the example of scripture itself, Latimer drew from the pastoral wisdom and authority of Augustine and Chrysostom, whose works affirmed priests' sacred responsibility to speak God's truth. By invoking such prominent preaching exemplars, Latimer utilized the past to criticize the present, hoping to convince Henry to acknowledge the corruption of the English clergy.

> But here mark their shameless boldness, which be not ashamed, contrary to Christ's doctrine, to gather figs of thorns and grapes of bushes, and to call light darkness, and darkness light, sweet sour, and sour sweet, good evil, and evil good, and to say that that which teacheth all obedience should cause dissension and

---

[25] J.J. Scarisbrick, *The English Reformation and the English People* (Oxford, 1984), 59-60; MacCulloch, "Henry the VIII and the Reform of the Church," 160; Marshall, "Evangelical Conversion in the reign of Henry VIII," 21-24.

[26] Foxe, *Acts and Monuments*, iv.677. See the discussion on the printing of the Bible in Andrew Pettegree, "Printing and the Reformation: the English exception" in ed. Marshall and Ryrie, *The Beginnings of English Protestantism* (Cambridge, 2002), 160-69.

strife. But such is their belly-wisdom, wherewith they judge and measure everything, to hold and keep still this wicked mammon, the goods of this world, which is their God, and hath so blinded the eyes of their hearts, that they cannot see the clear light of the sacred scripture, though they babble never so much of it (Works, II.297-98).

A key aspect of Latimer's strategy was to persuade Henry to see himself as God's instrument of reform, as a member of the mystical body of Christ who was charged with responsibility for preserving and keeping its lesser members. While God had called the king to his office of high majesty and regal power, he remained, "a mortal man, in danger of sinning, having the corrupt nature of Adam . . . in no less need of the merits of Christ's passion" (Works, II.309).

Latimer therefore urged Henry to consider Christ's ministry, Christ's words, and the message Christ sent his disciples to preach. Christ's golden rule, "the tree is known by the fruit," requires that true preachers be distinguished by their personal godliness, a commitment to preaching the truth of scripture, and a willingness to sacrifice and suffer for its message. These virtues were displayed by Christ, who was of humble lineage and without the goods, power, and treasures of the world. "It were to long to write how poor Joseph and the blessed Virgin Mary took their journey from Nazareth to Bethlehem, in the cold and frosty winter." Christ's poor beginning marked the means and goal of his human life, even though by his godly power he could have had all the goods and treasures of the world. His poverty of spirit, however, was foretold in the words of David, "If riches, promotions, and dignity happen to a man, let him not set his affiance, pleasure, trust, and heart upon them" (Works, II.300). Christ's true preachers are identified by participation in the suffering and rejection that accompany his message: "Lo, I send you forth as sheep among wolves." They are despised by worldly men, reputed as fools for their message, driven from town to town, until at the last, they lose both goods and life: "For where the word of God is preached, there is persecution . . . and where there is quietness and rest in worldly pleasure, there is not the truth" (Works, II.303).

Latimer advised that the wickedness of worldly men not prevent Henry from fulfilling his godly purpose. He warned that England's prelates were like the wicked counselors in I Samuel 10, whose worldly wisdom led to the destruction of the entire Amorite realm of Hammon, even though David sent his servants to advise him; however, it is Christ, the "right David," who has sent his true preachers to heal the weak, sick souls of England.

Only a few of Henry's servants favored the provision of vernacular scripture, and these were overruled by the action of the majority who, in Latimer's view, threatened the spiritual health of the realm: "For such is their manner to send a thousand men to hell, ere they send one to heaven." Latimer urged Henry to reconsider his previous judgment that prohibited books had caused insurrections and acts of disobedience; and that these troubles should rightly be attributed to the failure of curates to perform their duties. Just as the presence of

Christ was not the cause of the fall of Judas, neither should the scriptures be blamed for the evil, self-willed citizenship of England (Works, II.306-7).[27]

The letter concludes with an admonition for Henry to recall the story of King David, who once changed his mind by abandoning plans to construct a temple when Nathan announced God's displeasure: "He was not ashamed to revoke and eat his words." Assuming the role of the prophet Nathan to England's King David, Latimer expressed hope that Henry would continue to be a defender of his faith and a minister of his gifts, trusting in God to defend the faith by his power, "as all the stories of the Bible make mention" (Works, II.308).[28]

Latimer communicated by his speech what he preached with his pen. In early 1531 he was accused of spreading Protestantism, promoting vernacular scripture, and criticizing clergy who failed to preach and lead by moral example. He responded to these charges in a letter to William Hubberdine, an adherent of the old learning, by offering a persuasive account of scripture's power to engender new faith. According to Latimer, when the message of scripture is plainly spoken and humbly received it becomes the instrument by which the Spirit evokes faith in the presence of Christ, "the word of God that lasteth forever, and may sustain no change."

> For to begin withal; ye call the scripture the new learning, which I am sure is older than any learning which ye wot to be old. But if you will say, that it is not Scripture that ye call new, but other books lately put in English, I answer that Scripture was the first which you and your fautors condemned; besides that those other, for the most, teach nothing but that which is manifest in the Scripture and also plain in the ancient doctors. I speak not of your old doctors, Duns and St. Thomas, Halcot, Bright, and others, but Augustine, Jerome, Chyrsostom, Ambrose, Hilary, and such other, which, in like manner be called new doctors, as the scripture of new learning; as Tully, new Latin; as the text of Aristotle, new philosophy; and likewise of all sciences. And so this appeareth your first lie, that ye call the Scripture new doctrine; except that ye would call it new, either because it makes the receivers of it new men, or else that it was now newly received into the world (Works, II.318-9).[29]

---

[27] Here Latimer is presumably referring to the underground spread of prohibited literature during the 1520s by evangelicals, humanists, and Lollards. See Brigden, *London and the Reformation*, 82-128; Margaret Aston, *Lollards and Reformers: Images and Literacy in Late Medieval Religion*, chapters 5-7; Andrew Pettegree, "Printing and the Reformation: the English exception," 165-70; A.G. Dickens, *The English Reformation*, 46-105; Rupp, *The English Protestant Tradition*, 1-15.

[28] On the use of Old Testament Kings as models for Henry' self-image see King, *English Reformation Literature*, 161-76; Rex, *Henry VIII and the English Reformation*, 173, "If there was any consistency to the various policies which Henry imposed on his church, it is to be found in the image of kingship which he adopted together with the royal supremacy."

[29] On Latimer's use of Christian Antiquity see J.K. Yost, "The Christian Humanism of

Latimer declared that his "new" message was actually the familiar words of St. Paul, the word of scripture, the only rule of faith. Drawing a distinction made by Erasmus regarding the authority of church teaching and scripture as teacher, Latimer attributed the surprising effects of his sermons to the Spirit of Christ, the divine schoolmaster who enacts saving faith by the Word communicated through the words of preachers who are called, sent, and authorized.

> Faith is of hearing, and not of all manner of hearing, but of hearing the word of God: which faith, also, is the first fruit of the Spirit of God . . . which Spirit if we have, so beareth St. Paul that we be Christ's men . . . Which only is that which lay-people desire; utterly contemning all men's draughts, and all men's writings, how well learned they may be; only contented with their old and new schoolmaster, the Holy Spirit of God, and the minister thereto of him elect, and of him sent (Works, II.328-9).

Moreover, in the latter part of 1531, William Sherwood, a priest in residence near West Kington, charged Latimer with rash judgment and a lack of charity after hearing a sermon in which Latimer allegedly claimed that all bishops, popes, and ecclesiastics were thieves and robbers, "the hanging of whom all the hemp in England would hardly suffice." Latimer reportedly asserted that in the church were more goats than sheep; that it was hard to say where the true church was to be found; that whoever confessed, "Jesus is the Son of the living God" was Peter; and that Matthew 16 was the story of not only the pope and the priesthood, but of every Christian.

Latimer's letter to Sherwood, a conservative, reveals his fundamental disagreement with traditional religion concerning the nature of faith and, most importantly, the role of preaching for its cultivation. Latimer posed two questions: "Is confessing what the church believes sufficient when one does not know how the church believes?" and, "Is it sufficient for one to believe with the church, but without faith?" He answered,

> I affirm that a Christian, that is, a person received by baptism into the number of Christians, if he live not according to his profession, but yield himself up to the lusts of the flesh, is no more a Christian, as touching the inheriting of eternal life which is promised to Christ's people, than a Jew or a Turk; yea rather his condition at that day will be worse than the others', if ye allow that Peter spoke truly, 'It is better not to know the way of truth than having known it.' (Works, II.315).

Latimer viewed his remarks as a pastoral response to "false Christians" whose presence in the church was the consequence of clergy malpractice. Echoing the practical wisdom of Erasmian humanism, his aim was to provide instruction for living what is taught and professed in the church, since doctrine must be translated into life. Citing a homily by Augustine on I John, Latimer identified

---

the English Reformers" (PhD diss., Duke University, 1965), 265-99.

false Christians as anti-Christ and concluded: "It is the duty of a preacher to exhort his hearers, that they may be Christians after such sort, that suffering here together with Christ, they may reign with him in heaven; teaching them that to be otherwise a Christian is to be no Christian at all" (Works, II.317).

Latimer's preaching also provoked a storm of controversy in London, which had been the center of evangelical activity since the 1520s, since that city presented the largest concentration of people to be converted. As Brigden notes, "The faithful were fired and organized to proselytize, and they made London the storm center of their mission. To the reformers, preaching was the way whereby the Word might be illumined for the people, and though risk was acute, preach they did."[30] In 1531 Latimer preached at St. Mary Abchurch, invited by merchants on behalf of many people who were anxious to hear him: "They not only shewed themselves, but also many other, to be very desirous to hear me, pretending great hunger and thirst of the word of God and ghostly doctrine." Speaking from Romans 6:14, "For ye are not under the law, but under grace," he announced that holiness and righteousness were more pleasing to God and efficacious for salvation than pilgrimages, devotions to the saints, and the like. The most inflammatory points of Latimer's sermon were his attacks against bishops for their use of informants to prosecute cases of alleged heresies, and his assertion that, they should be guided by equity and charity rather than the law.[31] This was dangerous rhetoric, especially since Stokesley, Bishop of London, had recently intensified his campaign against heresy, leading to the burning of Thomas Bilney, Latimer's close friend from his Cambridge days.[32]

Latimer defended his Abchurch sermon in letters to Sir Edward Baynton, lord of the manor of Bromham, near West Kington, and Ann Boleyn's vice-chamberlain. The letters were presumably written to an evangelical sympathizer who corresponded with Latimer at the request of conservative clergy.[33] In the first letter Latimer justified his presence at Abchurch, invoking the authority of his license as a university preacher of the realm. He feigned surprise that such a busy prelate as Stokesley would be troubled by such an insignificant matter.

> I marvel not a little how my lord bishop of London, having so broad, wide, and large a diocese committed unto his cure, and so peopled as it is, can have leisure for preaching and teaching the word of God to his own flock . . . can have leisure either to trouble me, or to trouble himself with me, so poor a wretch, a stranger to him, and nothing pertaining to his cure (Works, II.325).

---

[30] Brigden, *London and the Reformation*, 111.
[31] Foxe, *Acts and Monuments*, vii.484-5; Chester, *Hugh Latimer*, 71-72; Demaus, *Latimer*, 126-27.
[32] Dunnan provides a relevant discussion of the relationship between Latimer and Bilney in "The Preaching of Hugh Latimer: A Reappraisal," chapter 4.
[33] Chester, *Hugh Latimer*, 75.

Latimer took refuge behind the text of scripture, surmising that if the Apostle had been heard by the Bishop of London, he too, "would have born a faggot at Paul's Cross for his heresy." The thought of such an occurrence prompted a sarcastic barb: "Oh! It had been a godly sight, to have seen St. Paul with a faggot on his back, even at Paul's Cross, my Lord of London, bishop of the same, sitting under the cross."

This imaginative encounter between the Apostle and the Bishop of London depicted Stokesley, a respected conservative scholar and defender of orthodoxy, but one who rarely preached, as an opponent of the gospel: "Me seems it were more comely for my lord to be a preacher himself, having so great a cure as he hath, than to be a disquieter and a troubler of preachers, and to preach nothing himself." Latimer ridiculed Stokesley for this failure, expressing desire that the bishop visit his [Latimer's] "little bishopric at West Kington. . . . For I have preached and teached but according to Holy Scripture, holy fathers, and ancient interpreters of the same, with the which I think my lord of London will be pacified." He concluded that both God and Stokesley would be pleased by his preaching, since it aimed to eliminate abuse from devotional practices and voluntary works (Works, II.330-33).[34]

Significantly, Latimer acknowledged that the disturbing message of the Abchurch sermon should be attributed to a change of mind affected by his return to "the three Ancient Creeds and the things of scripture." New learning, therefore, derived from familiar sources had inspired a transformation of understanding. While he once thought the pope to be lord of all the world, scripture had persuaded him otherwise; while he once believed the pope's dispensations to pluralities, benefices, and absences sufficed for the consciences of clergy, scripture had taught him otherwise; while he once thought the pope held authority over the status of those in purgatory and the large amounts of money bestowed that way, new learning had persuaded him otherwise; while he once thought that if he had become a friar and wore a cowl he would not be damned, he had come to abhor such superstition; while he once believed that images of saints had power to help him, this teaching no longer deceived him.[35]

According to Latimer, this change was the fruit of "continual prayer, continual study of scripture, and the communing with men of more right judgment, matters as weighty as my life is worthy." He expressed hope that God would strengthen him for the task of preaching and suffering for the

---

[34] On Stokesley's infrequent preaching, see Wabuda, "The Provision of Preaching in the Early English Reformation," 87.

[35] Yost emphasizes the role played by Christian humanism in Latimer's change of mind and the development of his thinking. Yost, "The Christian Humanism of the English Reformers," 265-300; Yost, "Hugh Latimer's Reform Program, 1529-36," *Anglican Theological Review*, 53 (1971), 103-14. On the use of scripture and the Fathers for theological authority during this period see Wooding, *Rethinking Catholicism in Reformation England*, 84-92; Ryrie "Evangelical Conversion," 30-33.

edification of listeners, and that Stokesley would amend his ways to join him: "I pray God that both he [Stokesley] and I may both discharge ourselves, he in his great cure, and I in my little, to God's pleasure and safety of our souls. Amen" (Works, II.334).

Baynton also reported in his letter that "certain friends" had called for Latimer to reform his manner of preaching since, "teaching which causeth dissension in a Christian congregation is not of God."[36] While making allowances for the word of God to create dissension among the unchristened, Baynton's conservative friends insisted that Latimer had stirred contention among Christians, thus breaking the bond of faith established through baptism.[37] They requested that Baynton urge Latimer to seek unity with both his words and behavior.

Latimer responded to what he characterized as, "false reports of a malignant church." He reasoned that if his words provoked objections, his objectors must be disposed towards foolishness rather than the wisdom of God. With a stroke of irony, he described himself as a "wretched fool," asserting that Baynton would do better to follow the teaching of his friends, "such great men as they appear to be." With an additional disclaimer, Latimer shrewdly excused himself from answering their objections, stating that his small cure kept him occupied with great business, but without the help of, "priest, scholar, or learned man" (Works, II.334-35).

Baynton had also communicated that some objected to excessive certainty in Latimer's preaching. Responding that God communicates truth through the certainty of faith, Latimer declared that his preaching was according to the measure given for his hearers' benefit. All preachers must "speak with certainty" or else they risk being perceived as doubtful and unsure. Christ's preachers speak simple wisdom to edify their people, rather than subtle, learned arguments that may cause them to "wander and to waver" in their faith.

> . . . as whether, if Adam had not sinned, we should have stockfish out of Iceland: how many larks for a penny, if every star in the elements were a flickering hobby: how many years a man shall lie in purgatory for one sin, if he buy not plenty of the oil that runneth over our lamps to slake the sin withal; and so forget hell, which cannot be slaked, to provide for purgatory (Works, II.338-39).

As an alternative to "learned" preaching, Latimer suggested that Baynton consider the simplicity of his [Latimer's] words, "true faith and fruits of the same, which be the good works of God." While denying that he preached to divide congregations, he acknowledged that certain views may be divisive: the opinions supporting Henry's "Great Matter," St. Paul's Epistle to the Galatians,

---

[36] According to Foxe's account Baynton wrote two letters to Latimer, Foxe, *Acts and Monuments*, vii.490; Chester, *Hugh Latimer*, 74-75.

[37] On the central importance of the social bonds of peace in the late medieval church, see John Bossy, *Christianity in the West: 1400-1700* (Oxford, 1985), 57-75.

the *Paraphrases* of Erasmus, and the writings of St. Jerome. Moreover, the message of faith and its capacity for bearing fruit is dependent upon not only the words of preachers, but also the faithful hearing of listeners. The word of God is neither heard nor works in congregations satisfied with their christened status; it requires a desire to hear God speak, Christian people committed to living into the promises of their baptism, "to renounce Satan, his works, his pomps" (Works, II.340-41).[38]

Citing the wisdom of the New Testament, Jerome, Chrysostom, and Augustine to support this line of argument, Latimer asserted that the unity of a Christian congregation is the fruit of faithful obedience, "that attendeth to the commandments." Divisiveness may actually be a signal that truth has been rejected, since many congregations are "rocked and locked" asleep by false prophets who confess Christ with their mouths but deny him with their acts, "wearing "satin, silk, and velvet." True prophets who speak the commandments of God, out of love for God, are to be distinguished from clergy characterized by, "rings, mitres, and rochets." With a final touch of irony, Latimer urged Baynton to refrain from repeating his criticisms lest they create dissension in a Christian congregation: "Jesu mercy . . . God make us all Christians after the right fashion!" (Works, II.349-51).

In 1532 Latimer was summoned by Stokesley to appear at St. Paul's, London to account for his divisive preaching. A commission comprising Archbishop Warham and Bishops Lee, Gardiner, and Fisher examined him for almost three months. After many sessions, the commission prepared sixteen articles on traditional religion for Latimer's subscription. He refused and received a sentence of excommunication from the Convocation of Clergy. Upon being placed in custody at Lambeth Palace, Latimer addressed a defiant letter to Archbishop Warham, excusing himself for declining to sign the articles and defending his preaching.[39]

Latimer insisted upon the distinction between an obligation to obey God's commandments and voluntary works, images, pilgrimage, praying to saints, and the remembrance of souls in purgatory. He pressed Warham to acknowledge that intolerable abuses existed throughout the church, and demanded that the bishop explain why preachers should be recommending works that cause the Christian religion to suffer loss. He went so far as to lament conditions in Warham's jurisdiction, including the prelate's silence regarding preachers who passed over abuses, and a failure to encourage those who dared to speak the doctrines of God. Concluding that his interrogators had acted unjustly, Latimer offered a brief apology for his preaching.

---

[38] Central to the message of Erasmus' *Enchiridion* was the efficacy of the sacrament of baptism for Christians to overcome the powers of sin, evil, and the devil, *CWE* 66:24-37.

[39] Chester, *Hugh Latimer*, 76-80; Foxe, *Acts and Monuments*, vii.456-58.

> If any man has any fault to object against my preaching, as being obscure or incautiously uttered, I am ready to explain my doctrine by further discourse: for I have never preached any thing contrary to the truth, nor contrary to the decrees of the fathers, nor, as far as I know, contrary to the catholic faith; all which I can prove to be true by the testimonies of my enemies and calumniators. I have desired, I own, and do desire, a reformation in the judgment of the vulgar (Works, II.355).

Latimer conceded that while voluntary works may be lawful, they require moderation to prevent abuse, to promote obedience to God's commandments, and to bring eternal life. He insisted that love of God is not displayed in zeal for voluntary works, but is truly displayed in keeping the words of Christ: "He that hath my commandments and doeth them, he it is that loveth me." In light of this dominical teaching, Latimer informed Warham, "I had rather that some things [devotional practices] were never done at all . . . which diminishes the regard to real duty" (Works, II.355).

Latimer was careful to emphasize the distinction between divine and ecclesiastical authority, a conviction shared by many who hoped for the overthrow of papal authority and the reform of church practices: "I cannot but be blameworthy, not to obey the fathers and leaders of the church. But it is their duty meantime to take care what, and to whom, they give commandment, since there are occasions in which we must obey God rather than men" (Works, II.356).[40]

To the surprise of many, Latimer received absolution three days later, with the provision that he confess to having preached indiscreetly, and that he subscribe to several moderate articles concerning consecrations and sanctifications, benedictions in the church, and preaching licensed by bishops. While waiting to sign these articles, he provoked more controversy by writing to Thomas Greenwood of St. John's, Cambridge, a conservative opponent from the days of the *Sermon on the Cards*. He informed Greenwood that any misbehavior by his listeners should not be attributed to his preaching, and that he would not change his message: ". . . and I will with all diligence, according to my promise in my *scriptis*, do all that is in me to reprove their infirmity" (Works, II.356-57). The matter was finally resolved on April 22, when an

---

[40] Erasmus wrote to Paul Volz in the *Prefatory Letter* to the *Enchiridion*, "Moreover, he who obeys a man who summons him to follow Christ obeys Christ and not man. And he who endures men who are all sham—cruel domineering men who teach not what makes for religion but as what bolsters their own tyranny—displays the patience of a Christian only as long as the commands they issue make him only unhappy and not ungodly too. Other wise, he will do better to meet them with the apostle's answer on his lips: 'We ought to obey God rather than men,'" *CWE* 66:23. On the issue of authority and obedience in the 1530s see Wooding, *Rethinking Catholicism in Reformation England*, 51-81; W. Bernard, "The Piety of Henry VIII" in ed. N. Scott Amos, A. Pettigree and H. van Nierop, *The Education of a Christian Society* (Aldershot, 1999), 63-66.

unexpected submission ordered by the king, was received from Latimer, enabling the bishops to publicly humiliate him.[41]

Although excommunicated by convocation in 1532 for speaking against purgatory, pilgrimages, and the intercession of saints, Latimer continued to enjoy the protection of the crown. In addition to voicing his continued support for Henry's divorce, his sermons became increasingly polemical in tone, attacking the sacerdotal status of the clergy and the traditional cult of saints, images, and purgatory. In 1533 his aggressive reformist preaching placed him at the center of conflict in Bristol.[42] Cranmer had already licensed Latimer to preach in his province, a decision the archbishop defended in a letter to Richard Sampson, conservative Dean of the Royal Chapel: "And whereas master Latymer, a man of singular learning, virtuous example of living, and sincere preaching of the word of God, hath lately been endangered, and suffered great obloquy; and also I myself, for justly licensing him to preach with the precincts and limits of my province, have been likewise misreported."[43] With Cranmer's backing, Latimer dared to preach more boldly than he had at Abchurch, using his license to gain access to pulpits throughout the region surrounding his West Kington parish.

During the season of Lent 1533, Latimer preached in Bristol at the invitation of clergy, merchants, and Mayor Clement Bays. Skeeter's research shows that a network of reform-minded sympathizers who contributed to the controversy supported Latimer. Several conservative clergymen joined together to preach against him in protest, including William Hubberdine, Edward Powell, and Friar John Hilsey, who eventually was converted by Latimer's evangelical message.[44] These opponents accused Latimer of speaking against purgatory, pilgrimages, veneration of saints, images, and the Virgin Mary. Strype's account of the controversy includes a letter from Richard Brown, a priest who registered his complaint with the chancellor of the diocese, Dr. Thomas Bagard, who was attending convocation. Brown accused Latimer of doing much damage and sowing much error among the "good Catholic people of Bristol," and of preaching opinions that were "fully against the determinations of the church."[45]

Brown's letter also reveals that a major point of attack against Latimer was aimed to challenge his authority to preach within his own diocese. Brown sent this letter to Bagard, chancellor to Bishop Ghinucci of Worcester, an absentee Italian prelate. After consulting with Cromwell and in light of Latimer's

---

[41] Chester, *Hugh Latimer*, 80-82.

[42] Chester, *Hugh Latimer*, 84-93; Elton, *Policy and Police*, 112-20; Wabuda, "The Provision of Preaching," 100-103; Martha C. Skeeters, *Community and Clergy: Bristol and the Reformation, 1533-1570* (Oxford, 1993), 38-46.

[43] Thomas Cranmer, *Writings*, 308-309.

[44] Richard Rex, "The friars in the English Reformation" in ed. Peter Marshall and Alec Ryrie, *The Beginnings of English Protestantism* (Cambridge, 2002), 46-54.

[45] John Strype, *Ecclesiastical Memorials* (Oxford, 1822) I.248-49.

previous submission, Bagard was permitted to inhibit all preachers without his own license. Reform-minded individuals in Bristol, including the mayor, merchants, and sympathetic clergy, rallied to Latimer's defense, registering their complaints against his conservative opponents. Cromwell responded favorably and induced Bagard to lift his inhibition against Latimer who, while continuing to preach around Bristol, collaborated with Cranmer to control pulpits in the region, promoting reformists and suppressing conservatives.[46]

In a letter to Ralph Morice, a fellow evangelical, Latimer claimed that his preaching at Bristol was according to Christ's word and for the purpose of remedying abuses and bringing glory to Christ. He concluded the ensuing conflict over his possession of a bishop's license, was created by jealous conservatives who wished to evade any malice they harbored against the truth. He admitted to claiming, "our Lady was a sinner," but added, "I did reason after this manner: that either she was a sinner, or no sinner." He determined, however, that because his opponents' malice was so great they would have reproved whatever he said or have belied him to say whatever they reproved. Responding to the charge that he taught, "saints are not to be worshipped," he accused his opponents of spreading falsehood, since he had shown a variety of meanings concerning saints, even defining them as, "laymen's books for remembrance of heavenly things" (Works, II.358-59).[47]

While he did not deny the practice of pilgrimage, he insisted that it must be properly performed, without superstition, idolatry, false faith, or trust in images or shrines. Moreover, pilgrimage must be kept in proper economic proportion so that debts are paid, restitution and provisions for wife and children made, and duty to poor neighbors discharged. As for his comments on the *Ave Maria,* Latimer protested, "Who can think that I would deny it?" But he drew a clear distinction between the *Pater Noster*, which was given by Christ, and the *Ave Maria*, a greeting to Mary, but not a prayer.

Concerning fire in hell, Latimer inquired, "Who could say or think so?" While acknowledging that he had challenged questions about its material properties, he announced that God's grace is able to set one free from its grip. Although he considered the teaching of purgatory to have brought thousands to hell, he stated he would rather be there "than in the Lollard's Tower, the bishop's prison, for divers skills and causes," since purgatory offers relief from moral responsibility, "and nothing there can break one's charity." As for purgatory,

> Debts have not been paid, restitution of evil-gotten lands and goods hath not been made, Christian people are neglected and suffered to perish; last wills unfulfilled and broken, God's ordinance set aside . . . Thus we have gone to hell with masses, dirges, and ringing of many a bell . . . If purgatory were purged of all that it hath

---

[46] Wabuda, "Provision of Preaching in the Early English Reformation," 100-103.
[47] On the use of images as laymen's books see King, *English Reformation Literature*, 39-40.

gotten by setting aside restitution and robbing of Christ, it would be but a poor purgatory, so poor, that is should not be able to feed so fat, trick up so many idle and slothful lubbers (Works, II.360-62).

Latimer's defense of his Bristol sermons reveals a theological course that dispels any doubts concerning his increasingly evangelical commitments. His sermons signaled a deepening dissatisfaction with the old religion and its resistance to change, plus a widening of the gap between himself and a broad Catholic consensus that was growing in support of the king's divorce. He affirmed that Christ had already taught Christians what to believe and how to believe to grant freedom from false faith and power for obedience to his commandments. He insisted that his preaching at Bristol had followed the clear, plain word of Christ in Romans, "We being justified by faith, have peace with God," and I John, "We know we are translated from death to life, because we love the brethren" (Works, II.364-65).

The establishment of Henry's royal supremacy in 1534 brought a dramatic increase in practice of the importance of the spoken word, set forth in the ideal of Erasmus, as an instrument for communicating change and commanding obedience within the realm.[48] This royal "rhetoric of obedience" was anticipated in 1533 when Richard Sampson, Dean of the Royal Chapel, published an oration that vindicated Henry and confuted the doctrine of papal power.

> A king is appointed for the punishment of evildoers, and for the prayse of the good; whom he regardeth, defendeth, advanceth . . . This power hath he of God. The matter is playne enough. The Scriptures are evident: for it is the Word of God, which teacheth us to obey this power. It exempeth no man in this world. Wither is there found in holy scripture one jote or tittle that maketh free any disobedient and wicked person from the power of the king.[49]

The word of God became the basis not only for the supremacy itself, but also for the paramount duty of Christian obedience which subjects owed their king. As Sampson affirmed, "The word of God is obedience to the king rather than the pope." Strype reveals the stark contrast, which was perceived between papal and royal authority.

> The Pope was now reckoned among many as Anti-Christ, for the opposition he made by his creatures to the Gospel, and for overthrowing the laws of it by his dispensations and traditions, and for his pride and affectation of superiority over all Princes and Bishops throughout the world.[50]

Following the act of parliament that gave the supremacy to the king, Henry immediately sent letters to every bishop, requiring that they "preach the sincere

---

[48]   Wabuda, *Preaching During the English Reformation*, 92-99.
[49]   Strype, *Ecclesiastical Memorials*, I.238-39.
[50]   Strype, *Ecclesiastical Memorials*, I.240. On the increasing use of a rhetoric of obedience see Rex, *Henry VIII and the English Reformation*, 25-26.

word of God; and to declare that this style and title of supreme head belonged to the crown and dignity of this realm." Detailed directions soon followed that supported Henry's divorce and the imposition of the royal supremacy.[51]

One of the earliest and most influential of the Henrician efforts to provide material for the nation's pulpits was the Bidding Prayer of 1534, a document written by Cranmer and other bishops who hoped to accomplish change by utilizing a familiar liturgical form. All preachers were to pray for Henry as the supreme head of the Catholic Church of England, Queen Anne his wife, and Princess Elizabeth, daughter and heir to both. All preachers (except those in court) were to pray for the clergy and temporality, and for the souls of the dead. Cranmer also ordered that clergymen must preach once to their greatest audience "against the usurped power of the bishop of Rome." Attempting to prevent political dissent and hinting that no doctrinal issues were to be reviewed, Cranmer mandated that for one year no clergyman should preach on purgatory, priestly marriage, justification by faith, pilgrimages, or forged miracles. Instead, they were to "purely, sincerely, and justly preach the scripture and word of Christ, and not mix them with men's institutions." They must not preach that any man had the power to dispense God's law. Furthermore, where Henry's divorce had been detracted, all preachers were to declare the justness of Henry's second marriage, "as nigh as their learning can serve them," from the articles provided for their use.[52]

Cranmer needed preachers to declare the king's supremacy, to support his divorce from Catherine, and to advance the cause of reform. His extensive influence enabled him to license and promote sympathetic clergymen to benefices and to appoint reformist preachers to strategic pulpits within the whole province of Canterbury, including his own diocese.[53] By virtue of the *Act of the Exoneration from Exactions Paid to the See of Rome*, passed in 1534, the Archbishop of Canterbury was empowered to grant dispensations that had been previously issued by the Papal Curia. A special archepiscopal court was established, the Faculty Office, which was granted the concession of licensing preachers to speak throughout the realm, even in the northern province.[54]

Cranmer denied that his sermons or those of his licensees were neither heretical nor opposed to orthodox doctrine and practice. He argued instead in favor of reformation or alteration of abuses in the church. An urgent need for preachers to advance support for the supremacy caused the regime to protect some who held views, which under other circumstances, might have been seen

---

[51] In this section I have followed Wabuda, "Provision of Preaching," 29-82; idem, *Preaching During the English Reformation*, 54-55, 93; Elton, *Policy and Police*, 217-61; Block, *Factional Politics*, 33-106.
[52] Cranmer, *Writings*, 460-62; Wabuda, "Provision of Preaching," 33-34.
[53] Block, *Factional Politics*, 50-58.
[54] Wabuda, "Archbishop Cranmer's Early Patronage of Preachers" in ed. Paul Ayris and David Selwyn, *Thomas Cranmer: Churchman and Scholar* (Woodbridge, 1993), 76-77.

as falling outside acceptable bounds.[55] Circumstances were changed in early 1534 with the passage of the *Act for Punishment of Heresy*, the first Reformation statute concerned with preaching in the entire realm. The act argued that canon law denied Henry jurisdiction in his own realm while sweeping away some of the canonical foundations of heresy law. In addition, the *Act for the Submission of the Clergy* put canon law and Convocation under Henry's control.[56]

Cranmer presumably was aware of the potential for harm to the evangelical cause when he appointed Latimer to preach at court on the Wednesdays of Lent, 1534. The archbishop corresponded with Sampson, Dean of the Royal Chapel, who was to make the arrangements. Despite his enthusiastic oration in support of the king in the previous year, Sampson, a conservative, was deeply suspicious of Latimer's evangelical rhetoric, as his response reveals.

> I favour him in my mind for his learning. I pray God it may be moderate. The signs are not most pleasant, since that his teaching moveth no little dissension among the people wheresoever he cometh, the which is either a token of new doctrine or else negligence in not expressing of his mind more clearly to the people.[57]

Cranmer therefore sent a long letter to Latimer, admonishing him to expound the gospel, the epistle, or some other passage of scripture according to its true sense and meaning. He was to make no mention of his controversial past nor was he to discuss those issues. He also was to be moderate in his manner of speech so he would not slander opponents. Finally, Cranmer ordered Latimer to limit his sermons to an hour or hour and a half, lest the king and queen grow weary. He even invited Latimer to London before Ash Wednesday in order to monitor the sermons in advance.[58]

The Lenten preaching went well enough; Henry appointed Latimer to the position of court chaplain at the urging of Cromwell and Dr. Butts, the Royal Physician. Strype states that Latimer was "often put up to preach before the king," speaking boldly at court and throughout London, and recommending reformist preachers for licensing. After a particular court sermon evoked accusations of seditious preaching, Latimer responded in a typically straightforward manner: "What form of preaching would you appoint me to preach before a king?" According to Strype, Latimer spoke plainly to Henry concerning the care and feeding of the king's horses at several abbeys, criticizing his practice on moral grounds since the revenues used to care for the horses should have been used to comfort the poor. When challenged by a nobleman for speaking against the king's honor, Latimer presumably replied,

---

[55] McCulloch, *Cranmer*, 124-35.
[56] Wabuda, "The Provision of Preaching" 32-33.
[57] *LP:* vii.32 cited in Block, *Factional Politics*, 54.
[58] Cranmer, *Writings*, 297-98.

"that God hath appointed a sufficient living (Henry's) for his state and degree, both lands and other customs. But to extort and take away the right of the poor is against the king's honor."[59]

Cranmer also sought Latimer's assistance for the supervision of preachers. Since the archbishop had not yet issued provincial injunctions for preaching, Latimer was awarded a commission to visit all preachers licensed by Cranmer and, to be certain "they should neither preach any thing which might seem prejudicial to the said matrimony, whereby the king's issue might come into question or doubt amongst vulgar people, nor likewise reprehend in their sermons any such ordinances, act, or statutes, heretofore made, or by the said high court of parliament hereafter to be ordained."[60] To accomplish this task Cranmer delegated the responsibility for administering injunctions to Latimer: "I will that you for my discharge therein, in my name and for my behalf, do take upon you the administration of these said injunctions for all such as hath already had or hereafter shall have my license to preach at your said request and instance.[61]

In 1535 Latimer's evangelical preaching, his support for Henry's divorce and supremacy, and patronage of Anne Boleyn and Cromwell, were key factors in his nomination for the episcopacy.[62] Wabuda has demonstrated that bishops did not preach frequently prior to the establishment of the royal supremacy, with Fisher of Rochester and Longland of Lincoln being notable exceptions. Latimer's election to the see of Worcester, which positioned him to become the evangelicals' model of a preaching bishop, coincided with the execution of Fisher, England's exemplary preaching prelate for more than 30 years.[63]

As the most prominent preacher of the Henrician Reformation, Latimer was a participant within a larger drama envisaged by Cromwell, its chief political and lay religious broker, and Cranmer, its chief pastor.[64] Together, they placed unprecedented emphasis on the duty of bishops to preach and to promote preaching, since the primary challenge for the "imperial kingship" and its official program was whether it would be accepted in the localities. To this end, Cromwell launched and sponsored a media and preaching campaign that recognized the pulpit first, and then the press.[65] In June 1535 Cromwell sent a

---

[59] Strype, *Ecclesiastical Memorials*, I.261-63; Chester, *Hugh Latimer*, 100.

[60] Cranmer, *Writings*, 308-309.

[61] Cranmer, *Writings*, 297.

[62] Chester, *Hugh Latimer*, 103-105; MacCulloch, "Henry VIII and the Reform of the Church," 169-71; E.W. Ives, *Anne Boleyn* (Oxford, 1986), 310-11; Bernard, *The King's Reformation*, 279-91.

[63] Wabuda, "Provision of Preaching in the English Reformation," 104-12; Kenneth Carlton, *Bishops and Reform in the English Church, 1520-1559* (Woodbridge, 2001), 82-88.

[64] Wabuda, "Provision of Preaching in the Early English Reformation," 29-46; Elton, *Policy and Police*, 171-216.

[65] See the discussion of Cromwell in Block, *Factional Politics*, 59-106.

circular letter in the name of the king to the bishops of England and Wales concerning the imposition of the supremacy. Elton concludes that the circular letter marked the foundation of the policy, which would characterize the remainder of the reign, during which the government continually intervened to tell clergymen what to preach.[66] No longer was the archbishop the main channel of instruction, but rather the lay vicegerent was, acting for the king. As vicegerent, vicar general, and special commissary to the king, Cromwell held in his own right virtually unlimited jurisdiction in ecclesiastical affairs. As long as he continued to enjoy Henry's favor, Cromwell, personally, possessed,

> . . . full power and authority from time to time to visit, repress, redress, reform, order, correct, restrain, and amend all such errors, heresies, abuses, offenses, contempt's, and enormities, whatsoever they be, which by any manner spiritual authority or jurisdiction ought or may lawfully be reformed, repressed, ordered, redressed, corrected, restrained, or amended, most to the pleasure of Almighty God, the increase of virtue in Christ's religion, and for the conservancy of peace, unity, tranquility of this realm: any usage, custom, foreign laws, foreign authority, prescription, or any other thing or things to the contrary hereof notwithstanding.[67]

Cromwell's circular ordered the bishops to preach the sincere word of God and the king's title of supreme head on every Sunday and high feast through the year. The frequency with which the clergy were now expected to preach was an innovation, as canon law had specified quarterly sermons, though some clergy had indeed preached more often. The bishops were to charge, "abbots, priors, deans, archdeacons, provosts, parsons, vicars, curates, and all other ecclesiastical persons" to preach the royal supremacy in all churches on Sundays and feast days, and to command all schoolmasters to teach the same to their students. Prayers mentioning the bishop of Rome were to be erased out of mass-books and other books used in churches. The circular was restated in a printed order to sheriffs and justices of the peace on 9 June. It was treated as a proclamation in London, where it was written into episcopal register. At Michalemas, Henry sent for the bishops at Winchester, and reiterated the June circular. He ordered them to go to their dioceses to preach the royal supremacy and explain why the bishop of Rome had been excluded from his jurisdiction in England.[68]

From 1535-38, when the evangelical cause enjoyed its greatest advances, Cromwell was a driving force for change, bestowing his favor upon reformers who emphasized living faith, the primacy of the Bible, and the high value of preaching the word. He made his stand against conservative opponents by

---

[66] The circular has not survived, but Elton has summarized its content from responses by recipients and a later circular to lay authorities. Elton, *Policy and Police*, 231-35, 239-40. See Elton's discussion of Cromwell's policy of persuasion, 231-62.

[67] *English Historical Documents*, ed. C.H. Williams (London, 1967), 746.

[68] Elton, *Policy and Police*, 231-35; Wabuda, "Provision of Preaching," 35-36; Cranmer, *Writings*, 325-28.

placing the authority of the Bible against objectionable aspects of traditional teaching and devotional practices. Moreover, he actively pursued possible avenues of accommodation with the Lutherans until Henry would have no more.[69] However, Cromwell's most important contribution to reform was overcoming the resistance of conservatives against the printing and distribution of an official English Bible.[70] As architect of policy and a patron of church officials, Cromwell's actions evinced his concern for the spiritual welfare of ordinary people. He blended articles, letters, injunctions, patronage, and the creation of a new ecclesiastical office in an attempt to address parochial needs and rally support to further reform of church and commonwealth.[71]

Cromwell also used his influence over episcopal appointments and licenses to ensure the preference of reformers since, as vicegerent of spirituals; he possessed the power to issue injunctions to all the bishops and clergy, and to enforce them at visitations. His first injunctions in 1536 ordered clergy to defend the royal supremacy in sermons; to teach children the Lord's Prayer, Ten Commandments, and other articles of faith out of scripture; to abandon pilgrimages, to keep chancels in good repair, and to give money for educational purposes. His injunctions in 1538 went further by encouraging moderate iconoclasm and by reviling rituals and beliefs not justified by scripture. Cromwell ordered images that were objects of pilgrimage or superstitious veneration to be stripped from churches on the grounds of idolatry; prohibited the burning of candles for saints and the dead; recognized the Bible as the chief authority for faith, requiring an English translation to be placed in every parish; and instituted registers to record baptisms, marriages, and burials in every parish to reduce disputes over descent and inheritance.[72]

The two formularies of faith issued during Cromwell's vicegerency, the *Ten Articles* (1536), and the *Institution of a Christian Man*, or the *Bishop's Book* (1537) embraced assumptions and forms of Lutheranism, but not their conclusions.[73] These attempted to strike a theological balance that would be acceptable to Henry, who in his desire to maintain unity and agreement in the church made concessions to both conservatives and evangelicals. Since a progressive and reforming intention combined with unequivocally Catholic doctrine, these statements could be interpreted as signaling either a forward or backward direction for the realm. Significantly, while these formulations sought reform and renewal without challenging accepted Catholic beliefs, they

[69] Rupp, *The English Protestant Tradition*, 89-127.
[70] Guy, *Tudor England*, 178-210; Guy, "Thomas Wolsey, Thomas Cromwell and the Reform of Henrician Government," 13-34; Elton, *Reform and Reformation*, 273-95.
[71] Block, *Factional Politics*, 107-108.
[72] Wabuda, "Provision of Preaching," 39-40; idem, *Preaching During the English Reformation*, 99-102; Rex, *Henry VIII and the English Reformation*, 91-92.
[73] Alec Ryrie, "The Strange Death of Lutheran England" in *JEH* 53.1 (January, 2002), 64-68. Ryrie refers to the Henrician reforms as "Lutheranism without justification."

defended accepted practices on the basis of scripture rather than tradition.[74]

More importantly, these formulations introduced a new idea: the issuing of official sermons or homilies that could be read to guide the beliefs of the nation. Each of the *Ten Articles* contains the formula, "We will that all bishops and preachers shall instruct and teach . . ." While each article in the *Bishop's Book* asserts, "We think it convenient that all bishops and preachers shall instruct and teach the people committed unto their spiritual charge."[75] The ambivalence of the two doctrinal formulations invited a diversity of interpretations in addition to an increase of preaching, a situation that presented Cromwell with the challenge of maintaining stability while advancing reform. It was plain that by the mid-1530s England was neither moving in an evangelical direction nor holding fast to its traditional orthodoxy, a situation that undoubtedly pleased Henry.[76] However, the slow pace of reform tested the patience of Latimer who had hoped to tip the balance towards further and faster change. He expressed his exasperation to Cromwell following the protracted wrangling of 1537 that produced the *Bishop's Book*.

> For verily, for my part, I had liever be poor parson of West Kington again, than to continue thus Bishop of Worcester . . . Forsooth it is a troublous thing to agree upon a doctrine in things of such controversy, with judgments of such diversity, every man (I trust) meaning well, and yet not all meaning one way (Works, II.379-80).

Although Cranmer assumed what may be described as a secondary role to Cromwell in guiding the evangelical campaign, he proved effective in utilizing his authority for licensing and imposing reformist preachers, especially in the diocese of London and at Paul's Cross. With the backing of Cromwell and the assistance of Hilsey, who succeeded Fisher as Bishop of Rochester in 1535, Cranmer undermined Stokesley's authority to gain control of the strategically important pulpit. During early 1536, on seven consecutive Sundays Cranmer, Hilsey, Longland, Tunstall, Shaxton, Salcot, and Latimer, a mixture of conservatives and evangelicals, all preached against papal supremacy and in favor of the royal supremacy. While maintaining a balance of perspectives among these preachers, Cranmer was actually setting the stage for post-papal orthodoxy which he hoped would come to fruition through negotiations with the Lutherans.[77] As Elton notes, "From the point of view of propaganda and persuasion, the only pulpit that really mattered was that at the Cross outside of St. Paul's."[78]

---

[74] Wooding, *Rethinking Catholicism in Reformation England*, 63-67.
[75] Wabuda, "Provision of Preaching," 37-39.
[76] MacCulloch, "Henry VIII and the Reform of the Church," 174-75.
[77] Neelak Tjernagel provides a detailed account of the negotiations in *Henry VIII and the Lutherans* (Saint Louis, 1965), 34-107.
[78] Elton, *Policy and Police*, 213-16; Wabuda, "Provision of Preaching in the Early English Reformation," 115-27; idem, *Preaching During the English Reformation*, 40-

A chronicler's report of Latimer's Paul's Cross sermon on March 12, 1536 shows how far Cranmer was willing to allow his preachers to go to prepare for the planned dissolution of the monasteries. Latimer repeated his polemic against the abuses of traditional religion, the corruption of clergy and monks, and added a qualification that some might be redeemable for preaching in the new church under construction.

> He saide that byshopis, abbatis, prioris, parsonis, canonis resident, prisits, and all, were stronge thevis, ye dukis, lordis, and all; the kyng, quod he, made a marvelles good acte of parliament that certayne men sholde sowe every of them ij acres of hempe, but it were allto litle, were it so moche more, to hane the thevis that be in England. Byshopis, abbatis, with soche other, shold not have so many servauntes, nor so many dysshes, but to god their first foundacion, and kepe hospitalytie to fede the nedye people, noe jolye felowis with goldyn chaynes and velvet gownes, ne let theym not onis come to the owis of religion for repase; let theym call knave byshope, knave abbat, knave prior, ye fede non of theym all, nor their horses nor dogges, nor yet sett men at lybertye; also eat fleshe and whit mete in Lent, so that it be don without huryng of weke consciences, and without sedition, and lykewise on Fridays and all dayes . . . The byshope of Canterbury seythe that the kingis grace is at a full poynte for fryers and chauntry pristis, that they shall swaye all that, savyng tho that can preche.[79]

The evangelicals intensified their efforts in June 1536 when Cranmer appointed Latimer to deliver the keynote address to convocation, and where Cromwell, a layman, was appointed to preside over the clergy as vicegerent of spirituals. Many of the conservative clergy who assembled at St. Paul's must have been outraged since, four years earlier, their preacher for the day had been tried for heresy and humiliated before a bishops' committee of Convocation.[80] Among these was Stokesley, who opened the proceedings by celebrating the mass.[81] Conservatives had been heartened in the spring by the fall of Anne Boleyn, a leading patron of evangelicals, and the news that Convocation would address problems created by doctrinal innovation. Some conservatives had even begun to talk of reconciliation with Rome after the death of Catherine of Aragon earlier that year.[82]

48, on Latimer, 130-37; MacCulloch, *Thomas Cranmer*, 150-52; Millar Maclure, *The Paul's Cross Sermons: 1534-1642* (Toronto, 1958); McRae, *God speed the plough*, 28-29.

[79] Maclure, *The Paul's Cross Sermons*, 27.

[80] Rex, *Henry VIII and the English Reformation*, 145-47.

[81] On Cranmer's promotion of Latimer see Susan Wabuda, "Setting forth the Word of God: Archbishop Cranmer's early patronage of preachers," 75-82; idem, "Bishops and Homilies: 1520-1546" in *Sixteenth Century Journal* XXV.3 (1994), 551-66; Joseph Block, "Thomas Cromwell's Patronage of Preaching" in *Sixteenth Century Journal* VIII.1 (1997), 37-50.

[82] MacCulloch, *Thomas Cranmer*, 159-60.

Latimer's powerful performance at Convocation must have confused these signals; his two-act sermon articulated the ambitious reform agenda envisaged by Cromwell and Cranmer, and summoned the clergy to make sweeping changes in the religious system the majority hoped to preserve. While Latimer's invective against clergy was intensified by his elevated view of priestly importance, his singular focus on their failures as spiritual leaders betrayed an anticlericalism that aimed to relativize their presumed status and function. Brigden calls this the true anticlericalism, the antisacerdotalism of heresy, denying the essential place and function of the clergy who, in Latimer's view, had usurped the place of preaching and God's word in salvation.[83]

Latimer began the *First Sermon Before the Convocation of Clergy* in a diplomatic tone. His *exordium* alerted the audience to the gravity of the occasion, his obligations as speaker, and his unworthiness to stand before them. He announced that his remarks would be base upon a notable sentence of Christ: "The children of this world be more prudent and politic than the children of light in their generation." In addition, he would speak with fear, trusting Christ to guide his use of words.

While acknowledging such a learned group should require no additional instruction, Latimer expressed hope they would join him in marveling at Christ and the relevance of his words. He asked that they define three things: "What prudence is; what the world; what light; and who be the children of the world; who of light: and what they signify in Scripture." The sermon theme, "I marvel if by and by ye all agree, that the children of the world should be wiser than the children of the light," would be developed by means of Luke 16, the *Parable of the Rich Man and his Unjust Steward* (Works, I.34).

Latimer's exposition of the parable enacted the sermon theme: "Brethren, because these words are so spoken in a parable, that yet they seem to have a face and a similitude of a thing done indeed, and like an history, I think it much profitable to tarry some what in them" (Works, I.35). His purpose was to invite the clergy into the parable to recognize themselves as the unjust stewards Christ was calling to repentance.

> For if ye inwardly behold these words, if ye diligently roll them in your minds, and after explicate them and open them, ye shall see our time much touched in these mysteries. Ye shall perceive that God by this example shaketh us by the noses and pulleth us by our ears. Ye shall perceive very plain, that God sitteth before our eyes in this similitude what we ought to flee, and what we ought soonest to follow" (Works, I.34-35).

Latimer portrayed Christ as the rich man speaking to the clergy, as the good man of his house, the church. The clergy were his vicars; his word and sacraments were gifts that should be fed diligently to his people. They were

---

[83] Brigden, *London and the Reformation*, 67-68; see the discussion of anticlericalism in Marshall, *The Catholic Priesthood and the English Reformation*, 232-36.

called to examine themselves in light of Christ's generosity, the richness of his mercy, the abundance of his gifts, and the treasure of his blessings.

> But, I pray you, what is to be looked for in a dispenser? That he be found faithful, and that he truly dispense, and lay out the goods of the Lord . . . that he give meat in time; and not sell it; meat I say, and not poison . . . This is to be looked for, that he be one of whom God hath called and put in office, and not one that cometh uncalled, unsent for; not one that of himself presumeth to take honor upon him (Works, I.35).

With this assertion, Latimer probed deeper to inquire, "Who is a true and faithful steward? I pray you, ponder and examine this well, whether our bishops and abbots; prelates and curates, have been hitherto faithful stewards or no? Go ye to tell me how your conscience leadeth you" (Works, I.36). He confronted the clergy with evidence that sounded an alarm sufficient for their heeding: the word of God was adulterated like minting counterfeit coin and mingled with the words of men; there was false teaching about Christ; forgiveness was purchased with money; costly images were being worshipped; will works were being taught rather than the works of mercy; and the ambiguous, doubtful nature of the doctrine of purgatory was dispensed by false dissipaters (Works, I.37). Most significantly, the true image of Christ, seen in the hungry, the cold, the homeless, and the poor, was neglected.

The English clergy were portrayed as the unjust stewards to whom Christ was speaking: "Thus the evil is much better set out by evil men, than the good by good men; because the evil be more wise than the good in their generation" (Works, I.38). Latimer announced God's judgment against their unfaithfulness, immorality, and arrogance. "What is this I hear of you? . . . Oh, what do I hear from you?" He accused the clergy of failing to preach, voicing contempt for priests who neither taught scripture nor cared that it was understood. He acknowledged that while many were politically astute and aligned themselves with Henry's supremacy, God's expectation for them was to lead the realm toward religious reform: "Have ye thus deceived me, or have ye deceived yourselves" (Works, I.39)?

Latimer's polemic created an imaginative courtroom scene to place the defenders of traditional religion on trial for ingratitude, abuse, and deception. He declared their failure to act faithfully was the source of Christ's displeasure; that Christ's word and sacraments offered sufficient evidence for their judgment and damnation. Revealing that his purpose was to paint a vivid image of Christ in his listeners' minds, Latimer summoned the clergy to repent: "Come forth then, let us see an account of your stewardship. A horrible and fearful sentence; ye may no longer have my goods in your hands. A voice to weep at, and to make men tremble!"(Works, I.39). He concluded with a call to pray for his words, to seek God in the Lord's Prayer, and to intercede on behalf of the king, the clergy, the laity, and the dead (Works, I.40).[84]

During the afternoon session Latimer continued his call to repentance with a vivid depiction of particular clerical vices: "Nay this grieved Christ that the children of this world should be of more policy than the children of light; which thing was true in Christ's time, and now in our time is most true" (Works, I.41). The children of darkness persecute the children of light, they are wise in the ways of politics, but they wreak hurt and harm like their father, the Devil (Works, I.42). A familiar proverb, "an evil crow, an evil egg," attributed these traits to the serpent who begets lyings, deceits, perjuries, discords, and manslaughters. This is the fecundity of the Devil, their mother World, Discord, and her children: Lady Pride, Dame Gluttony, Mistress Avarice, Lady Lechery, Dame Subtlety and Hypocrisy. According to Latimer, even the Devil's children are present, "in courts, cowls, cloisters and rochets." They are good, obedient children, "how religious, how mocking, how monking"(Works, I.44).[85]

The traditional dispositions shared by the majority of the clergy required Latimer's strong polemic to provoke their self-examination: "Had it not been better we had not been called together at all? For as the children of this world be so evil, so they breed and bring forth things evil; and yet the more there be of them in all places, or at least they be more politic than the children of light in their generation" (Works, I.45). He challenged the wisdom of their actions during the previous seven years, mocking them as "great fathers" whose "great acts" were to burn a dead man's body for heresy, and who apprehended a good man, "raked over the coals" for failing to subscribe to articles denying the supremacy of the king. Latimer thus urged the clergy to examine their actions in light of divine judgment: "What one is put forth, whereby Christ is more glorified, or else Christ's people made more holy?"(Works, I.46).

Speaking by means of stark antitheses, Latimer depicted the children of light and the children of darkness: the offspring of light work simply, faithfully, and plainly; the children of darkness have worldly policy, foxly craft, lion-like cruelty, power to do hurt, doing all things fraudulently, deceitfully, guilefully. Moreover, the children of light set forth the word of God diligently and continually to bear fruit, patience and prayer, pulling down will-works and rebuking abuses. On the other hand, the children of darkness arm themselves with lies, money, frauds and deceit to enjoy, "fat feasts and jolly banquets."[86]

---

[84] See the discussion on bidding prayers and reform in Wabuda, *Preaching During the English Reformation*, 57.

[85] On the symbolic display of virtues and vices by medieval preachers see Owst, *Literature and Pulpit in Medieval England*, 81-107. On the harshness of Tudor polemic see Rainer Pineas, *Thomas More and Tudor Polemics* (Bloomington, 1968), 1-11.

[86] Latimer is obviously deploying Epideictic, the praise and blame of qualities of character in order to instruct, remind, and evoke approval and disapproval from his hearers. For a good discussion of Epideictic in Renaissance rhetoric see Shuger, *Sacred Rhetoric*, 172-90.

Most alarming was that the children of darkness were nowhere stronger than among prelates: "From top to toe overwhelmed with darkness, darker than is the darkness of hell" (Works, I.47).

Latimer reserved his strongest attack for devotional practices imposed by papal authority, actions abused by the clergy: "canonizations, expectations, pluralities and unions, tot-quots and dispensations, pardons, stationaries, jubilaries, pocularies for drinkers, manuaries for handlers of relicks, pedaries for pilgrims, oscularies for kissers." His fiercest criticism, however, was reserved for the practice of purgatory.

> But yet they that begot and brought forth that our old ancient purgatory pick-purse; that was swaged and cooled with Franciscan's cowl, put upon a dead man's back, to the fourth part of his sins; that that was utterly to be spoiled, and of none other but of our most prudent lord pope, and of him as oft as him listed; that satisfactory, that missal, that scalary; they, I say, that were the wise fathers and genitors of this purgatory, were in my mind the wisest of all their generation, and so far pass the children of light (Works, I.50-51).

Traditional religion had failed to deliver what it promised. Purgatory was a "pleasant fiction," "an abusive monster" but finds no one, "a cowlish deliverance, scalary loosings, papal spoilations and other such figments" (Works, I.51).[87] Rather than concluding with the failures of the past, Latimer summoned the clergy to consider the future, to lift up their heads, to open their eyes, "to spy what things are to be reformed in the Church of England." A series of questions pointed the way forward to the reform of religious practice.[88]

> Is it so hard, is it so great a matter for you to see the abuses in the clergy, in the laity? What is done in the Arches? (Canterbury) Nothing to be amended? Do they correct vice or else defend it; something being well corrected in other places? What do men do in bishop's consistories? Shall you often see the punishments assigned by the laws executed, or else money redemptions used in their stead? How think you of the ceremonies of the Church of England, of the superstition and estimation of them? Do you see nothing in our holidays? See ye nothing brethren? God seeth all the holidays to be spent miserably in drunkenness, in glessing, in strife, in envy, in dancing, dicing, idleness and gluttony. What think ye of these images that are more than their fellows in reputation? . . . Do you think that this preferring of picture to picture, image to image is the right use, and not rather the abuse of images? Last of all, what think ye of matrimony? Is all well here? What of baptism? What think ye of these mass-priests, and of the masses themselves? What say ye? Be all things here so without abuses, that nothing ought to be amended? How have we been so long a-cold, so long slack in setting forth

---

[87] Latimer had previously expressed his views on purgatory in the letter to Morice on the Bristol sermons. Latimer, *Works*, II.361-66.

[88] See the excellent discussion of Latimer's opposition to purgatory in Peter Marshall, *Beliefs and the Dead in Reformation England* (Oxford, 2002), 52-82.

so wholesome a precept of the church in England, where we be so hot in all things that have any gains in them, albeit they be neither commanded of us, nor yet given us counsel; as though we had lever the abuse of things should tarry still then, it taken away, lose our profit? (Works, I.52-55).

Latimer concluded the sermon on a somber note: "But God will come, God will come, he will not tarry long away. He will come and cut us to pieces. He will reward us as he doth the hypocrites . . . And let here be the end of our tragedy, if ye will (Works, I.57).

Latimer's vehement polemic transformed the St. Paul's pulpit into a stage for his dramatic rendering of scripture.[89] The accumulative force of his scriptural performance created sufficient rhetorical space to assert an alternative vision of priestly vocation: "Come go to; leave the love of your profit; study for the glory of Christ; seek in your consultations such things as pertain to Christ, and bring forth at the least somewhat that may please Christ. Feed ye tenderly, with all diligence, the flock of Christ. Preach the word of God" (Works, I.57).[90] The Convocation sermons were quickly printed; the first by Latimer to be preserved and distributed both in England and on the continent.[91]

Once Convocation was under way, the Lower House attempted to establish an agenda. They prepared a list of more than one hundred doctrinal errors that were submitted to the bishops for condemnation, *Mala Dogmata*, derived from English heretical writings and presumably, major points of Latimer's polemic against abusive practices.[92] This was not acceptable to the dominant party of bishops, and the controversy was resolved on 11 July when Foxe, Bishop of Hereford, produced a book of *Ten Articles* composed with the king's authority to resolve certain disputed doctrinal and ceremonial questions. As Rex states: "The *Ten Articles* were intended to forestall the dire consequences which it was feared would necessarily arise from religious division. Heresy and sedition

---

[89] On the use of drama by the evangelicals during Cromwell's administration see Seymour Baker House, "Literature, Drama and Politics," 196-98. The 1512 Convocation Sermon by John Colet presumably would been available as model for Latimer's use; on Colet's preaching see Christopher Harper-Bill, "Dean Colet's convocation sermon and the pre-reformation Church in England" in ed. Peter Marshall, *The Impact of the English Reformation: 1500-1640* (London, 1997), 17-36; Peter I. Kaufman, *Augustinian Piety and Catholic Reform: Augustine, Colet, and Erasmus* (Macon, 1982), 83-92. Kaufman notes that Latimer was one of the few sixteenth-century English reformers to acknowledge Colet; Latimer, *Works*, I.440; Wabauda, *Preaching During the English Reformation*, 28-29. Both Colet and Latimer deployed a well-worn genre of denouncing clerical sins and offering prophetic admonition for repentance and reform. For a discussion of medieval criticism and satire see Owst, *Literature and Pulpit in Medieval England*, 243-86.
[90] On the shift in pastoral status and function during the Henrician period see Marshall, *The Catholic Priesthood and the English Reformation*, 86-110; Wabadu, *Preaching During the English Reformation*, 82-91.
[91] Chester, *Hugh Latimer*, 114.
[92] Duffy, *The Stripping of the Altars*, 391.

were seen as two sides of the same coin in early Tudor England, as a result of the Lollard rising more than a century before. Whether the royal council was more afraid of a Protestant rising or a Catholic backlash is unclear."[93]

The material constituting the *Ten Articles* was divided into two types. The first was made up of principal articles commanded by God and necessary for salvation: the Creed; the sacraments of baptism, penance, and the altar; and justification. The other type was composed of laudable ceremonies not necessary for salvation, but of long continuance for the decent order of the church: the use of images; the honoring of saints, praying to saints; rites and ceremonies; and purgatory. Most historians have noted the influence of Lutheran views, especially since the *Ten Articles* mentioned only three sacraments, passing over the others in silence. Without rejecting confirmation, marriage, holy orders, or extreme unction, they implied that they were not necessary for salvation, or not even sacraments at all. Although they did not refer to consecration or transubstantiation, the *Ten Articles* declared that Christ's body and blood were actually present in the bread and wine. They maintained that Christians were justified by faith and works, and repudiated the superstitious use of images. The *Ten Articles* tried to find a middle way; preachers were notified that it was good and charitable to pray for souls departed and say masses, even if their present location and condition were left uncertain by scripture.[94]

Wabuda argues that the importance of the *Ten Articles* for preachers and clergy has been overlooked.[95] She notes that they were printed in a booklet and issued at least five times by the king's printer. In 1536 Cromwell's royal injunctions ordered the clergy to preach from the *Ten Articles* each Sunday for the quarter after the injunctions were released, and at least twice a quarter thereafter. The clergy were to specify which tenets were necessary for salvation, and which were not.[96] However, when Henry limited sermons for a year after Michaelmas in 1536, he ordered clergy to read them to their audiences but not to preach from them unless specially licensed. He also

<hr/>

[93] Rex, *Henry VIII and the English Reformation*, 147.
[94] For discussions of the *Ten Articles* see A.G. Dickens, *The English Reformation*, 207-209; MacCulloch, *Cranmer*, 161-66; Elton, *Policy and Police*, 246-49; Duffy, *The Stripping of the Altars*, 391-95; Rupp, *The English Protestant Tradition*, 109-15; N.S. Tjernagel, *Henry VIII and the Lutherans*, 163-78, 195-205, 240-47; Rex, *Henry VIII and the English Reformation*, 147-52.
[95] Wabuda, "The Provision of Preaching," 72-73; Eric Josef Carlson, "The Boring of the Ear: Shaping the Pastoral Vision of Preaching in England, 1540-1640" in ed. Larissa Taylor, *Preachers and Preaching in Reformations and Early Modern Period* (Leiden, 2001), 261: "Preaching, which had never received attention in earlier explications of the priestly office, was first among ministerial duties in every official statement from the commencement of the English Reformation." See also Marshall, *Catholic Priesthood*, 116-17.
[96] *Documents Illustrative of English Church History*, ed. Henry Gee and William Hardy (London, 1910), 270-71.

demanded that bishops read them, making the form of their use homilies which were to be read from the pulpit.[97]

The articles approved the veneration of images, the cult of the saints, and the practice of the intercession for the dead. However, the terms in which these were approved were carefully qualified. Images were "representers of virtue and good example," and were meant to be "kindlers and firers of men's minds." Although they could remain in churches, preachers were to ensure that the people were warned against idolatry. As for "censing of them, and kneeling and offering unto them, with other worshippings," which had "entered by devotion and fallen to custom," the people were to be instructed that such worship was in reality not offered to images, but only to God and in his honor "although it be done before the images, whether it be of Christ, or the cross, or of our Lady, or of any other saint beside." The article on Purgatory also modified traditional teaching, while retaining the belief that the dead benefit from the prayers of the living, but in the meantime,

> . . . it is necessary that such abuses be clearly put away, which under the name of purgatory hath been advanced to make men believe that through the Bishop of Rome's pardon souls might clearly be delivered out of purgatory, and all the pains of it, or that masses said at *Scala Coeli*, or otherwhere . . . or before any image, might likewise deliver them from all their pain, and send them straight to heaven.[98]

Additional matters of practical devotion were addressed. "Laudable customs, rites, and ceremonies" were defended in the form of holy water, holy bread, blessed candles, ashes and palms. Good Friday and Easter ceremonies of creeping to the Cross, the setting up of the sepulchre, as well as baptismal and other exorcisms were retained, but were given a didactic and symbolic interpretation. The sprinkling of holy water was explained not in terms of the water's power to banish demons or bring blessing, but "to put us in remembrance of our baptism and the blood of Christ sprinkled for our redemption," holy bread was presented not as a cure but "to put us in remembrance of the sacrament of the altar," candles at Candlemas not as defences against the power of evil or the disorder of the elements but "in memory of Christ the spiritual light." These explanations were to be impressed on the laity, and were "right necessary to be uttered from henceforth in our mother tongue always on the same day" they were performed. Presumably, the evangelicals were pleased with the statement redefining the purpose of

---

[97] Wabuda, "The Provision of Preaching," 73; idem, *Preaching During the English Reformation*, 11-12; *Certain Sermons or Homilies and A Homily against Disobedience and Wilful Rebellion* ed. Ronald B. Bond (Toronto, 1987), 4. "Formularies such as the Ten Articles and the Bishop's Book, clear examples of incipient protestantism, were both meant to be preached, and they serve as reminders that the reformers were adept at manipulating the pulpit as well as the press."

[98] *Documents of the English Reformation*, ed. Gerald Bray (Minneapolis, 1994), 174.

traditional practices: "None of these ceremonies have power to remit sin, but only to stir and lift up our minds to God."[99]

During the latter part of 1536, the disposition of the monasteries continued to be a major issue, since Henry lacked funds due to rising debts, growing inflation, foreign expeditions, and military expenditures. A team of visitors appointed by Thomas Cromwell prepared and delivered an unfavorable report to parliament on the state of the monastic life in England, resulting in the *Act of Dissolution* of 1536. This act was the beginning of a process that was completed in 1540 with the surrender of Waltham Abbey: the King needed revenue as much as reform.[100] The dissolution of the lesser monasteries provoked considerable resistance, although accounts of the Pilgrimage of Grace are varied. M.L. Bush writes,

> Two basic concerns sustained the Lincolnshire uprising and the Pilgrimage of Grace: the subversion of Christ's religion and the decay of the commonwealth. Both were neatly fused in the Pilgrim's oath, which termed the movement "the Pilgrimage of Grace for the commonwealth," and in the rebels' detestation of Cromwell as a reputed "destroyer of the commonwealth" and heretic. The threat to religion was seen as resulting from the infusion of heresy; the threat to the commonwealth lay in the Crown's seizure of the realm's wealth.[101]

Robert Aske, leader of protests in the North Country, declared: "For this pilgrimage we have taken it for the preservation of Christ's Church, of this realm of England, the King our sovereign lord, the nobility and commons of the same, and to the intent to make petition to the King's highness for the reformation for that which is amiss within this realm and for the punishment of the heretics and subverters of laws." There were echoes of Aske's sentiments in the south as well, with stirrings being felt in London.[102] Duffy argues that the symbol chosen by the Pilgrims of Grace—the Five Wounds of Christ—was an

---

[99] *Documents of the English Reformation*, . . . "Articles concerning the Laudable Ceremonies used in the Church," 171-74.

[100] Dickens, *The English Reformation*, 147-91; Haigh, *English Reformations*, 137-51; Haigh, *Reformation and Resistance in Tudor Lancashire* (Cambridge, 1975), 220-29; Doran and Durston, *Princes, Pastor and People*, 162-73; Ronald Hutton, "The local impact of the Tudor Reformations" in ed. Christopher Haigh, *The English Reformation Revised* (Cambridge, 1987), 114-38; MacCulloch, *Thomas Cranmer*, 168-72; Rex, *Henry VIII and the English Reformation*, 148-51.

[101] M.L. Bush "'Up the Commonweal': The significance of tax grievances in the English rebellions of 1536' EHR 106, (1991), 299-318; idem, *The Pilgrimage of Grace: A Study of the Rebel Armies of October 1536* (Manchester, 1999). See also C.S.L. Davies, "The Pilgrimage of Grace reconsidered," *PP* 41, (December, 1968), 54-68. Davies emphasizes the importance of religious ideology for giving the movement cohesion. See also the discussion in R.W. Hoyle, *The Pilgrimage of Grace and the Politics of the 1530s* (Oxford, 2001); Geoffrey Moorhouse, *The Pilgrimage of Grace: The rebellion that shook Henry VIII's throne* (London, 2002).

[102] Brigden, *London and the Reformation*, 248-52.

emblem of their loyalty to the whole medieval Catholic system. He concludes that Latimer had deduced correctly that the attack on the monasteries meant more than money but that the doctrine of purgatory itself and the whole religious and social system that supported it was under attack.[103]

In late October, and during the height of the protest by the Pilgrims, Cranmer and Cromwell appointed Latimer to preach at Paul's Cross, the most important pulpit in the realm.[104] Latimer began the sermon with a brief introduction, which reflected, either his familiarity with the preaching place or the urgency of his task. Taking Ephesians 6:1-10 as his text, he offered a simple exposition of its theme, "But put on all the armour of God, that ye may stand," and its purpose, "Now cometh he forth to and comforteth them, and teacheth them to be bold, and to play the man, and fight manfully. For they must fight with valiant warriors as appeareth afterward in the text."[105]

Latimer identified himself and the Paul's Cross congregation with Paul and his readers in Ephesus, "he teacheth them that in Christ we be all brethren, according to the saying in this same chapter 'God is no acceptor of persons'" (Works, I.25). He then summarized the apostle's message: "Our battle, saith St. Paul, is against princes, potestates . . . that is, against devils . . . Against these we wrestle, against spiritual wickedness in *coelestibus*, that is, in the air; or we fight against spiritual wickedness in heavenly things"(Works, I.25-26). Inscribing his traditionalist opponents into the text of Ephesians, Latimer identified the pope and his prelates in England as powerful weapons of the devil "who hath shot at some good Christian men, that they have been blown to ashes" (Works, I.27). Moreover, he accused members of monastic communities of clothing themselves in religious garb rather than the truthfulness of chaste hearts: "Ye must live rightly in God's Law, clothed righteously in this armour, and not in any feigned armour, as in a friar's coat or cowl" (Works, I.29).[106]

The primary claim of the sermon, however, was directed against the men of the North Country, the Pilgrimage of Grace. Its function was to expose their errors and to attribute their activity to the devil, thus dissuading sympathizers from joining their cause: "They make pretense as though they were armed in God's armour, gird in truth, and clothed in righteousness . . . they deceive the poor, ignorant people, and bring them to fight against both the king, the church and the commonwealth . . . they arm them with the sign of the cross, and go

---

[103] Duffy, *The Stripping of the Altars*, 248, 395-405. See the good discussion on dissolution in Jones, *The English Reformation*, 58-94.

[104] Millar Maclure, *The Paul's Cross Sermons*, 1-4. For a discussion of the crisis and its threat to the Crown see MacCulloch, *Thomas Cranmer*, 169-72.

[105] Erasmus' *Enchiridion*, a manual for Christian warfare based on Ephesians 6, appeared in English in 1533. For a discussion of its translation and popularity see David Daniell, *William Tyndale: A Biography*, 64-74; McConica, *English Humanists and Reformation Politics*, 145.

[106] Blench discusses the Reformers' attacks against monks and other polemical commonplaces against traditional religion, *Preaching in England*, 263-77.

clean contrary to him that bore the cross, and suffered those wounds . . . They rise with the King, and fight against the King . . . they rise with the church and fight against the church . . . they rise for the commonwealth and rise against the commonwealth . . . they go about the commons each to kill other, and to destroy the commonwealth." Latimer's judgment was clear: "Lo, what false pretense can the devil send amongst us!"(Works, I.29).

Latimer's use of Ephesians 6 cast the Pilgrims as enemies of the gospel and its gifts: peace, obedience, humility and quietness, true obedience to the King, and love for neighbors (Works, I.30). He attributed the insurrections to the failure of bishops to enforce injunctions in their dioceses and to teach the *Ten Articles* to their people Latimer concluded the sermon by challenging traditionalists' objections: "But ye say it is new learning. Now I tell you it is the old learning. Yea ye say, it is old heresy new scoured. Nay, I tell you it is old truth, long rusted with your canker, and now new made bright and scoured . . . But how hath this truth over rusted with the pope's rust"(Works, I.30)?

MacCulloch argues that Cranmer saw the pilgrimage as the turning point in the English Reformation. Cranmer drew parallels with the Peasants' War, a defining moment for the continental evangelicals, when their authorities were established as protectors against religious and social radicalism. As he explained in correspondence with evangelicals on the Continent: "Finally you may perceive that those same bishops and presiding of the faction, so many as lately abounded to excess, whom we considered unbending and stiff-necked, now look humbled to the ground and oppose us less. Briefly, as that Peasants' War produced a lasting peace for you, there is hope that so will this for us."[107] By 1537 everyone in England knew where they stood; there was little room for the moderate Catholic humanism of the decade's earliest years.

In 1537-38, as Cromwell's program of reforms advanced, Latimer returned to Worcester to implement the Royal Injunctions.[108] Upon leaving London, he wrote to Cromwell: "I pray God preserve you, and send you hither shortly again, that we might end and go home, into our diocese, and do some good there" (Works, II.375). Latimer began an episcopal visitation at the end of July and issued injunctions in October, which was the first formal effort by a bishop to enforce the Royal Injunction of 1536: that every religious house and every church should provide itself with an English Bible. Latimer's injunctions survive in two forms; one is addressed to the prior and convent of St. Mary's Worcester, the other is addressed to all parsons, vicars, and curates of the diocese. While both sets of injunctions provide a perspective for understanding Latimer's view of his diocese and its need of reform, the injunctions to the clergy offer the clearest picture of his primary aim: to make room for fruitful

---

[107] MacCulloch, *Cranmer*, 156.

[108] Chester, *Hugh Latimer*, 122-43; Demaus, *Latimer*, 267-337. For a good discussion of Latimer's patronage of preaching in Worcester, see Wabuda, "Provision of Preaching," 105-12.

preaching and hearing of God's word (Works, II.240-44).

The injunctions begin with a similar greeting: "Hugh, by the goodness of God, bishop of Worcester, wisheth to all his brethren Curates grace, mercy, peace, and true knowledge of God's word, from God our Father and our Lord Jesus Christ." Describing the ignorance and negligence that he discovered among the clergy, Latimer prescribed a program to eradicate idolatry, superstitions, and enormities, and to produce obedience to the word of God, the king, and their bishop. A fundamental principal was that each clergyman was to have the whole Bible, or least the New Testament, in Latin and English, by Christmas. At least one chapter was to be studied each day by comparing Latin text to English text, and proceeding in a continuous manner through each biblical book. In addition, each of the clergy was to posses a copy of the *Institution of a Christian Man* to provide guidance for the study of scripture, preaching, and teaching (Works, II.242-3).

The remaining injunctions spell out what Latimer hoped to see realized through guided scriptural study. Parishioners were to be excited from will-works to works of charity and mercy, and inspired to pursue peace, love, and avoidance of wrath. Preaching was to receive the highest priority over other observances, ceremonies, and processions. To ensure that sermons not be eclipsed by other liturgical practices, Latimer limited bead-telling to the prescription set forth in Cranmer's 1534 injunction. In addition to preaching, priests were to teach children, equipping them to recite the *Pater Noster* prior to receiving the sacrament of the altar and to instruct them to read English so they will learn, "how to believe, how to pray, and how to live to God's pleasure." The laity, moreover, was to be encouraged to read good books in Latin and English, while the clergy were to learn, teach, and recite the *Pater Noster*, the Creed, and the Ten Commandments (Works, II.244).

Latimer also contributed to the enforcement of official injunctions against "intolerable abuses" of images, pilgrimages, and relics, participating in acts of iconoclasm that gave material expression to his polemical preaching.[109] Cromwell's injunctions for the Church of England opened a phase of sustained hostility towards much of the apparatus of traditional popular religion in the wake of the Convocation, which had approved the *Ten Articles*.[110] The changes undermined the basis of popular religion and put into circulation, "a rhetoric of idolatry." The evangelicals saw themselves as prophets participating in a Deuteronomist-like assault against false images, led by a king who saw himself in the image of Old Testament godly princes David, Josiah, and Hezekiah.[111]

The exposition of the Ten Commandments in the 1537 *Bishop's Book* is notable for its adoption of the "Reformed" rather than the Catholic enumeration: where the medieval tradition included the prohibition on graven

---

[109] See the discussion in Aston, *England's Iconoclasts*, I.161-72.

[110] Aston, *England's Iconoclasts*, I.222-25.

[111] Rex, *Henry VIII and the English Reformation*, 9-10.

images under the general heading of the first commandment (to worship God alone), it now became the second commandment in its own right. The purpose of this was to make an issue out of the veneration of images and the cult of the saints and thus to provide a firm theological basis for the campaign which followed soon after. Henrician iconoclasm, which was justified, like Henry's supremacy, by appealing to the word of God, represented the replacement of visual images with verbal ones. It is no coincidence that the veneration of relics and images was abolished in the same injunctions that ordered every parish church to buy an English Bible.[112]

In 1537 Latimer ordered the stripping of Our Lady of Worcester in the priory of St. Mary's, Worcester, in obedience to Cromwell's injunctions. In early 1538 he returned to London to participate in a public condemnation of relics and images, during which the famous Rood of Boxley, the "Rood of Grace in Kent," was smashed and burned at Paul's Cross, while Hilsey preached the sermon.[113] Latimer presided at the degradation of the Rood of Rumsbury, reportedly picking it up and hurling it out the west door of St. Paul's. The intensity of these events is reflected in Latimer's report to Cromwell on our Lady of Worcester: "She hath been the devil's instrument to bring many (I fear) to eternal fire: now she herself, with her old sister of Wilshingham, her young sister of Ipswich, with their other two sisters of Dorcestor and Pearce, would make a jolly visitor in Smithfield; they would not be all day burning!" (Works, II.395).[114]

Latimer also played a prominent role at the execution of John Forest, a member of the Observant Friars of Greenwich, the most conservative of the religious orders that opposed the king's divorce and royal supremacy.[115] In 1538 Forest was accused of using the confessional to encourage penitents to deny the supremacy and was charged with treason and heresy. At the urging of other imprisoned friars, he refused to abjure and to bear his faggot, despite Latimer's request that the audience, "pray heartily for God to convert the said friar from his said obstinacy and proud mind." Forest was executed before a crowd that was said to have numbered ten thousand.[116] Latimer preached a

---

[112] Rex, *Henry VIII and the English Reformation*, 91-93, 152; Duffy, *The Stripping of the Altars*, 406-409; Aston, *England's Iconoclasts*, I.226-30.

[113] *Original Letters*, II.606-607.

[114] Chester, *Hugh Latimer*, 130-31. On iconoclasm see Alexandra Walsham, *The Reformation of the Landscape: Religion, Identity and Memory in Early Modern Britain and Ireland* (Oxford, 2011), 94ff.

[115] See the discussion of Latimer's intense targeting of friars in Richard Rex, "The Friars in the English Reformation" in eds. Peter Marshall and Alec Ryrie, *The Beginnings of the English Reformation* (Cambridge, 2002), 46-58.

[116] Chester, *Hugh Latimer*, 131-33; Richard Rex, "The Friars in the Reformation," 56-59; Duffy, *The Stripping of the Altars*, 404; MacCulloch, *Cranmer*, 214; Aston, *England's Iconoclasts*, I.234; Brigden, *London and the Reformation*, 213, 226, 290-92.

sermon against idolatry promoted by a sacerdotal priesthood, speaking from a platform built especially for the occasion. He explained his intent in a letter to Cromwell.

> And sir, if it be your pleasure, as it is, that I shall play the fool after my customable manner when Forest shall suffer, I would wish that my stage stood near unto Forest; for I would endeavour myself to content the people that therewith I might also convert Forest, God so helping, or rather altogether working: wherefore I would that he should hear what I say, si forte, etc (Works, II.391-92).

In late 1538 Cromwell sent Latimer to suppress the Cistercian abbey of Hayles in Gloucestshire, a place that possessed a famous relic, a vial said to have contained a portion of the Most Precious Blood. The relic was a famous object of pilgrimage, the participants of which passed by Latimer's residence during his days as rector of West Kington. In a sermon preached at Paul's Cross Hilsey alleged that the vial contained duck's blood.[117] Latimer led the investigating commission and reported its findings to Cromwell.

> Sir, we have been bolting and sifting the blood of Hailes all this afternoon. It was wondrously closely and craftily inclosed and stopped up, for taking of care. And, verily, it seemeth to be an unctuous gum and compound of many things. It hath a certain unctuous moistness, and though it seem somewhat like blood when it is in the glass, yet when any parcel of the same is taken out, it turneth to a yellowness, and is cleavng like glue (Works, II.407-408).

As the Henrician Reformation continued to advance, Latimer's work to defeat superstitions of images and pilgrimages moved from criticism to abolition; his increasingly hostile actions revealed a willingness to stake all on a program of reform to create room for the Word throughout the realm. This vision was constituted by repeated emphasis on scripture, the eradication of abuses, and the removal of offending objects. For evangelicals the word and page, the word-pictures of Christ and the apostles were closer to the truth than any artistic form. The word in the hand, scripture heard or read, said or sung, bore a certainty that imagery could never have. It took Christians straight to Christ and was his spiritual testament. As Erasmus had affirmed, in the gospel Christ lived and breathed and spoke to believers. Veneration was due to words rather than corporal images; the divinity of Christ was to be reached through scripture.[118]

---

[117] Chester, *Hugh Latimer*, 133-34.

[118] Aston, *England's Iconoclasts*, I.196-97. Aston concludes of Latimer, "His position on this question [images] from the first moment when we can observe it is significant in not being aligned with any continental viewpoint. It belongs rather at this stage of events to the school of criticism which we think of as Erasmian" (169). Also see the discussion of Erasmus and images, 196-97. For a discussion of the influence of Erasmian literature on devotional reforms during Cromwell's viceregency see McConica, *English Humanists and Reformation Politics*, 189-90; Wooding,

Although the great majority of people either acquiesced or accepted the royal supremacy, the position of the Henrician church as a branch of Catholicism without Rome was inherently unstable. [119] The burning issues of the Continental Reformation, when joined with Henry's deep dislike of Protestantism, meant that the royal supremacy oscillated between evangelical and conservative positions. Henry's reformation remained broadly Catholic in nature, striving to carve out a space between uncooperative traditionalists and uncompromising radicals. Throughout the 1530s religious conservatives continued to hope that Henry would use his authority to defend Catholic beliefs, while evangelicals preferred to view their king as God's agent of reform. Towards the end of the decade, when the cumulative effects of the Pilgrimage of Grace, the threat of French invasion, and a growing sacramentarian and Anabaptist presence awakened Henry to the inherent dangers of continuing innovation, conservatives seized the opportunity to discredit Cromwell and the evangelicals. [120]

In 1539 Henry called a halt to further reforms and theological discussion with a new statement on six central points of doctrine. [121] The *Six Articles Act* affirmed royal support for the central Catholic doctrines of transubstantiation, communion in one kind for the laity, clerical celibacy, the inviolability of priestly vows of chastity, the validity of private masses, and the necessity of auricular confession. Reform had gone far enough for a King whose religious and political purposes had taken him so far down that road. [122] After debate and negotiation, the Houses of Parliament and the two of Convocation gave the required answers and the *Six Articles* were enshrined in statute. Denial of transubstantiation was to be punished by burning without opportunity for recantation; denial of any of the other articles was to be punished by hanging or life imprisonment. [123]

Rethinking Catholicism, 30-37. Bernard argues that Henry's reformation was basically Erasmian in attitude and scope, *The King's Reformation*, 235-43.

[119] See the discussion on "choosing" reformation in Norman Jones, *The English Reformation: Religion and Cultural Adaptation* (Oxford, 2002), 7-32.

[120] MacCulloch, "Henry VIII and the Reform of the Church," 168-70; Ryrie, "Counting sheep; counting shepherds: the problem of allegiance in the English Reformation," 91-106. In *The Gospel and Henry VIII* (248-58) Ryrie argues that at the end of Henry's reign there was a small but well placed group of evangelical leaders who during the reign of Edward VI were able to continue the reformist momentum from the mid-1540s.

[121] *Documents Illustrative of English Church History*, 303-19.

[122] Chester, *Hugh Latimer*, 140-61; Demaus, *Latimer*, 367-79; Foxe, v.187-236, vii.463; Dickens, *The English Reformation*, 216-21; Doran and Durston, *Princes, Pastors and People*, 15-17, 126-27; Duffy, *The Stripping of the Altars*, 420-47; King, *English Reformation Literature*, 21-25. See the extended discussion of Henry's role as a moderate religious and political reformer in Bernard, *The King's Reformation*, 595-606.

[123] MacCulloch, *Cranmer*, 243-59; Haigh, *English Reformations*, 152-56.

The bishops' debate over the *Six Articles* sealed Latimer's doom. He joined with Cranmer and Shaxton to argue stubbornly against the articles for three days. However, Lee, Gardiner, Tunstall, and Stokesley led the support for the proposals until Henry personally intervened on the fourth day, speaking in the house in support of the articles to confound the opposition. *An Act Abolishing Diversity of Opinions* sailed through both houses of Convocation and Parliament with little evangelical resistance; it was written into the books on June 28, representing a major setback for the reformers. Both Latimer and Shaxton resigned, or were forced to do so, three days later, presumably left unprotected by Cromwell, who was also fighting for his political survival.[124]

By summer's time, both Latimer and Shaxton were widely denounced by the common people as "false knaves and whoresons."[125] Because Latimer's resignation was made to appear as an act of protest against government policies, in particular those of the king, he was imprisoned for several months and silenced under order forbidding him to preach. So began Latimer's "silent years," a period lasting until the death of Henry in 1547 when a general pardon was declared on February 20, the coronation of young Edward VI.[126]

---

[124] Chester, *Hugh Latimer*, 146-50. Chester discusses the possible causes of Latimer's resignation, but does not find sufficient evidence for a definite conclusion. An account is given by Richard Hilles in correspondence with Heinrich Bullinger, *Original Letters*, II.214-15.

[125] Duffy, *Stripping of the Altars*, 420.

[126] Chester, *Latimer*, 160-62; Haigh, *English Reformations*, 164-67; MacCulloch, *Cranmer*, 351-65.

Chapter 3

God's Ploughman:
Performing the Gospel for England

"I have assayed to set forth my plough, to prove what I could do" (Latimer).

For listeners in Tudor England, a sermon by Hugh Latimer was a significant religious, social, and cultural event. During the Edwardian period, Latimer was arguably the most popular and persuasive preacher of the realm, announcing the word of God in a fresh, vibrant way to promote reform of the church and social order. His itinerant preaching ministry required that he address a variety of audiences, from the King's Court to common folk in the countryside, and, on occasion, appear before large gatherings at St. Paul's Cross, London.[1]

This chapter offers a fresh assessment of Latimer's *Sermon of the Plough*, which was delivered early in the Edwardian period from the outdoor pulpit at Paul's Cross London—the "broadcast house of the nation." Offering an exemplary performance of the gospel by means of familiar farming metaphors, Latimer presented himself as a model ploughman for the word of God. While hurling stinging criticism at traditional religion for its failure to produce a godly people in England, Latimer spoke to inspire action towards the future, for the renewal of the church and Christianizing of the social order.

Moreover, the *Sermon of the Plough* included Latimer's articulation of a radical redefinition of priestly status and its function within the church and society. This priestly role was neither predicated upon a supposedly sacramental character conferred at ordination, nor upon one's social or economic status, but on standards of personal godliness, and above all on one's disposition toward preaching the word of God to effect personal salvation and social regeneration.[2] Latimer's riveting call for the clergy of England to return

---

[1]   See the excellent discussion of the persuasive role of preaching in England and on the Continent during this time in Andrew Petegree, *Reformation and the Culture of Persuasion* (Cambridge, 2005), 10-39.

[2]   *The Works of Hugh Latimer: Sometime Bishop of Worcester, Martyr, 1555,* ed. George E. Corrie, 2 Vols. Parker Society (Cambridge, 1866), I.59-80. Hereafter, Latimer's works will be cited in the body of the text. While the Parker Society edition titles this work *The Sermon of the Plough*, there were three other sermons preached by Latimer at Paul's Cross in January of 1548, all of which are lost. Chester argues that the title of the whole series is "of the plow," while this one is specifically of "the plowers," that is, the clergy; and that, plowers (plural), is more appropriate

to their homiletic vocation deserves careful reconsideration in assessing his contributions to reform the Edwardian reforms.[3]

The death of Henry VIII in 1547 freed the reformers from the restraint of a king who, despite his reforming interests, remained attached to the traditional framework of Catholicism. Thomas Cranmer communicated this new reality at the coronation ceremony of Edward VI in February of that year, when he identified the young king as England's new Josiah whose task was to see God truly worshipped, idolatry destroyed, the tyranny of Rome banished, and all images removed. While Cranmer's charge to Edward provides a clue to the intentions of the new reign administered by Protector Somerset, it also provides a perspective for understanding Latimer's preaching context upon his return to the pulpit after an eight-year absence.[4]

During the summer of 1547, in the midst of a rising swell of support for reform, a visitation of the whole realm was announced. While the injunctions drawn up for the visitation reaffirmed the reform measures enforced by Cromwell during Henry's reign, they also represented a major shift towards Protestant sensibilities. The Royal Visitation was put into effect in September 1547 and extended into the next year, bringing the most sweeping religious changes England had seen to date. Thirty commissioners were named for the whole country, each being equipped with copies of the injunctions and the *Book of Homilies*, which were to be distributed to the parish clergy for Sunday public reading. The commission held far-reaching powers and aggressively pursued its work, enforcing the destruction of images, the extinguishing of lights, and the abolition of abused ceremonies, diametrically counterpoising image and word.[5] In December 1547 a new *Chantries Act* passed stating that the purpose of the institution and its practices were wrong: "phantasising vain opinions of purgatory and masses satisfactory, to be done for them which be departed." The *Chantries Act* justified their abolition on religious grounds, but also provided the Crown with an opportunity to confiscate immense resources.[6] Eamon Duffy describes how loyal traditionalists might have perceived events in 1547-48.

All over England churchwardens cooperated in the removal and destruction of images and the suppression of traditional services, but this cooperation should not be read as approval. Tudor men and women had stoically endured many religious changes in the reign of Henry. They had seen the monasteries and friars go, the shrines pillaged, the lights in the parish churches snuffed out, the abolition of many of the traditional feast days. There had been Protestant preaching, even, in some places, image breaking and burning. But these early Edwardian changes

---

than plough (singular), given the antithetical structural design of the sermon. See Chester, *Selected Sermons of Hugh Latimer* (Charlottesville, 1968), xxxi.
[3] McRae, *God speed the plough*, 24.
[4] MacCulloch, *Thomas Cranmer*, 351-75; Haigh, *English Reformations*, 168-73.
[5] Aston, *England's Iconoclasts*, I.258.
[6] Dickens, *The English Reformation*, 230-42.

were recognized as something new, something different.

Duffy highlights reactions to these radical changes with an example from a churchwarden's records: "the tyme of scysme when this Realm was devyded from the Catholic Churche, the second year of King Edward the syxt, when all godly ceremonyes and good usys were taken out of the Church within this Realme."[7]

In a time of crisis, as the injunctions impacted parishes and the situation threatened to spiral out of control, Cranmer called upon Latimer to preach at Paul's Cross in January 1548 to address the people face to face. Only one survives of a possible eight sermons Latimer may have preached at Paul's Cross during that time, that of January 18, 1548. In this sermon Latimer summarizes the previous three: reporting on his defense of the *Royal Injunctions* and Somerset's policies; his affirmation of the *Book of Homilies*; his call for more teachers and schools; his attack upon the adoration of images; his plea for the use of the vernacular in worship; his explication of the nature of the cross.[8]

The preaching point at Paul's Cross, where diverse crowds gathered representing the high and low of the realm, provided Latimer with a strategic location, a stage for which his dramatic preaching style was ideally suited to present a reformist message to the popular imagination. Although he served as Bishop of Worcester under Henry VIII, Latimer primarily saw himself as a prophet and evangelist whose strongest desire and central duty was pastoral in nature, to win souls and to transform the social life of the whole nation. The goal of his preaching was to allow the biblical message to convict and convert even more than to inform, to engage listeners with the word of God mediated through scripture and embodied in sermon.

Latimer thus linked imagination and affectivity to the work of reason, utilizing rhetorical means for the persuasion of the soul, and for affecting change of the whole person in all its relations for obedience to God's call. Following the practice of Erasmus and other Christian humanists, Latimer viewed theological language as a means for transforming life according to the subject matter of Scripture.[9] This practical perspective led him to adopt preaching strategies that he employed through a plain, vernacular style informed by biblical speech, enabling him to cross social barriers in a manner uncommon for high-ranking ecclesiastical officials.[10] The constraints of wealth

---

[7] CWA, cited in Duffy, *The Stripping of the Altars*, 460-62. See also the discussion of changes in practice in Norman Jones, *The English Reformation: Religious and Cultural Adaptation* (Oxford, 2002).

[8] Chester, *Hugh Latimer*, 162-65.

[9] John N. Wall, *Transformations of the Word: Spenser, Herbert, Vaughn* (Athens, 1988), 17-18.

[10] Blench, *Preaching in England*, 37-49, 87-95, 142-56. See M. Dowling, "John Fisher and the preaching ministry," *Archive for Reformation History*, Yearbook lxxxii

and power which were inherent to many who held episcopal office did not inhibit Latimer, as the wealth that had accrued to him during his tenure as bishop only served as a means to implement those convictions of social righteousness that he preached.[11] During the reign of Edward VI, the preaching of Latimer and other reformers took on strategic significance, with Latimer's sermons playing such an important role they were collected and printed almost immediately, enhancing his reputation as a founding father of the English national church.[12] Augustine Bernher, Latimer's secretary and biographer, wrote that during the days of Edward, "he began to set forth his plough and to till the ground of the lord" (Works, I.111).

English Reformation scholarship has tended to underestimate the dramatic subversive and reconstructive potential of sixteenth-century reforming discourse and its antecedent reformist traditions. In England, however, as on the continent, preaching for the reform of Christian faith and life proved central, continuing and expanding a homiletic trend that emerged during the fourteenth and fifteenth centuries and which took a dramatic leap during the Henrician period under the direction of Cromwell and Cranmer.[13] Reformers exploited sermons effectively, taking over the mendicant tradition of publicly attacking the corruption of church and society. They utilized the pulpit to teach new doctrine, to introduce new practices, to articulate new visions, and to move their listeners to adopt them.[14]

A significant example of both confidence and fear related to the efficacy of preaching was the assembling of the first *Book of Homilies*. It was issued in 1547 as a means of communicating and controlling the central convictions of the reform, defining a vision of evangelical faith and life that would be capable of transforming the realm into a Christian commonwealth under the royal supremacy.[15] Thus changes in religious ideas, practices, language, and identity which were begun and achieved during Edward's reign, were in no small part due to the work of preachers. Claiming scripture as their authority and model, reformist preachers were, in the words of Patrick Collinson, "living in the pages

---

(1991), 287-309. Dowling describes Fisher's humanistic emphasis on scripture, but also highlights his learned citations from classical authors, something that is absent in Latimer's sermons. See also Claire Cross, *Church and People*, 81-101.

[11] Felicity Heal, *Of Princes and Prelates: A Study of the Economic and Social Position of the Tudor Episcopate* (Cambridge, 1980), 164-66.

[12] Andrew McRae, *God speed the plough*, 64.

[13] See Chapter 2 for my discussion on the Crown's deployment of preaching during the 1530s.

[14] Peter E. McCullough, *Sermons at Court: Politics and religion in Elizabethan and Jacobean preaching* (Cambridge, 1998), 51-59; R.N. Swanson, *Church and Society in Late Medieval England* (Oxford, 1989), 347-61; Blench, *Preaching in England*, 87-94.

[15] *Certain Sermons or Homilies*, ed. Ronald B. Bond (Toronto, 1987).

of the Bible."[16]

John Wall argues persuasively that the English Reformation was driven in large part by the printing, distribution, and use of religious books as instruments of religious and institutional reform, and as vehicles for the dissemination of Edwardian policies and intentions for the spiritual welfare of the people.[17] The story of the English Reformation may, in part, be seen from the perspective provided by its great books: *The English Bible*, the *Book of Homilies*, Erasmus' *Paraphrases of the New Testament*, and the *Book of Common Prayer*.[18] The *Royal Injunctions* which were promulgated in July, 1547, required every parish church in England to have the "whole Bible, of the largest volume in Englishe," Erasmus' *Paraphrases on the Gospels and Acts*, and a collection of twelve sermons, known as the *Book of Homilies*, for use in reading, study, and preaching. By making Scripture available in the language of the people, Cranmer intended to construct a renewed Church of England built upon a theology of the Word and with the conviction that biblical speech, when properly presented in its various forms, contains the power to transform the world in which it is spoken, heard, and obeyed.[19]

The *Book of Homilies* represented Cranmer's ambition to issue a collection of sermons to remedy the shortage of reliable preachers in the church. This culminated in a plan under Edward that was begun during the reign of Henry VIII, having predecessors in the various occasional addresses issued by Cromwell, the format of the *Ten Articles*, and the 1537 *Bishops' Book* which aimed to provide insufficiently trained priests with a doctrinal summary and framework for biblical interpretation and sermon construction. Cranmer's concern in the homilies, then, was to establish the nature of salvation as God's free gift of faith, while demonstrating that this affirmation would not lead to a

---

[16] Patrick Collinson, *The Birthpangs of Protestant England* (New York, 1988) 1-11; Peter Marshall, *The Catholic Priesthood and the English Reformation* (Oxford, 1994), 86-107.

[17] John N. Wall, "Godly and Fruitful Lessons: The English Bible, Erasmus' Paraphrases, and the Book of Homilies" in ed. John Booty, *The Godly Kingdom of Tudor England: Great Books of the English Reformation* (Wilton, 1981), 47-138; John N. King, *English Reformation Literature*, 122-30. For my understanding of the background, content, and purpose of the *Book of Homilies* I am indebted to the work of John N. Wall, "The Vision of a Christian Commonwealth in the *Book of Homilies*" (PhD diss., Harvard University, 1979). On the use of print by the Edwardians see Andrew Petegree, "Printing and the Reformation: The English Exception" in eds. Peter Marshall and Alec Ryrie, *The Beginnings of English Protestantism* (Cambridge, 2002), 157-73.

[18] John N. Wall, *Transformations of the Word*, 1-34. On the influence of Erasmus during the Edwardian perod see Gregory D. Dodds, *Exploiting Eramus: The Erasmian Legacy and Religious Change in Early Modern England* (Toronto, 2009), 6-10.

[19] Wall, "Godly and Fruitful Lessons," 47-58; Wabuda, *Preaching During the English Reformation*, 144-45.

collapse of morality, since good works still formed an essential part of the Christian life. Yet the homilies also represent a significant shift in theological emphasis, since a whole range of traditional practices were eliminated and the range of works was redefined and narrowed.[20]

While resembling medieval homiliaries, books of model sermons on which ignorant parish priests would rely when discharging their duty of regular preaching; the Edwardian homilies introduced a new economy of salvation in which sermons, *ex opere operata*, played the central part. This theological orientation established them as significant agents of religious change and control, as instruments for promoting new faith and learning deriving its authority from two sources, a *Preface* issued in the name of the king, and in the thirty-second Injunction that anticipated significant religious change.

> Because through lack of preachers in many places of the King's realms and dominions the people continue in ignorance and blindness, all persons, vicars, and curates shall read in their churches every Sunday one of the homilies, which are and shall be set forth for the same purpose by the king's authority, in such sort as the shall be appointed to do in the preface of the same.[21]

This injunction made reading of the homilies for all but the few licensed preachers of the realm a binding responsibility. Moreover, the *Book of Homilies* was published not only to assist non-preaching prelates, but also to serve as an instructing and regulating guide for learned preachers such as Latimer. The *Book of Homilies* provided a guide for evangelical doctrine and life, a doctrinal framework which was practically ordered according to essential topics derived from scripture to ensure homiletic "quality control" across the realm.[22] This was of great importance during a time of commotion and change, when conservative priests resisted Edward's reforms, and when the tolerant atmosphere created by Somerset's policies encouraged maverick preachers or "gospellers."[23] *Certayne Sermons or Homilies, appoynted by the Kinges Majestie, to be declared and redde, by all persones (parsons) Vicars, Curates, every Sundaye in their Churches, where they have Cure* were published to address these challenges, demonstrating Cranmer's desire that there be weekly pastoral instruction for the transformation of parishioners' lives by means of

---

[20] *Homilies*, 3-6; Wabuda, *Preaching During the English Reformation*, 144-45.

[21] "The Edwardian Injunctions, 1547" in ed. Gerald Bray, *Documents of the English Reformation* (Minneapolis, 1994), 256. On the practical Edwardian Reforms see Kenneth Fincham and Nichols Tyacke, *Altars Restored: The Changing Face of English Religious Worship* (Oxford, 2007), 1-73.

[22] *Homilies*, 6-7. On the regulative function of doctrine as grammar see George Lindbeck, *The Nature of Doctrine: Religion and Theology in a Postliberal Age* (Philadelphia, 1984), 91-107. On the need for Protestants to develop regulative norms for biblical interpretation in the sixteenth-century see David C. Steinmetz, *Luther in Context* (Bloomington, 1986), 86-91.

[23] Brigden, *London and the Reformation*, 442-43.

scriptural language spoken in the vernacular.

Moreover, the homilies were initially experienced through the ear, not the eye, and with the authorization of the *Book of Common Prayer* which was issued in 1549 they provided regular opportunities for English people to be incorporated into scripture's drama of salvation, the most vital impulse for re-fashioning church and nation.[24] Nicholas Ridley acknowledged the practical aim of the homilies that was in keeping with medieval precedence, asserting that some were "in commendation of the principal virtues that are commended in scripture,"and "others against the most pernicious and capital vices that useth (alas!) to reign in this realm of England."[25]

John King points out that homily, "conversation, instruction," corresponds to sermon, "*sermo*," or "word," but ultimately derives from "crowd, or "mob," reflecting the outdoor circumstances under which Jesus, Paul, and the apostles preached. By analogy with the incarnation, the plain style of the homilies paradoxically unites the highest and the lowest, the heavenly and the earthy, in a plain, modest style that corresponds to its subject matter; revelation, instruction, and persuasion for Christian living in the world. King argues that the world of Edwardian England addressed by the homilies was diverse, and that its complexity parallels that of the Elizabethan stage. This world was represented by the large crowds that congregated at Paul's Cross, London, reflecting the "high and low" audiences envisioned by Cranmer in compiling the homilies, revealing the "high to low" movement of the Word through the learned but earthy preaching exemplified by Latimer.[26]

Wall concludes the *Book of Homilies* called for Christian action nourished by faith and leading to eternal life. In this important matter, the homilies follow the biblical vision conveyed in the *Enchridion* of Erasmus but enlarged its framework to include society as a whole. The *Book*, then, is both a religious and political document, representing a move towards greater reform in the church and greater consolidation of power for its enactment in the hands of a godly prince. For this reason, the scope of the homilies is defined by the *Preface* in terms of moving the people "to honor and worship almighty God, and diligently to serve hym." This means serving the king "with all humilitie and subjeccion," . . . "godly and honestly, behaving themselves toward all men." A vision of a Christian commonwealth is being evoked, a vision of national life which embodies imitation of Christ through the virtue of charity. This way of life was modeled after the Erasmian *philosophy of Christ*, while also moving beyond traditional religious ceremonial and devotional practices to

---

[24] MacCulloch, *Tudor Church Militant*, 12.

[25] Nicholas Ridley, *Works*, ed. H. Christmas (Cambridge, 1841), 400.

[26] John N. King, *English Reformation Literature*, 123-27. These views echo those set forth by Erasmus. See the *Paraclesis,* 97-108. See the discussion of how reform was capable of overcoming the "high and low" division of English Society, "Introduction" in eds. Peter Marshall and Alec Ryrie, *The Beginnings of English Protestantism* (Cambridge, 2002), 2-4.

embrace a regeneration of all aspects of society.[27]

Because the Bible was the chief source for the rhetoric of the homilies, their aim was to imitate the language of scripture, particularly its figures and examples, thus replacing religious images with the image of the Word—*pictura* with *scriptura*.[28] This biblically-derived style rendered the sermons more forceful and vivid, increasing their clarity and immediacy while grounding teaching in the soil of scripture. The vision of a Christian commonwealth, as it was conveyed by the homilies, offered fitting and persuasive models for imitation, since the production of an obedient Christian citizenry would be the test of a true and lively faith. Thus a whole way of life unfolds throughout the ordering of the homilies, calling listeners to knowledge of scripture through the story of God's redeeming acts, and eliciting faith expressing itself through charity in accordance with God's commandments.[29]

The first homily communicates this over-arching purpose, making clear the *Book* is Bible-centered and draws its inspiration, scope, and style from scripture, "the heavenly meate of our soules." Through reading and hearing— devouring and absorbing its message—Christians are transformed into the Word they digest and energized to do what it says for attaining salvation: "The words of holy scripture . . . have power to convert through God's promise, and to be effectuall, through God's assistance."[30] The aim of the homilies, then, was transfiguring the lives of obedient listeners by enfolding them into the story of biblical history so that living faith and charitable acts would lead to the formation of a Christian commonwealth.[31]

A primary purpose of Latimer's preaching at Paul's Cross was to promote the use of the *Book of Homilies* by speaking in its support, modeling its use, and embody its message. In speaking as an authorized voice of the Edwardian church, Latimer drew from scripture as his source and the homilies as his guide in crafting the *Sermon of the Plough*, which demonstrates considerable flexibility and practical wisdom in extending aspects of official Edwardian teaching to his diverse Paul's Cross audience. Students of the English Reformation have not paid sufficient attention to Latimer's homiletic achievement. By allowing the biblical scope, substance, and style of the homilies to inform and shape the rhetoric of the *Sermon of the Plough*, Latimer established himself as an exemplar for preachers and their people. Moreover, Latimer's presence in London was especially significant, since the center of England's national life had been deeply divided over religion for several decades, so that its pool of prospective priests had decreased since the advent of reform. Exemplary models, those who were capable of attracting and inspiring

---

27 Wall, "Godly and Fruitful Lessons," 90-93.
28 John N. King, *English Reformation Literature*, 152-60; Margaret Aston, *England's Iconoclasts: Laws against Images*, I.125-36.
29 Bond, *Certain Sermons or Homilies*, 3; Wall, "Godly and Fruitful Lessons," 95-103.
30 Wall, "Godly and Fruitful Lessons," 124-25; *Homilies*, 62.
31 *Homilies*, 66-67.

a preaching priesthood, were important for the advancing a new world of English religion in which the Word was to be more central than the sacraments, and in which the status and function of the clergy would be profoundly changed.[32]

In determining the theme of the *Sermon of the Plough*, Latimer chose texts utilizing metaphors of ploughing and sowing to signify the powerful eruption of judgment and mercy in the spoken word (Works, I.59). This choice of familiar farming images identified Latimer with a company of preachers who traced their homiletic roots to the authority and example of scripture which was modeled in the lives and speech of the prophets, the apostles, and most importantly, by Christ. This tradition, which defined preaching as a humble activity, similar to ploughing and sowing, for the ministry of the Word, was represented in patristic and medieval sermons through such figures as: Hilary, Jerome, Augustine, Bede, John Chrysostom, Gregory the Great, Rabanus, Richard and Hugh of St.Victor, Bonaventure, Albert, Aquinas, and John Fisher.[33] By planting himself in this tradition, Latimer hoped, in distancing himself from the circumstances of the immediate past, to articulate a prophetic call for personal regeneration and social righteousness.

Preaching by means of figurative language provided Latimer with a degree of exegetical and homiletical flexibility for applying Scripture to the changing circumstances of his audiences and for engaging a diversity of listeners. Although he expressed opposition to allegorical interpretations of Scripture as favored by his traditionalist preachers, he remained open to discovering, within limits, multiple meanings for his preaching, as he explained in a 1552 sermon on the *Parable of the Laborers*. Dismissing allegorical interpretations that applied the parable to the successive ages of world history, Latimer declared,

> Some there are which would have an allegory of it. But all agree in this point, namely, that it is not requisite in a parable to expound every word of the same. For every parable hath *certum statum*, "a certain scope," to the which we must have respect; and not go all about to set all words together, or to make a gloss for the same; for it is enough for us when we have the meaning of the principal scope; and more needeth not (Works, II.198-99).[34]

Moreover, Latimer's selection of the *Parable of the Sower* (Luke 8) created an allusive association with the *Piers Plowman* tradition, which may provide another clue for understanding his preaching. With this allusion to the humble,

[32] Brigden, *The Reformation in London*, 392-93; Marshall, *The Catholic Priesthood and the English Reformation*, 229-30; MacCulloch, *The Later Reformation in England*, 95-96.

[33] Stephen L. Wailes, *Medieval Allegories of Jesus' Parables* (Berkeley, 1987), 96-103; Ordelle G. Hill, *The Manor, the Plowman, and the Shepherd* (Selinsgrove, 1993), 45-52.

[34] Blench, *Preaching in England*, 1-49, surveys changes in biblical interpretation during this time period.

down-to-earth figure of Piers, who himself is never mentioned in the sermon, Latimer seized an opportunity for identifying himself with a critical but orthodox name that was known by many but at the same time, distancing himself from traditionalist clergy—whom he portrayed as arrogant, greedy, and negligent in their call to preach. The figure of the ploughman was rich and varied in its historical meanings; it could be associated with constant, honest labor, Christian virtue, simplicity of life and speech, or the voice of God condescending and speaking to affect the salvation of common people. In addition, the activity of the ploughman echoes the Genesis narrative, of humanity created to inhabit the garden of creation, of its fall into sin, and of God's curse upon Adam to work the land by the sweat of his brow. The plough was also associated with the restoration of Israel as a covenant people as marked by their return from exile to the promised, land. Most important was the character of the ploughman, which served as a figure of Christ, and the plough, which served as a figure of the cross. Together, these two figures depicted the power of the gospel at work, rooting up sin in the soul and planting the seeds of godliness which leads to salvation.

Latimer presumably would have had access to a rich storehouse of religious imagery for addressing his fellow citizens as a humble ploughman of the New Jerusalem he hoped would be achieved through Edward's reforms.[35] This type of discourse arguably found its literary origin in Langland's *Piers Plowman*, the most crucial text in a loose but important tradition dating from the fourteenth century. Tudor England reformers did not hesitate to use, amend, or re-contextualize this tradition of criticism and complaint for sermons in support of their religious and social vision.[36] Although the *Sermon of the Plough* echoes the commitment of medieval preachers who called for a social embodiment of

---

[35] For a survey of complaint literature and the *Piers Plowman* tradition see McRae, *God speed the plough*, 1-57; David Aers, *Chaucer, Langland and the Creative Imagination* (London, 1980), 1-61; Margaret Aston, "Lollardy and the Reformation: Survival or Revival?" *History* 49 (1964), 149-70; idem, *Lollards and Reformers: Images and Literacy in Late Medieval Religion* (London, 1984), 220-29; Anne Hudson, "The Legacy of Piers Plowman" in *A Companion to Piers Plowman*, ed. John A. Alford (Berkeley, 1988); John King, *English Reformation Literature*, 11-12, 262-63, 323-24; Hudson, *The Premature Reformation* (Oxford, 1988), 465-517; Hudson, *Lollards and their Books* (London, 1985), 227-48; Owst, *Literature and Pulpit in Medieval England*, 98-100, 210-470; Robert L. Kelly, "Hugh Latimer as Piers Plowman" in *Studies in English Literature* 17 (1977), 12-26; David Birch, "Early Reformation English Polemics" in ed. James Hogg, *Elizabethan and Renaissance Studies* 92.7 (Salzburg,1983), 8-62; *The praier and complaynte of the ploweman unto Christe* ed. Douglas H. Parker (Toronto, 1997), 14-78; Helen C. White, *Social Criticism in Popular Religious Literature of the Sixteenth Century* (New York, 1944), 1-81; H. Leith Spencer, *English Preaching in Late Medieval England* (Cambridge, 1996), 475-86; D.S. Dunnan, "Hugh Latimer: A Reassessment of his Preaching" (PhD diss. Oxford,1991), 179-202.

[36] Hudson, *Premature Reformation*, 500-507; *The praier and complaynte*, 53-78.

the gospel, it also presents its listeners with a fresh vision of society, as reordered under the word of God, and for the manifestation of evangelical faith and lie.[37]

> During the brief reign of Edward VI, preachers, poets and pamphleteers revitalized and reshaped preexistent traditions of social complaint. Latimer, whose reformist views and polemical style drew him to the forefront of this movement, applied the weight of tradition to the new context in his 'Sermon of the Plough', preached at Paul's Cross in 1548 . . . His insistence on the figure of the ploughman, however, draws attention to its rhetorical potential, at a time when the government of Edward Seymour, Protector Somerset, was giving new impetus to Protestant reform.[38]

In addition to the indigenous literature of complaint that was circulated during the reign of Edward VI, a number of polemical works from the continent—that of Tyndale, Erasmus, and Luther being the most influential—were disseminated in England during the 1520s and 1530s. These works had certain similarities with the reformist views of John Wyclif and the Lollards, which provided grist to the mill for sermons by Protestant reformers.[39] Preachers made effective use of these commonplace attacks to voice their complaints on a variety of relevant issues. Their polemic singled out clergy corruption, wealth, arrogance and privilege; the excesses and greed of the preaching friars; papal authority; the Real Presence; penance, confession, purgatory, and other practices of external devotion. These complaints were often combined with demands for the free circulation of the Bible in English to increase lay knowledge and responsibility in a society that was dominated by the authority and activity of clergy.[40]

Henry's commitment to elements of Catholic orthodoxy limited the extent of

---

[37] Owst devotes the last chapter of his work to the social ideal of the Piers tradition and medieval preaching. See Owst, *Literature and Pulpit in Medieval England*, 548-93.

[38] McRae, *God speed the plough*, 30.

[39] For a survey of literature imported from the continent to England see James McConica, *English Humanists and Reformation Politics* (Oxford, 1965), 106-30; E.G. Rupp, *Studies in the Making of the English Protestant Tradition* (Cambridge, 1949), 1-62; Carl R. Trueman, *Luther's Legacy: Salvation and the English Reformers*, 1525-1556 (Oxford, 1994), 31-120; William A. Clebsch, *England's Earliest Protestants* (Yale, 1964), 1-45; Donald D. Smeeton, *Lollard Themes in the Reformation Theology of William Tyndale* (Kirksville, 1986), 1-30; Swanson, *Church and Society in Late Medieval England*, 330-52; Carl Trueman and Carrie Euler, "The Reception of Martin Luther in Sixteenth—and Seventeenth—Century England" in eds. Polly Ha and Patrick Collinson, *The Reception of Continental Reformation in Britain* (Oxford, 2010), 63-81; Patrick Collinson, "The Fog in the Channel Clears: the Rediscovery of the Continental Dimension to the British Reformation" in eds. Ha and Collinson, *The Reception of the Continental Reformation in Sixteenth—and Seventeenth—Century England* (Oxford, 2010), xxvii-xxxvii.

[40] Hudson, *Lollards and their Books*, 248.

Latimer's reformist preaching during the 1530s.[41] However, following the King's death in 1547 and with the accession of Edward VI, the newly established religion moved towards a more reformed position than ever, freeing Latimer and other evangelicals to intensify their attacks on traditional authority, doctrine, and practices. Edward's accession initiated the execution of a full-blown, root-and-branch campaign that would radically transform the social distribution of power in both church and society, since the reformers were eager to respond to demands of the laity for their increased participation in decision-making and leadership.[42]

Latimer's *Sermon of the Plough* was, in principle, addressed to the whole realm and with two primary ends in mind: to establish sufficient authority for the acceptance of Edwardian measures for reforming clergy and lay vocations; and to reestablish himself as a prophetic voice, an evangelist, and public "opinion-maker" for the church and crown.[43] The strategic importance of the *Sermon of the Plough* was heightened by the fact that it was Latimer's first significant pulpit appearance after eight years of officially imposed silence for his expression of reformist views during the Henrician period—ending on February 20, 1547, the day of Edward's coronation. Latimer was soon licensed under ecclesiastical seal for his return to the pulpit with full authority to preach throughout the realm.[44]

The sermon also marked Latimer's return to the Paul's Cross pulpit, a place where any sermon was a major social event.[45] Since medieval times the pulpit was often used to announce new government policies concerning religion. For this reason, Paul's Cross, which retained an ancient association with the defense of orthodoxy, proved itself exceptionally useful to the sixteenth-century reform by lending an aura of authority to its proclamation. During the period from 1534-54, Paul's Cross was the most important vehicle of persuasion used by the government, providing a kind of theater for preachers, a stage for pulpit performances and means of delivering religious and political proclamations that both interpreted and directed England's future under the rule of divine and human kingship.[46] Maclure's description of this important

---

[41] Susan Wabuda, "'Fruitful Preaching' in the Diocese of Worcester," 49-55.

[42] Claire Cross, *Church and People 1540-1660: The Triumph of the Laity in the English Church* (Trowbridge, 1976), 9-100; Maculloch, *Thomas Cranmer*, 429-441.

[43] I am indebted to the work of Peter Matheson on public opinion, propaganda, and persuasion during the Continental Reformation: "The sermons of Luther, or Muntzer, or Bucer, for example, are themselves immensely complex, and evidence a whole spectrum of intentions, including pedagogical and pastoral ones as well as proclamatory or exhortatory ones." Peter Matheson, *The Rhetoric of the Reformation* (Cambridge, 1998), 27-59.

[44] Chester, *Hugh Latimer*, 162.

[45] Chester, *Hugh Latimer*, 156-65; Dickens, *The English Reformation*, 226-55.

[46] Maclure, *The Paul's Cross Sermons*,16-20, 147-48; Wabuda, *Preaching During the English Reformation*, 40-48.

preaching point is worth quoting at length.

> The Cross is an octagonal structure of wood, mounted on a stone base, with stone steps leading up to it, surmounted by an ogee-shaped roof, on which is set an ornamental cross. The whole structure is of a fourteenth-century memorial type. The preacher stands between two of the supporting pillars; to his right, prominently placed, is an hourglass; on the wall beneath him is a coat of arms, possibly of the Bishop of London. The cross is enclosed by a low wall of brick within which sit a number of privileged persons. The walls of the transept and choir, facing the cross, are built up with covered galleries, the "houses" as they were called, in which the dignitaries are seated: King, Queen, Prince of Wales, members of the Privy Council, the Lord Mayor and Aldermen. The main body of the audience is seated on forms in something like a "garland or ring" as Bishop King termed it during his sermon of 1620. There is a solid group of what are presumably meant to be the crafts in their liveries, with a sprinkling of fine gentlemen and citizens' wives. If we look at the scene as a whole, it reminds us of the Elizabethan theater: groundlings and notables, pit and galleries, and, in the midst, the pulpit as stage. Indeed it was a theater; . . . sermons, proclamations, processions, and penances were all theatrical.[47]

The *Sermon of the Plough*, then, was Latimer's debut as a major actor in the Edwardian Reformation, an epic contest unfolding between polar opposites, for which one aim was to destroy the old world of devotion and to implement the new program of religious life promised by the emerging evangelicals.[48] The setting at Paul's Cross afforded several means of persuasion to Latimer's

---

[47] Maclure, *The Paul's Cross Sermons*, 3-4.

[48] Here I follow MacCulloch's interpretation of the Edwardian Reformation in dramatic terms. "We are beginning a consideration of this religious revolution with a cast list, since we are to be spectators at a drama: a drama of six years' span. Edward's reign and the Reformation which it encompassed is a story of an adventure. . . . The dramas of the Edwardian Reformations were biblical in more senses than one. The rebuilt Church was evangelical in essence. The assignment for evangelicals was a treasure hunt for the *euangelion*, the good news to be found in the New Testament, and the excavators were impatient of the centuries of church experience, which overlay it. Yet spokesmen for the Edwardian revolution were also drawn to the Old Testament, where they could view other kingdoms battling against great odds to hear the message of God," MacCulloch, *Tudor Church Militant*, 9-14. A considerable body of scholarship relates preaching and drama during the Henrician and Edwardian Reformations. My exposition of Latimer's preaching attempts to recapture the dramatic character and movement that is intrinsic to the biblical drama. See Owst, *Literature and Pulpit in Medieval England*, 471-547; Bryan Crockett, *The Play of Paradox: Stage and Sermon in Renaissance England* (Philadelphia, 1995), 5-7, 32-40; Janette Disson, *Language and Stage in Medieval and Renaissance England* (Cambridge, 1998), 11-27, 72-87; Paul Whitfield White, *Protestantism, Patronage, and Playing in Tudor England* (Cambridge, 1993), 1-9, 40-130, 169-71; Glynee Wickham, *Early English Stages: Their Plays and their Makers 1300-1660* (London, 1991), I.128-34.

preaching: 1) his previous London appearances and reputation; 2) his allusion to Piers, the humble preacher-ploughman of scripture, a type of Christ who was a recognizable figure from homiletic and literary traditions; 3) the aura of orthodoxy lent by the history of his preaching space; 4) enthusiasm for reform by sympathetic members of his audience, especially citizens of London and surrounding regions where Edward's reformation had begun to take root.[49]

Latimer justified his sermon theme by establishing its scriptural basis: Luke 7:5, "He that soweth, the husbandman, the ploughman, went forth to sow his seed," and Luke 9:62, "No man that putteth his hand to the plough and looketh back is apt for the kingdom of God" (Works, I.59-60). The way forward to God's kingdom, "putting the hand to the plough," determines the pattern and progress of the sermon. The first part interprets the metaphors of the plough and the work of its humble ploughman as the activity of the word of God through faithful preachers with whom Latimer identifies. The second part alerts listeners to the presence of England's most formidable prelate-ploughman, the devil himself, with whom Latimer identifies traditionalist clergy, who, in their resistance to reform, had refused to preach.[50]

Latimer utilized the figurative language of scripture for depicting two categories of personalities, or ploughers—one arrogant, the other humble—and who were engaged in a spiritual warfare for England's soul.[51] Dramatic interpretation of this type was common practice in the sixteenth century, since most of the English reformers were familiar with apocalyptic rhetoric which enabled them to articulate the urgency of their mission and to inspire hope for its fulfillment. In this they were one with many prominent Continental reformers and also in continuity with late medieval traditions, both dissenting and orthodox.[52] It was Lollardy that presumably played an important part in contributing to English Reformation rhetoric, since its traditions of anti-papal exegesis were ready for use in its oral and literary forms. Sixteenth-century

---

[49] MacCulloch, *Tudor Church Militant*, 59, "Their [evangelicals] support came from people who did not matter in politics: Cambridge dons, a minority of clergy and a swathe of people below the social level of the gentry, all concentrated in south-east England. The projected Edwardian Reformation could not expect enthusiastic support from the majority of lay people in positions of power, gentry and nobility. Likewise, few bishops would cooperate wholeheartedly with the dismantling of traditional religion."

[50] Richard Bauckham, *Tudor Apocalypse: Sixteenth century apocalypticism, millenarianism and the English Reformation from John Bale to John Foxe and Thomas Brightman* (Oxford, 1978), 11-112.

[51] Robert Wuthnow, *Communities of Discourse: Ideology and Social Structure in the Reformation, the Enlightenment, and European Socialism* (Cambridge, 1989), 13-15, "The discursive field refers to a symbolic space or structure within the ideology itself . . . definition by some fundamental opposition of binary concepts is often evident."

[52] Ephraim Radner, "Doctrine, Destiny, and the Figure of History" in ed. E. Radner and G. Sumner, *Reclaiming Faith: Essays on Orthodoxy in the Episcopal Church* (Grand Rapids, 1993), 65-79; Davies, *A Religion of the Word*, 181-82.

reformers could seize upon this vision, carefully sifting and proposing specific correlations between events and images described in scriptural representations of history's course. Latimer presumably would have read the biblical parables in a historicist manner, interpreting his context as an arena of divine intervention and a summons to radical repentance, thereby infusing his preaching with eschatological urgency and contemporary relevance.[53]

After a brief recap of the topics covered during the previous *Sermons of the Plough*—what doctrine should be taught in Christ's Church—Latimer announced that his intention was to declare who should preach and teach Christian doctrine, and who should sow God's word in God's field (Works, I.59). This was a subject of great importance for the medieval church, and which was addressed by pastoral treatises, sermons, and handbooks to provide practical wisdom in relation to the theological and moral virtues—the character required of those who are called to preach. This topic was also of critical concern in England for Christian humanists such as Erasmus, and for the Protestant reformers, since, to a large degree, theology and homiletic instruction in the late medieval church had been divorced from pastoral practice, the social embodiment of faith, and obscured by excessive emphasis on technical skill for the art of sermon construction.[54] Yet the preacher's wisdom and holiness was a matter of perennial concern. New Testament writers addressed this topic, especially through the *Pastoral Epistles*, and during the fifth century Augustine discussed the matter at length in the first handbook for Christian preachers, *On Christian Doctrine*, in which he wrote,

---

[53] The homily, *An Exhortation to Obedience*, asserts of the pope: "The Bishop of Rome teacheth immunities, privileges, exempcions, and disobedience, most clearly agaynst Christes doctrine and S. Peters. He ought, therefore, rather to be called Antichriste and the successor of the Scribes and Pharisees" (*Homilies*, 168). For discussions of English apocalypticism, see Curtis V. Bostick, *The Anti-Christ and the Lollards: Apocalypticsm in Late Medieval and Reformation England* (Leiden, 1998), 1-2, 51-56, 177-95; K.R. Frith, *The Apocalyptic Tradition in Reformation Britain 1530-1645* (Oxford, 1979); Marjorie Reeves, *The Prophetic Sense of History in Medieval and Renaissance Europe*, Variorum Collected Series (Aldershot, 1999), 40-72.

[54] Servais Pincaers, O.P., *The Sources of Christian Ethics*, trans. Sr. Mary Thomas Noble, O.P. (Washington, 1995), 240-59; Mary E. O'Carroll, SND, *A Thirteenth-Century Preacher's Handbook: Studies in MS Laud Misc. 511* (Toronto, 1997), 1-74; James J. Murphy, *Medieval Rhetoric: A History of Rhetorical Theory From Saint Augustine to the Renaissance* (Berkeley, 1974), 85-127, 292-332. This was a critical issue for many in England during the early sixteenth-century. See McConica, *English Humanists and Reformation Politics*, 13-105. On Erasmus' desire for the practical embodiment of wisdom, see Pierre Hadot, *Philosophy as a Way of Life*, ed. Arnold I. Davidson (Oxford, 1995), 33; Romanus Cessario, O.P., *Christian Faith & The Theological Life* (Washington D.C., 1995), 132; Peter Marshall discusses expectations of priestly holiness in *The Catholic Priesthood and the English Reformation* (Oxford, 1994), 96-117.

But for us to be listened to with obedient compliance, whatever the grandeur of the speaker's utterances, his manner of life carries more weight . . . There are plenty of people, after all, who seek an excuse for their bad lives in those of their very own leaders and teachers, replying in their hearts, or even bursting out with it and saying to their faces, "Why don't you yourself do what you are telling me to do?" Thus it happens that they do not listen obediently to someone who doesn't listen to himself, and that they despise the word of God being preached to them along with the preacher.[55]

Moreover, in the *Pastoral Rule*, Gregory the Great instructed priests on their conduct and speech.

The ruler should be exemplary in conduct, that by his way of life he may show the way of life to his subjects, and that the flock, following the teaching and conduct of its shepherd, may proceed the better through example than words . . . His voice penetrates the hearts of his hearers the more readily, if his way of life commends what he says"[56]

Writing in the thirteenth century, Humbert of Romans, Preacher General of the Dominicans, offered practical wisdom regarding the character of preachers in the *Treatise on the Formation of Preachers*.

So if preaching is to be meritorious for the preacher as well as beneficial to those who listen to it, the preacher must avoid preaching without authority, he must not be a notorious sinner, he must not deviate from the truth, what he does must accord with what he says, he must be more interested in spiritual gain than worldly profit, he must not preach with a view to doing other people down, he must not upset his hearers with foolish words, he must not give occasion for any evil, he must not be without evidence of doing penance, and his motivation must not lack charity.[57]

Erasmus similarly exhorted those in holy orders regarding their life and speech in the preface to the *Enchridion*.

Let Christ remain that which he is, the center with a number of circles surrounding Him. Do not remove the target from its own central position. Those who are nearest to Christ, priests, bishops, cardinals, and popes, and all whose

---

[55] Augustine, *Teaching Christianity: De Doctrina Christiana*, trans. Edmund P. Hill (New York, 1996), IV.60.

[56] St. Gregory the Great, *Pastoral Care*. Ancient Christian Writers, ed. and trans. Henry Davis, S.J. (New York, 1950), 21.

[57] Humbert of Romans, "Treatise on the Formation of Preachers" in *Early Dominicans: Selected Writings*, ed. Simon Tugwell, O.P. (New York, 1982), 184. Tugwell states that what is different about the nature of Humbert's work from the *ars praedicandi* of the medieval period is his emphasis on the spirituality and character of the preacher rather than skill or technique. See his introduction in *Early Dominicans: Selected Writings*, 181-82.

duty it is to follow the Lamb wheresoever He shall go, let them embrace what is so pure, and as far as they can, let them transfer this to those nearest to them.[58]

The character of preachers and their preaching, for instructing and enlivening the church, was the subject of Latimer's introduction, "For preaching of the gospel is one of God's plough-works." Biblical metaphors depict the activity of pastors among their people: "God's ploughland, God's field, is the faithful congregation and the preacher is the sower, the one who sows God's field with God's seed, God's word found in the Bible." A true prelate "is that man, whosoever he be, that hath a flock taught of him; whosoever hath any spiritual charge in the faithful congregation, and whosoever he be that hath cure of souls" (Works, I.59-60).[59] Latimer acknowledged this interpretation of the priesthood would be radical for many, an offensive departure from the familiar application of farming parables to monastic vows and practice. He viewed these established interpretations as a "racking of the scripture" and attributed their continued acceptance to a refusal to read scripture in a prophetic and self-critical way, as the expression of pride which was preventing many from perceiving the presence of God's future which was being revealed in their midst (Works, I.60).[60]

To incite an acceptance of preaching as the primary instrument of reform, Latimer likened the preacher to the ploughman, since each must labor in all seasons of the year and with special tasks in each season. Just as the ploughman first plows and then tills, breaks, ridges, harrows, manures and weeds, so too, must the prelate tarry in bringing parishioners to right faith bearing fruit in good works. This was articulated in the *Book of Homilies*.

> A faith that embraceth Christ, and trusteth in his merits; a lively faith, a justifying faith; a faith that maketh a man righteous, without respect of works: as ye have it very well declared and set forth in the Homily . . . now casting them down with the law, and with threatenings of God for sin; now ridging them up again with the gospel, and with the promises of God's favour: now weeding them, by telling them their faults and making them forsake sin; now clotting them by breaking their stony hearts and by making them supplehearted and by making them to have

---

[58] *Christian Humanism and the Reformation: Selected Writings of Erasmus*, ed. John C. Olin (New York, 1982), 117.

[59] See Hudson's discussion of Lollard ecclesiology with its central emphasis on preaching scripture. *Premature Reformation*, 314-58; Malcolm Lambert, *Medieval Heresy: Popular Movements from the Gregorian Reform to the Reformation* (Oxford, 1992), 241-46; see also "The Nature of the Church" and "The Duty of the Priesthood" in *Selections from English Wycliffite Writings*, ed. Anne Hudson (Toronto, 1997).

[60] The exercise of prudence and adherence to the standard of decorum were important matters for Renaissance Humanists who appropriated medieval teaching on moral theology and the tradition of classical rhetoric. Victoria Kahn, *Rhetoric, Prudence, and Skepticism in the Renaissance* (Ithaca, 1985), 29-54.

hearts of flesh; that is soft hearts, and apt for doctrine to enter in; now teaching them to know God rightly and to know their duty to God and their neighbors; now exhorting them, when they know their duty, that they do it and be diligent in it (Works, I. 62).

In addition, the *Book of Homilies* drew from the wisdom of John Chrysostom.

Whatsoever is required to salvacion of man is fully conteyned in the Scripture of God. He that is ignoraunte maye there learne and have knowledge. He that is harde harted and an obstinate synner shall there finde eternall tormentes, prepared of Gods justice to make him afraied and to mollifye him. He that is oppressed with misery in this world shal there find relief in the promises of eternal life, to his great consolacion and comfort. He that is wounded by the devil unto death shall find there medecine, wherby he may be restored agayn unto health. If it shal require to teach any truth or reprove false doctrine, to rebuke any vice, to commend any vertue, to geve good counsail, to comfort or exhort, or to do any other thyng requisite for our salvacion, all those things, we may learne plentifully of the Scripture.[61]

The Edwardians' robust confidence in scripture and its authority for preaching—which is manifested by living faith in Christ and godly obedience—strengthened Latimer's appeal for an increase of financial support: "Great is their [preachers'] business, and therefore great should be their hire" (Works, I.62). Financial provision for resident preachers and itinerant evangelists was desperately needed for the meat of scripture, rather than mere "dainties," to nourish the people through a steady diet of gospel teaching.[62] Latimer attributed this lack of preaching to the clergy's involvement in political and economic affairs, and to their habitual dependence upon the church's penitential practices for financial gain. "Many make a strawberry of it (preaching), ministering it once a year, but such do not the office of good prelates" . . . "And how few of them there be throughout this realm that give meat to their flock as they should do, the Visitors can best tell. Too few; Too few" (Works, I.62). According to Latimer, activities unrelated to the task of ploughing-preaching had prevented non-resident and non-preaching clergy from fulfilling their priestly vocation: "They hawk, they hunt, they card, they dice; they pastime in their prelacies with gallant gentlemen, with their dancing minions, and with their fresh companions, so that ploughing is set aside." Such examples of pastoral negligence evoked moral indignation: "Cursed be he that

---

[61] *Homilies*, 62.

[62] On economic changes and support in relation to the clergy see Felicity Heal, "Economic Problems of the Clergy" in ed. Felicity Heal and R. O'Day, *Church and Society in England: Henry VIII to James I* (London, 1977), 99-119; idem, *The English Clergy: The Emergence and Consolidation of a Profession* (Leicester, 1979), 24-32, 232-49; idem, *Of Prelates and Princes: A Study of the Economic and Social Position of the Tudor Episcopate*, 1-19, 126-67.

doth the work of God negligently and guilefully!" . . . "A sore word for them that are negligent in discharging their office, or have done it fraudulently; for that is the thing that maketh the people ill."

According to Latimer, many non-preaching prelates who had turned away from their parishes misjudged the difficulties inherent in the preacher's task. This had caused them to lose heart upon encountering stony ground, and in their disappointment, to inquire of their vocation, "What shall I look for among thorns, but pricking and scratching? What among stones, but stumbling? What among serpents, but stinging?" (Works, I.64-66). Latimer' criticism was similar to a plough striking hard, rocky soil.

> They are so troubled with lordly living, they be so placed in palaces, couched in courts, ruffling in their tents, dancing in their dominions, burdened with ambassages, pampering of their paunches, like a monk that maketh his jubilee; munching in their mangers, and moiling in their gay manors and mansions, and so troubled with loitering in their lordships, that they cannot attend it. They are otherwise occupied, some in king's matters, some are ambassadors, some of the privy council, some to furnish the court, some are lords of the parliament, some are presidents, and comptrollers of mints (Works, I.67).

In order to provide an alternative vision, Latimer invoked the authority of the apostles, whose choice had been to preach rather than to lord: "For Paul was no sitting bishop, but a walking and a preaching bishop . . . he left behind him the plough going still." He challenged the propriety of prelates in the rule of political matters and lamented their poor management of government affairs: "What is their charge, what is their duty?" Should we have ministers of the church to be comptrollers of the mints? Is this a meet office for a priest that hath the cure of souls?" Alluding to the wisdom of St. Paul in I Corinthians 6, Latimer accused "worldly prelates" of depriving the church of preaching and contributing to its spiritual malnourishment (Works, I.68).[63]

In addition to calling for repentance, Latimer appealed for an increase in opportunities for equipping the laity to manage the affairs of the realm, which would free priests and prelates to return to their pastoral calling, and most important, to preaching: "If there be never a wise man, make a water bearer, a tinker, a cobbler, a slave, a groom, a yeoman, or a poor beggar, lord president" (Works, I.68.).[64] According to Latimer, the realization of England's spiritual and social reform would occur only through a return of clergy and laity to their

---

[63] On the role of medieval clergy in political and economic affairs see Swanson, *Church and Society in Late Medieval England*, 27-139. For a summary of medieval criticisms directed towards clergy see G.R. Owst, *Literature and Pulpit in Medieval England* (New York, 1961), 81-101; see Dickens, *The English Reformation*, 61-80, 321-25.

[64] On increased lay education and participation in the leadership of the realm see Claire Cross, *Church and People*, 81-100; Rosemary O'Day, "Hugh Latimer, Prophet of the Kingdom" *Historical Research* LXV.158 (London,1992), 263-64; Fritz Caspari, *Humanism and the Social Order in Tudor England*, 1-15.

respective vocations as affirmed by St. Paul in I Thessalonians: "'Let everyman do his own business, and follow his calling.'" Latimer concludes: "Let the priest preach, and the nobleman handle temporal matters. I would all men would look to their duty as God hath called them; and then we would have a flourishing Christian commonwealth" (Works, I.70).[65]

Latimer's prescription for the realm's cure was strong medicine indeed, since it viewed the absence of preaching as a failure of pastoral duty which was even more life-threatening than a ploughman's refusal to work the land: "And as it is necessary to have this ploughing for the sustenance of the body, so we must have also the other for the satisfaction of the soul, or else we cannot live ghostly" (Works, I.66). Drawing an analogy from the two types of ploughing, Latimer joined social reform with religious renewal, and extending his moral criticism to the practice of enclosure which was eliminating large amounts of open, common land. Both humanists and reformers viewed the practice of enclosure as a ruthless expression of greed, sin that was a hindrance to both bodily and church ploughing. Latimer diagnosed the two forms of sin, spiritual and material manifestations of enclosure, as a disease which afflicted the whole realm—greed and pursuit of idolatry—and which required radical treatment: clergy must get their ploughs to moving, preaching as they should for the creation of living faith and the flourishing of righteousness into a godly commonwealth (Works, I.66-7).[66]

The practices of ploughing and enclosure served material and metaphorical purposes in Latimer's discourse. On the one hand, they enabled him to identify particular conflicts related to agrarian practices in England; on the other hand, they signified a larger reality disclosed in common, earthy forms of life: a battle that was being waged between true and false images of religion and life, which was caught in the cosmic struggle between God and the devil. The images of ploughing and enclosing also served Latimer's prophetic goal which was the overcoming of abusive practices and the creation of corporate faith in Christ.

---

[65] O'Day, "Hugh Latimer, Prophet of the Kingdom," 276. "In such a commonwealth, all men and women will follow the vocations to which God has called them and, diligently working within them, they will prosper." Latimer gives no indication of his source in emphasizing vocation. The Preface to the *Book of Homilies* states that their purpose is to move the people to "honor and worshippe almighty God and diligently serve hym, ever on accordyne to their degree, state, and vocacion" (*Homilies*, 56).

[66] On the problem of enclosure, its material and metaphorical importance during the Edwardian period see the following discussions: McRae, *God speed the plough*, 23-117; Dickens, *The English Reformation*, 179-80, 246-51; Roger Manning, *Village Revolts: Social Protest and Popular Disturbances in England, 1509-1640* (Oxford, 1988), 27-39; White, *Social Criticism*, 27-28; C.G. Clay, *Economic Expansion and Social Change: England 1500-1700*, 2 Vols. (Cambridge, 1984), I.222; Whitney R.D. Jones, *The Mid-Tudor Crisis 1539-1563* (London, 1973), chapter 5; idem, *The Tudor Commonwealth 1529-1559* (London, 1970) 70-71; Joan Thirsk, *The Rural Economy of England: Collected Essays* (London, 1984), 35-36.

Familiar imagery provided fresh means for announcing a new social order, the creation of faithful ploughmen at their respective vocations: clergy preaching the Word, magistrates enforcing the law, and parishioners performing the Word through acts of mercy towards the neighbor (Works, I.68-69).[67]

Latimer's admonition to the laity was especially appropriate, since many had enriched themselves through the dissolution of monasteries and chantries, from transfer or sale of episcopal lands and church property, and by depriving the poor of relief and preachers of their livings.[68] Singling out London, England's most important city, Latimer called its people to account for their sins, to repent, and to participate in God's renovation of their common life.[69] The city of London had given birth to the English Reformation; it was where the new faith initially was evangelized, the New Jerusalem where it was showcased under its Christian prince, the Mount Zion from which its evangelical message was spread, and where its enthusiasm for reform was rekindled. As bishop of London, Nicholas Ridley observed that, from London "goeth example . . . into all the rest of the king's majesty's whole realm."

Addressing the moral failure of London,[70] Latimer accused its people of being rich, proud, malicious, and merciless. He compared them with the citizens of Nebo in the days of the prophet Jeremiah, declaring that London possessed more pride, cruelty, covetousness, oppression, and superstition than even that ancient city. Echoing the prophetic call of Jeremiah: "I say repent, O London; repent, repent! I think if Nebo had had the preaching that thou hast they would have been converted" Latimer's diagnosis was severe. London had never been so ill, with so little pity and compassion for the poor, the hungry and the sick, with such meager desire for supporting education and godly learning. Latimer's appeal was to the citizens of London for amending their lives and for its prelates to begin preaching by setting their ploughs at work for the ground to bring forth fruit (Works, I.65).

Latimer devoted the majority of the second half of the *Sermon of the Plough* to depicting the labors of the devil, the chief rival of all true preachers, who continued to work through the influence of traditionalist clergy, their teaching and practices. He inquired, "Who is the most diligentest bishop and prelate in all England, that passeth all the rest in doing his office?" His answer describes the weapons which were being used by the devil for his work of ploughing:

---

[67] O'Day, "Hugh Latimer, Prophet of the Kingdom," 263-64; McRae, *God speed the plough*, 28-36.

[68] Heal, *Of Prelates and Princes*, 1-179; Dickens, *The English Reformation*, 167-81, 230-47; Joyce Youings, *The Dissolution of the Monasteries* (London, 1971), 117-30; MacCulloch, *Tudor Church Militant*, 8; Claire Cross, *Church and People*, 53-100.

[69] On the strategic importance of London for the reformation of the realm see Susan Brigden, *London and the Reformation* (Oxford, 1989), 1-5, 458-587, 633-37; MacCulloch, *Tudor Church Militant*, 99-111.

[70] Brigden, *London and the Reformation*, 469-90; Davies, *A Religion of the Word*, 206-209.

superstitions and popery in the form of candles, beads, censing, images, ashes, holy water, and other inventions which take the place of books, the Bible, and the gospel (Works, I.70-71).[71]

The evangelicals viewed such traditional practices as obscuring the glory of Christ's cross and hindering its power from affecting the faith and life of the people. They were especially vehement in their attacks on the significance of purgatory, since the commitment of resources for the maintenance of images and holy places had contributed to a decrease in works of mercy, and in feeding and clothing the poor.[72] The need for such expressions of mercy was especially critical during the Edwardian reign, since demand for poor relief seriously depleted local funds. The effects of enclosure, inflation, rack-renting, military expenditures, population growth, and the loss of monastic charity had created a crisis of poverty that was viewed with alarm. Latimer appealed for a decrease of popular investment in the old religion—Satan's "cockle and darnal"—and an increase of ploughing, for evangelical preaching that would bear fruit in acts of charity to the poor.

> Down with Christ's cross, up with purgatory pick purse, up with them, the popish purgatory, I mean. Away with clothing the naked, the poor and impotent; up with decking images, and gay garnishing of stocks and stones: up with man's traditions and his laws, down with God's traditions and his most holy word . . . Oh that our prelates would be as diligent to sow the corn of good doctrine, as Satan is to sow cockle and darnel (Works, I.70-2).

Latimer's warning was to be aware of traditionalist clergy, ex-monastics, ex-friars, and former chantry priests who continued encouraging loyalty to Catholic teaching and resistance to Protestant reforms.[73]

> *Circuit*, he goeth about in every corner of his diocess; he goeth on visitation daily, he leaveth no place of his cure unvisited; he walketh round from place to place, and ceaseth not. *Sicut leo*, as a lion, that is, strongly, boldly, and proudly; stately and fiercly with haughty looks, with his proud countenances, with his stately braggings. *Rugiens*, roaring; for he letteth not slip any occasion to speak or to roar out when he seeth his time. *Quaerens*, he goeth about seeking, and not sleeping, as our bishops do; but he seeketh diligently, he searcheth diligently all corners, where as he may have his prey. He roveth abroad in every place of his diocess; he standeth not still, he is never at rest, but ever in hand with his plough, that it may go forward. There was never such a preacher in England as he is. Who is able to

---

71 On the educational program of the reformers, see the essays in *The Godly Kingdom of Tudor England: Great Books of the English Reformation* ed. John E. Booty (Wilton, 1981).

72 The homily, "of Good Woorkes," lists forms of counterfeit religion, including the traditional practices condemned by Latimer (*Homilies*, 112); Davies, *A Religion of the Word*, 175-83, 214-20.

73 On the conflict among the clergy, see Brigden, *Reformation in London*, 392-404.

tell his diligent preaching, which every day, and every hour, laboureth to sow cockle and darnel, that he may bring out of form, and out of estimation and room, the institution of the Lord's Supper and Christ's Cross? (Works, I.71-72).

To bring about the effective plucking of Satan's "cockle and darnel" from his listeners' minds, Latimer defined the Sacrament of the Altar as a remembrance of Christ's once-for-all sacrifice, rather than a sacrifice which is repeatedly offered by a priest.

For he was a continual sacrifice, as I said, in effect, fruit, operation, and virtue; as though he had from the beginning of the world, and continually should to the world's end, hang still on a cross; and he is fresh hanging on the cross now, to them that believe and trust in him, as he was fifteen hundred years ago, when he was crucified (Works, I.73).

Latimer's hoped to subvert the image of priestly celebration of the mass and a related web of practices which constituted traditional religion. Declaring these forms of devotion as idolatrous, he compared them to the serpent, lifted up by Moses in the wilderness, and a sign of Israel's judgment, "to evacuate Christ's death, and to make of it small efficacy and virtue" . . . "Woe to thee, O devil, woe worth thee, that hast prevailed so far and so long; that hast made England to worship false gods, forsaking Christ their Lord."

Calling the realm to turn from its idolatry, Latimer announced the finality of Christ's death, the message of the cross which is capable of producing living faith, salvation, and righteousness: "If Christ by his death draweth all things to himself, and draweth all men to salvation, and to heavenly bliss, then the priests at the mass, the popish mass, I say, what can they draw, when Christ draweth all, but lands and goods from the right heirs? (Works, I.73-74).[74] Latimer's preaching anticipated a major shift in the church's worship, in addition to a radical realignment of pastoral authority and practice which would soon be implemented through a new *Ordinal,* an *Order of Communion,* and the *Book of Common Prayer.*[75] These new arrangements would be grounded within a theology of the Word that related the authority of preaching much more closely to the sacramental efficacy of Baptism and the Mass.[76]

Laboring as God's ploughman at Paul's Cross, Latimer sowed the seed of

---

[74] See the homily, *of the Salvacion of All Mankynde, Homilies,* 85. "Nevertheless, because fayth doth directely sende us to Christ for remission of our synnes, and that by faithe geven us of God."

[75] On the authority and activity of the priesthood in late medieval England see Marshall, *The Catholic Priesthood and the English Reformation,* 108-40; Duffy, *The Stripping of the Altars,* 53-130. On the dependence of Cranmer's pastoral and liturgical reforms on transformation by the Word in its various forms, see MacCulloch, *Thomas Cranmer,* 367-430; Wall, *Transformations of the Word,* 5-50.

[76] Marshall, *The Catholic Priesthood and the English Reformation,* 233-36; Steinmetz, "The Intellectual Appeal of the Reformation" 467-69.

the Word for the renewal of the realm.[77] Because this vision of preaching was dependent upon the crown for its support and realization., Latimer warned of "blanchers" in the King's Council, presumably conservative Bishops such as Bonner of London and Gardiner of Winchester, who actively lobbied for slower and less radical reforms, accommodated for peaceful acceptance by the people.[78] Latimer compared traditionalist bishops to those who were advisors to Israel's King Hezekiah, but were unable to prevent idolatry from being destroyed (Works, I.76).

MacCulloch has argued that the Edwardian Reformers, outside the court and council chamber, drew their chief support from Cambridge dons, a minority of the clergy, and an unknown number of people below the social level of gentry. The Edwardians could not count on widespread support from the majority of laypeople in positions of power, nor could they expect more than a few bishops to cooperate with the dismantling of traditional religion, although they would not be able to accomplish much without them. A major preoccupation during the early years of Edward's reign was to conciliate the conservative bishops in order to gain grudging consent for step-by-step progress in reformation as a safeguard against more extreme radicals.[79] Gardiner and Bonner were the most formidably aggressive spokesmen among the conservative clergy, since Gardiner had played a major role in arranging Latimer's ban from preaching during the latter years of Henry's reign.[80]

Gardiner openly expressed concern over Edward's minority, suggesting that further religious changes be deferred until the king became of age: "I think silence best, with reverence to the authority of our late sovereign, whose soul God pardon, and therein to remain, till our sovereign lord that now is, come to his perfect age, whom God grant to find such people as his father left, not altered with any innovation."[81] Bonner joined Gardiner in enforcing the *Six Articles of Religion*, which were still in effect, to regulate religion and to embarrass the evangelicals, with Bonner's diocese of London requesting and receiving a commission to continue making inquiries and prosecuting under the authority of the *Six Articles Act*.

---

[77] Bryan Crockett, *The Play of Paradox: Stage and Sermon in Renaissance England*, 5-36. It is interesting that Crockett, in the context of a study primarily devoted to acting, drama, and the theatre, provides a clear interpretation and discussion of the significant shift in the locus of sacramental activity from the mass to the sermon.

[78] On conservative resistance by the bishops see MacCulloch, *Thomas Cranmer*, 363-409; *The Letters of Stephen Gardiner* ed. J.A. Muller (Cambridge, 1933, Westport, rpt., 1970), 286-314; Foxe, *Acts and Monuments*, v.23-269; for an account of Bonner, see Foxe, v.716-96; Brigden, *London and the Reformation*, 447-49; Glyn Redworth, *In Defence of the Church Catholic*, 248-83; On Edward's council see D.E. Hoak, *The King's Council in the Reign of Edward VI* (Cambridge, 1976), 115-29.

[79] MacCulloch, *Tudor Church Militant*, 68; Davies, *A Religion of the Word*, 197-98.

[80] MacCulloch, *Tudor Church Militant*, 59; Chester, *Hugh Latimer*, 159.

[81] *Letters of Gardiner*, 210-11.

Moreover, when the royal visitation was announced for the summer of 1547, both Bonner and Gardiner protested, pointing to the fact that the teaching of Edward's official homilies on justification disagreed with the *Six Articles* of the late king. In a letter to the council, Gardiner argued against the homily of salvation,

> . . . That the people should be taught only faith justifieth; with this addition, how this manner of teaching of 'only faith justifieth' is old and ancient, and that who impugneth the doctrine of only faith, as it is in this last book taught, is not to be reputed a true Christian man. Which is a terrible speech and a marvelous to be published in this realm to the condemnation of our late sovereign lord, the condemnation of ourself, and the prejudice of the truth, to affirm that ancient which is not ancient, and call that the teaching of Holy Scripture, which Holy Scripture doth not maintain.[82]

Bonner insisted that royal visitors show their commission, stating that he would observe the injunctions only, "if they be not contrary and repugnant to God's law and the statutes and ordinances of the Church.[83] Winchester wrote to Cranmer, "although his body [Henry's] no longer liveth among us, yet his memory should in such sort continue in honor and reverence, as your Grace should not impute to him now that was not told him in his life."[84] A consequence of these stalling tactics was that Bonner and Gardiner were eventually imprisoned for their failure to cooperate with the crown.[85]

In January 1548, the government formulated a eucharistic policy, the "Act against Revilers of the Sacrament and for Communion in Both Kind's," to prevent debate or dissent from spinning out of control. The Act prompted two meetings between Somerset and Gardiner that coincided with the time when Latimer was to preach at Paul's Cross.[86] The attention shown to Gardiner, who persisted in his refusal to conform, may have triggered Latimer's attack against the conservative bishops during the *Sermon on the Plough*. Redworth comments, "Their [evangelicals] distrust of Gardiner was fueled to the point where they actually saw Winchester as a threat to their regime by his inability to accept or comprehend their assumptions about such things as the nature of the community of true believers . . . its role in society, its wealth, the function of its clergy and laity." Gardiner did not even share their vocabulary, their "world view . . . [which] was provided by an all-encompassing concern with the potentially transforming effects of the gospel on both individuals and the social order."[87] Interestingly, these major disagreements had their roots in the

[82] *Letters of Gardiner*, 362.
[83] Foxe, *Acts and Monuments*, v.724.
[84] *Letters of Gardiner*, 310.
[85] Elton, *Reform & Reformation*, 339-40.
[86] On the turmoil created in London by debate over the sacrament, see Brigden, *London and the Reformation*, 433-42; Redworth, *In Defence of the Church Catholic*, 258-59.
[87] Redworth, *In Defence of the Church Catholic*, 260.

Henrician period, which accounts for Gardiner's opposition to Erasmus' *Paraphrases*, the *Book of Homilies*, his doubts concerning the sufficiency of the English Bible to serve as a layman's book, and his belief that its text had been corrupted by the process of human transmission and translation.[88]

> For, albeit the authority of the Scripture dependeth not upon man, yet the ministration of the letter, which is writing and speaking, is exercised, and hath been from the beginning delivered, through man's hand, and taught by man's mouth; which men the Scripture calleth holy men; and that is, contrary to liars.[89]

Gardiner, moreover, voiced opposition to government-sanctioned iconoclasm during the royal visitation. Upon receiving a report from Portsmouth, where it was reported that images of Christ and the saints "had been most contemptuously pulled down and spitefully handled," Gardiner wrote to Edward Vaughn, commander of the garrison.

> And if we, because we can read . . . shall pull away the books [images] from the rest and would our letters only in estimation, and blind all them, shall not they have just cause to mistrust what is meant? And if the cross be a truth, and if it be true that Christ suffered, why may we not have a writing thereof, such as all can read, that is to say, an image?[90]

Despite challenges from conservative resistance and changing popular opinion, after just one year in power Somerset and his Protestant colleagues had accomplished everything needed for further progress toward purifying the church. Serious opposition had been eliminated in the Privy Council, justification by faith had been established in the *Book of Homilies*, traditional devotional practices curtailed, heresy legislation repealed, and the acceptance of clerical marriage secured.[91] John King considers the timing of Latimer's return to the Paul's Cross pulpit in early 1548 as marking a symbolic beginning of the true English church, a celebration of the transition from the Old Law to the New Law at the advent of Christ. This was continued during Candlemas, when the bearing of candles was left off throughout the whole of London, when the use of ashes was omitted on Ash Wednesday, and when the bearing of

---

[88] Redworth, *In Defence of the Church Catholic*, 164-67, 258-63; Paul O'Grady, *Henry VIII and the Conforming Catholics*, 120-35.

[89] Foxe, *Acts and Monuments*, vi.40.

[90] Foxe, *Acts and Monuments*, vi.27. For a revisionist account of Gardiner which argues that his desire was to support the Reformation but without violating the rule of law during Edward's minority see Redworth, *In Defence of the Church Catholic*, 248-85; MacCulloch, *Cranmer*, 375-77; on Edwardian iconoclasm see Aston, *England's Iconoclasts*, I.259-60.

[91] MacCulloch, *Tudor Church Militant*, 59, 81; Haigh, *English Reformations*, "It was the Protestants who really made the running in 1548, forcing the pace of change by their books, sermons, and agitation." 173; Norman Jones, *The English Reformation*, 154-170.

palms was left out on Palm Sunday. In addition, the institution of a revised English service was implemented at St. Paul's Cathedral on Whitsunday (Pentecost), thus coinciding with the celebration of the birth of the church through the descent of the Holy Spirit upon the apostles.[92]

Latimer concluded the *Sermon of the Plough* with an appeal to Edward, a new Hezekiah, for promoting the glory of God across the realm; and for exhorting faithful prelates to apply their ploughs with diligence to the preaching of the Word: thus reform of the realm must follow reformation of religion.[93] The accession of a godly king would be providential for turning hope into reality.

> There is now very good hope that the king's majesty, being by the help of good governance of his most honorable counselors, trained and brought up in learning, and knowledge of God's word, will shortly provide a remedy, and set an order therein; which that it may be so, let us pray for him. Ye have great cause to pray for him (Works, I.77-8).

The *Sermon of the Plough* articulated a vision for clergy and laity in a re-formed Church of England—a social embodiment of the gospel which Latimer had announced, whose aim was to effect what he had prescribed by means of his words: "I have assayed to set forth my plough, to prove what I could do."[94] Depicting himself as God's ploughman and England as God's field, Latimer rendered a dramatic performance of a "new world" being brought to speech through the powerful activity of the Word. As Matheson comments, "The Reformation caught the popular imagination precisely because it presented the age-old Christian game with poetic, mythic, dramatic originality, with verve and panache."[95] Latimer's provided a convincing display of the power of preaching for addressing contemporary challenges and reconstituting the religious and political life of the realm. The significance of *The Sermon of the Plough* was attested by its immediate printing and distribution, which was followed by Latimer's appointment as preacher extraordinary to the king.[96]

---

[92] King, *English Reformation Literature*, 151.
[93] MacCulloch, *Tudor Church Militant*, 14-15; *Literary Remains of King Edward the Sixth* ed. J.G. Nichols 2 Vols. (Roxburghe Club, 1857), cciv. The "Homily on Rebellion" written in 1559, refers to Edward as "our Josiah" (*Homilies*, 214); Davies, *A Religion of the Word*, 177-82, 215-19.
[94] Robert Whiting, *Local Responses to the English Reformation* (New York, 1998), 117-81.
[95] Matheson, *The Rhetoric of the Reformation*, 241.
[96] Chester, *Hugh Latimer*, 164-65.

Chapter 4

Agent of the Word – Agent of the Court

As the diligence of this man of God never ceased, all the time of King Edward, to profit the church both publicly and privately . . . that God not only gave unto him his Spirit plenteously and comfortably to preach his word unto his church ... that if England ever had a prophet, he might seem to be the one (John Foxe, Acts and Monuments).

As preacher extraordinary of Edward's reign, Latimer continued the homiletic pattern of the *Sermon of the Plough*, sowing, proclaiming, and accommodating the Word for the court of England's boy-king. The editor of the *Sermons* describes Latimer's court sermons in terms of God's ploughman diligently at work: "He declared the message of the living God; he supplanted and rooted out all sins and vice; he planted and crafted in men's hearts plenteousness of all spiritual blessings in Jesus Christ our Lord" (Works, I.82).

This chapter discusses Latimer's role as an agent of both the Word and the Edwardian court, treating his preaching primarily as prophetic discourse and secondarily as propaganda for Edward's regime. This allows for a fresh hearing of Latimer's voice, since to limit discussion of the court sermons to their political import obscures Latimer's scriptural rhetoric to instruct, to engage, and most important, to convert his listeners. Latimer focused his discourse to give it presence and clarity and to establish identity between himself and his hearers, calling Edward and his courtiers to action in response to a moving parade of biblical narratives and images.[1]

Latimer's powerful sermons before Edward define him as both a biblical and social preacher, sounding a remarkable reforming ring that is particular in its content and national in its scope. Latimer's goal, from first to last, was to define and create a Christian commonwealth; a vision grounded in faith in the power of the Word for bringing this about. This lends a prophetic tone to the sermons, which were directed against idolatry on the one hand and social injustice on the other; thus, conspicuous throughout the sermons is Latimer's fear of God's

---

[1] See the excellent summary of Latimer's preaching provided by Rosemary O'Day, "Hugh Latimer: Prophet of the Kingdom" in *Historical Research* LXV.158 (1992), 258-76. This chapter, however, offers an exposition of the court sermons in context that goes beyond the brief analysis offered by O'Day. I follow the narrative provided by Chester, *Hugh Latimer*, 168-82.

wrath falling upon England if his call to revival should not be heeded. But everything to which Latimer calls his listeners must spring from the new, true faith that depends on the word of God, with preachers and preaching as the instruments through which salvation is announced and accomplished. Enjoying access to Edward his court and its pulpit, the ear of the press and the English people, Latimer confirmed that the future of the commonwealth was dependent on the renewal of the church, and that after centuries of silence, a new beginning was being given through the activity of the Word.[2]

An additional factor that presumably lent authority to Latimer's discourse was his authorship of the official homily, "An Homelie agaynst Contencion and Brawlynge."[3] The opening paragraph asserts, "But among all kydnes of contencion noe is more hurtfull then is contencion is matters of religion."[4] Echoing the message of Erasmus' *Paraclesis,* its rhetorical appeal for the creation of a Christian commonwealth was shaped by scripture.

> Is it not a shame for us that professe Christe to be worse then heathen people in a thynge chiefly perteyning to Christes religion? Shall philosophie perswade them more then Gods Woorde shall perswade us? Shall natural reason prevaile more with them then religion shall do with us? Shall mans wisdome leade them to that thynge whereunto the heavenly doctryne cannoty leade us? What blyndenesse, wilfulnesse, or rather madnesse is this?[5]

As John Wall notes, the homily offers a vigorous attack on religious disputes; its message is comprised primarily to confute. This polemical strategy, however, serves the overall vision of the *Book of Homilies* and the goal toward which its whole argument moves: to educate the people in active charity for the transformation of English society into a true Christian commonwealth.[6] Behind this call for England to realize this vision lay the urgency of obedience to God's will, which was summarized by Latimer: "We cannot be joynted to Christ our head, except we be glued with concord and charitie, one another. For he that is not in this unitie, is not of the church of Christ, which is a congregacion or

---

[2] Gottfried W. Locher, "Zwingli's influence in England and Scotland" in *Zwingli's Thought: New Perspectives* (Leiden, 1981), 359-62. Locher describes Latimer as Zwingli *revividus,* based on the replication of patterns evident in Zwingli's preaching (biblical and social). MacCulloch argues that this continental connection, primarily maintained by Cranmer, has been underestimated. "MacCulloch, *Tudor Church Militant,* 171-78; Davies, *A Religion of the Word,* 13-66, 199-209; McRae, *God speed the plough,* 32-35.

[3] *Homilies,* 191-201; See the convincing discussion of Latimer's authorship in John N. Wall, "The Vision of a Christian Commonwealth in the Book of Homilies of 1547: A Study of Christian Humanism and Early Tudor Religious Literature" (PhD diss. Harvard University, 1973), 32-33.

[4] *Homilies,* 191.

[5] *Homilies,* 197.

[6] Wall, *Transformations of the Word,* 121.

unitie together, and not a division."[7] This theme is consistent with the scope of Latimer's court sermons, since the need for harmony in the church and society—a Christian commonwealth—are not separate issues, but one requirement bearing the weight of the whole matter of salvation. The goal of the Christian life, therefore, is to live in obedience to God's commands, which means to live in unity and peace, an imitation of a divinely ordered creation.[8]

Latimer preached at Westminster Court during the Lenten seasons of 1548-1550. While the sermons of 1548 were not preserved, Latimer referred to them during his final Lenten sermon in 1550. According to Latimer, his words on the topic of restitution had evoked a dramatic response in the life of John Bradford. While engaged as secretary to Sir John Harrington, treasurer of the king's corps and buildings, Bradford was involved with Harrington in defrauding the government of 500 pounds. After hearing Latimer's preaching on restitution at court in 1548, Bradford apparently was so moved by contrition that he immediately wrote to Harrington to plead that they return the money. When Harrington balked, Bradford sought Latimer's counsel, the effect of which was to bring about payment by Harrington and Bradford's change of life for undertaking the study of divinity. Latimer recounted this story at court in 1550, bringing to memory the transforming effect of preaching and encouraging Edward to continue the promotion of preaching across the realm.[9]

Indeed, the dramatization of scripture's message for its revelatory and life-changing effects may best characterize Latimer's court sermons of 1549; homiletic performances which were delivered on seven successive Lenten Friday afternoons, with each being an enactment of the word of God for its particular time, place, and audience. When taken as a whole, the court sermons possess astounding accumulative persuasive force in keeping with the *ethos* of Edward's court, which provided the stage, scene, and audience for Latimer's renderings of the Bible's script.[10]

Coronation spectacle was an essential part of the public defense offered by the reformers on behalf of Edward to dramatize the transcendent origin of the young king's authority and supremacy. Speaking at Edward's coronation, Cranmer established precedence for a biblical and ideological interpretation of his sovereignty, thus conveying a message of hope for England's future and

---

[7] *Homilies*, 192.

[8] Wall, "The Vision of a Christian Commonwealth in the Book of Homilies of 1547," 137-33. See Wall's discussion of the *Book of Homilies* in, "Godly and Fruitful Lessons: The English Bible, Erasmus' Paraphrases, and the Book of Homilies," 92-138.

[9] Chester, *Hugh Latimer*, 165-66.

[10] See my discussion of Latimer's *Sermon of the Plough* and the relationship between drama and preaching in the previous chapter. See John N. King, *English Reformation Literature*, 271-318, for a detailed discussion of this relationship. King quotes Foxe, who emphasized the importance of "Printers, Playwrights, and Preachers" for the dramatic advance of the Reformation under Edward (277).

exhorting the young prince to build up a Christian commonwealth modeled on ancient Israel, where godly kings took the matter of reform into their hands:

> Your majesty is both God's vicegerent within your own dominions, and to see with your predecessor Josiah, God truly worshipped, and idolatry destroyed, the tyranny of bishops of Rome banished from your subjects, and images removed. These acts be signs of a second Josiah, who reformed the church of God in his days. You are to reward virtue, to revenge sin, to justify the innocent, to relieve the poor, to preserve peace, to repress violence and to execute justice throughout your realms.[11]

Sermons continued to be spectacular performances at the New Jerusalem of Edward's court, with the favor lavished upon Latimer's evangelical preaching assuming an important role in the unfolding drama of Somerset's protectorship. Royal iconography portrayed this drama, its *personae*, and its aim as a revolutionary act, a dynamic assault on the past, an apocalyptic struggle between Christ and anti-Christ. An illustration in Foxe's *Acts and Monuments* depicts the young king presiding over the royal court; in the house of God there is godly preaching and the austere but reverent performance of baptism and the eucharist. The peace of the new order, however, appears against a background of purposeful turmoil; a church building being stripped of popery, a bonfire being consumed of images, the agents of the Bishop of Rome fleeing for the English coast, salvaging whatever religious remains they can.[12]

Latimer figures into this drama within a woodcut calling attention to the Bible and its faithful preacher, which was first incorporated as a fold out in "The Seven Sermons of M. Hugh Latimer." This image later became an integral part of the *Book of Martyrs*, epitomizing the godliness of Edward's reign, inhering in scripture, its faithful preacher, and its attentive listeners. Latimer receives a place of prominence as court preacher in the Privy Gardens of Whitehall Palace where he and Edward appear to be on the same level, thus depicting a Protestant ordering of church and society and inverting medieval depictions of papal authority triumphing over emperors. Just as striking in this illustration is the presence of the laity; at the foot of the pulpit a woman reads the Bible. This defining image draws the preacher, in the figure of Latimer, to the center of a coherent reform movement based on the rule of vernacular scripture and an evangelical king extending into the life of common folk throughout the realm. Foxe highlights Latimer's court preaching by means of

---

[11] Thomas Cranmer, *Works*, II.127; Sidney Anglo, *Spectacle, Pageantry, and Early Tudor Policy* (Oxford, 1969), 275-300; King, *English Reformation Literature*, 161-69; Ernst Kantorowicz, *The King's Two Bodies: A Study in Medieval Political Theology* (Princeton, 1957), 9-21.

[12] MacCulloch, *Tudor Church Militant*, 9-10; John N. King, *Tudor Royal Iconography: Literature and Art in an Age of Religious Crisis* (Princeton, 1989), 90-101; Davies, *A Religion of the Word*, 197-200.

an allusion to the courage and eloquence of John Chrysostom: "The golden mouthe of thys preacher, long shut up before, was now opened agayne" . . . and that Latimer, "dispensed the fruitful woorde of the glorious gospel of Jesus Christ before the King and his whole courte, to the edification of many."[13]

The important study of Tudor court preaching by Peter McCullough[14] helps to recover the lost significance of a practice that made royal chapels one of the most important religious and political theaters in early modern England. An outdoor preaching place was created for Latimer, a substantial pulpit in what had been the Henrician Privy Garden, so that he would to be heard by four times as many listeners than normally stood in the King's Chapel. McCullough's research shows that the Whitehall preaching place provided a surface area of some 55,000 square feet, large enough to accommodate up to 5,000 people, a mixed audience that would include commoners, thus increasing the dramatic importance of court sermons. From the elevated windows of the Council Chamber protruding into the garden, the sovereign listened to the sermon, providing the preacher with a singular point of focus in the midst of the large crowds. This strategic pulpit stood in continuity with medieval preaching practice and the construction of outdoor pulpits, which usually were located on the hallowed grounds of churchyard cemeteries, convents, or monastery yards, with the most obvious example in medieval England being Paul's Cross, London. However, the significance of Whitehall was in its construction on secular rather than sacred ground, symbolizing the turn towards the Tudor subordination of church to crown, an arrangement creating a peculiar set of challenges for preachers who hoped to intrude upon the political sphere to claim it for the prophetic demands of God against the devil.[15]

This background serves to underscore the key role played by preaching at the court of Edward, an importance that increased with the king's call for weekly sermons.[16] Latimer's sermons complemented other court theatrical events with the peculiar drama of a one-man performance, providing religious and political discourse that addressed the regime's concerns: to destroy the old church of traditional devotion and to construct a new church on evangelical preaching and faith. Modeling itself on scripture, this program was represented in the biblical figures of King Josiah and King Solomon, who respectively purged the realm of Israel from idolatry and built a new temple for true worship of God. MacCulloch's assessment of the Edwardian Reformation and its

---

[13] Foxe, *Acts and Monuments* (1563), 1353.

[14] Peter E. McCullough, *Sermons at Court: Politics and Religion in Elizabethan and Jacobean Preaching* (Cambridge, 1998) On court preaching during Edward's reign and the establishment of the Whitehall pulpit, see 42-58; King, *English Reformation Literature*, 171-79.

[15] McCullough, *Sermons at Court*, 45-46. See the discussion on sermons and drama in Andrew Pettegree, *Reformation and the Culture of Persuasion* (Cambridge, 2005), 76-101.

[16] McCullough, *Sermons at Court*, 57.

leadership is relevant for understanding Latimer's role as its star preacher at court.

> There is much we may deplore about their six-year adventure under the boy-king, much that was negative, destructive and cynical in the revolution they released. However, we will misread their work and do injustice to their memories if we do not listen out for the genuine idealism, the righteous anger and the excitement, which were essential components of the play of King Edward.[17]

In contrast to this favorable view of the Edwardian period, historians have tended to focus on the economic and social problems of Somerset's presumably compromised and confused leadership from 1547-49. Latimer's court sermons are viewed as means of addressing these problems and for defending Somerset's administration and its policies. Latimer thus becomes the leading court prophet among Edward's Commonwealth men, a party or group of like-minded preachers and administrators devoted to a program of social reform in support of Somerset. The Commonwealth party message purportedly attacked evils arising from greed, especially in the practice of enclosure, as well as inflation and increased unemployment and destitution.

Following this line of interpretation, Geoffrey Elton comments on the court sermons: "It must be plain that the confused heaping up of delinquencies seen in the body politic constitutes at best only a general outburst of grieved spleen, devoid of either a reforming program or any rational understanding of what had gone wrong." Elton instead favors the policy set forth in Sir Thomas Smith's "Discourse of the Common Weal," which he refers to as, "the most notable piece of economic analysis in the sixteenth-century." According to Elton, Smith did not call for repressive laws or moral exhortations, but for a wise manipulation of the means of gain available, "so that the natural desire of individuals to better themselves should redound to the good of all." Compared with Smith, Latimer appears to be a conservative critic who, according to Elton, "was an old man with memories though still filled with passion" but woefully out of step with current events, and whose naïve view of England rendered his preaching rhetoric irrelevant.[18]

This chapter argues for a different perspective from which to view Latimer's court preaching, interpreting him as neither a carping critic nor designer of political plans and economic blueprints. To read the Lenten sermons in this manner flattens Latimer's prophetic discourse and empties his rhetoric of its

---

[17] MacCulloch, *Tudor Church Militant*, 9. For a different assessment of this period see Duffy, *The Stripping of the Altars*, 448-78.

[18] G. Elton, "Reform and the 'Commonwealth Men' of Edward's Reign" in *The English Commonwealth, 1547-1640*, ed. P. Clark and others (Leicester, 1979), 23-38; M.L. Bush, *The Government of Protector Somerset*, (1975), 61-70; A.B. Ferguson, *The Articulate Citizen and the English Renaissance* (Durham, 1965), 245-50; Christopher Haigh, *English Reformations*, 171-76; McRae, *God speed the plough*, 52-57.

biblically-derived aims and authority to reform the lives of his hearers. Rather than offering a program or techniques for the amelioration of social problems, Latimer's rhetoric of preaching lent relentless passion and energy to a much deeper religious revolution, a combination of prophecy, evangelism, and social vocation directed by God and advanced by the monarchy and its authorized preachers. Coincidentally, Latimer's Lenten series began as Parliament was adjourning from the session during which it approved the *Uniformity Act* that provided backing for the first *Book of Common Prayer*.[19] Arguably, this would have added even more urgency to Latimer's message: that a decisive break with the past had occurred, freeing England from oppressive religious tradition and its burdensome, abusive practices. At the heart of this program lay the conviction that God would act to resolve England's troubles, a program implemented through the preaching of the Word and obedience of the people in their respective callings, a sign of divine intervention in every aspect of society. Latimer therefore viewed his primary task as bringing the Bible to life, overcoming sin, and creating social righteousness through godly living, voicing moral indignation and a call to involvement in an ongoing process of dramatic change.[20]

An important factor overlooked by many historians is the substantial boost given to the evangelicals' emphasis on preaching, thanks to the efforts of Cranmer to promote Protestant international cooperation, an expression of his desire for England to stand at the center of a renewed evangelical Church at a time of military and political crisis for the reformed movement.[21] During the latter 1540s the fortuitous presence of "guests" from European persecution found a haven in England. Leading continental divines came at the invitation of Cranmer, among them Bucer, Peter Martyr, Fagius, Ochino, Dryander, Utenhove, Micronius, Musculus, ab Ulmis, a Lasco, Tremelius, Veron, Alexander.[22] Writing to Bucer in 1548, Cranmer encouraged him to seek refuge in the safe harbor provided by England.

---

[19] MacCulloch, *Cranmer*, 408.

[20] O'Day, "Hugh Latimer: Prophet of the Kingdom," 268. "We will never understand what Latimer and his fellow 'prophets' were about if we pooh-pooh the spiritual. Latimer was not preoccupied with society or the problems of an earthly polity in the manner of a reform party but one of those who lamented over man's fallen nature in a purposeless way. His analysis of the problems was not that of a materialist modern man. His remedy for the problems, which he perceived was not either. But it was nonetheless purposeful and thoroughgoing. He identified disease in the commonwealth-spiritual disease. He had a definite programme of religious reform. England should be God's and not the Devil's kingdom." See also King, *English Reformation Literature*, 161-71; McRae, *God speed the plough*, 33.

[21] MacCulloch, *Tudor Church Militant*, 78-79.

[22] W.K Jordan, *Edward VI: The Young King*, 189-205; C. Hopf, *Martin Bucer and the English Reformation* (Oxford, 1946); Davies, *A Religion of the Word*, 231.

Those, in the meantime, who are unable amidst the raging storm to launch out into he deep must take refuge in harbour. To you, therefore, my Bucer, our kingdom will be a most safe harbour, in which, by the blessing of God, the seeds of true doctrine have happily begun to be sown. Come over therefore to us, and become a laborer with us in the harvest of the Lord.[23]

Some of the exiles found positions in the universities, while others came to London, some to benefices there. Arriving in England they found, "fallow ground here, such as the Antichrist is wont to leave." In England, as in France and Italy, preaching was also neglected, while the clergy were "neither very learned, nor zealous in matters pertaining to Christ's kingdom."[24] In a letter to a Lasco, Cranmer revealed his vision for the refugees in England.

We are desirous of setting forth in our churches the true doctrine of God, and have no wish to adapt it to all tastes, or to deal in ambiguities; but, laying aside all carnal considerations, to transmit to posterity a true and explicit form of doctrine agreeable to the rule of sacred writings . . . We have therefore invited both yourself and some other learned men; and as they have come over to us without any reluctance, so that we scarcely have to regret the absence of any of them;[25]

Among those invited by the archbishop, two of Europe's greatest preachers, Italians Bernadino Ochino and Peter Martyr Vermigli, became refugees in England during the Interim of Charles V. Ochino and Vermigli had been members of Catholic orders in Italy where they regularly preached to large crowds, especially during the highest liturgical seasons such as Lent. It was said of Ochino, a Capuchin, that his court sermons had charmed even the Emperor, Charles V, who delighted in preaching with such "spirit and great devotion, which made the stones weep."[26] When Ochino preached throughout Naples in 1536, his manner of preaching and the power of his eloquence, "marvelously moved the minds of his hearers so much that the whole city ran to hear his sermons and attend him with exceeding press, and the other preachers were bereft of audience."[27]

Vermigli, who was an Augustinian Canon, saw similar success in his vocation as an expositor of scripture, combining an unusual union of moving eloquence with solid scholarship. Those who heard him returned with friends and family members, "to see and hear an excellent man, admired and celebrated

---

[23] *Original Letters*, I.20.

[24] *Original Letters*, II.536, 539; Brigden, *London and the Reformation*, 459-60.

[25] *Original Letters*, I.17.

[26] MacCulloch, *Thomas Cranmer*, 380-440; *Tudor Church Militant*, 87-96. Chester reports that Latimer was residing at Lambeth during the time these distinguished continental reformers arrived in England. Chester, *Hugh Latimer*, 169; Dickens, *The English Reformation*, 257-69. On Vermigli and Ochino in Italy see Philip McNair, *Peter Martyr in Italy* (Oxford, 1967), 116-293.

[27] McNair, *Peter Martyr in Italy*, 39.

for his learning and eloquence and for the integrity of his life in the city of Naples and throughout Italy."[28] In his *Life of Martyr*, Simler describes Vermigli's preaching experience in Italy.

> The less frequent the sermons, however, the larger and more crowded is the throng of people, especially in great and populous cities. Therefore those men who seem especially outstanding in learning and eloquence are chosen for this duty from all the congregations of monks. The Roman pontiffs have endowed the Congregation of the Canons of Saint Augustine with special privileges for these duties so that all from this congregation who have at some time been employed in this public duty of preaching enjoy the honors, titles, dignities, and privileges which are conferred on those whom the universities proclaim doctors in a solemn ceremony. These titles, which others hardly merit when they are already growing old, were conferred on Martyr when he was age twenty-six.[29]

Vermigli once wrote of the requirements for sustaining preaching at such a high level of excellence: "Besides inward grace, faith, and outward scripture, we have also need of admonitions and godlie sermons out of the word of God."[30]

Through the hospitality of Cranmer, both Ochino and Vermigli took up residence at Lambeth, where Latimer was already an established houseguest. Soon after their arrival, Ochino was authorized to set up an independent congregation in London serving mainly Italians, but also for other "strangers" who might choose to attend.[31] Ochino wrote enthusiastically to Musculus at Augsburg about possibilities in a new land: "There are in London more than five thousand Germans, to whom you may preach and administer the sacraments; and if you wish to lecture at Cambridge, you may do so."[32] Ochino, however, may be remembered best for his contribution to England's reformation literature, "A dialogue of the unjuste usurped primacie of the Bishop of Rome," which was translated by John Ponet and dedicated to Edward in 1549. The book's drama is framed in a series of conversational play-lets; explaining how the centuries old papal plot for world domination was being foiled by a syndicate of God, Henry VIII and young Edward himself. As MacCulloch comments, "The young king could savor the prospect of reading about himself and people he knew personally in the framework of a cosmic drama."[33] Edward's leadership marks the English as an elect nation in contrast to the curse that had fallen upon Rome as it was personified in Ochino. In Ochino's dramatic presentation, a young Josiah attacks and overcomes the

---

[28] McNair, *Peter Martyr in Italy*, 154.
[29] *Peter Martyre Vermigli: Life, Letters, and Sermons*, trans. and ed. John Patrick Donnelly, S.J., The Peter Martyr Library, Vol. 5 (Kirksville, 1999), 16-17.
[30] Cited in McNair, *Peter Martyr in Italy*, 119.
[31] MacCulloch, *Tudor Church Militant*, 79.
[32] *Original Letters*, I.336.
[33] MacCulloch, *Tudor Church Militant*, 27.

papal Antichrist by means of the conventional weaponry in Edwardian iconography—the Sword and the Book.[34]

Simler reports that Vermigli's presence in England was an important contribution to Cranmer's plan for abolishing papal religion and reforming the churches according to the word of God. Cranmer thus viewed Martyr as uniquely qualified for a teaching position because of his considerable learning and skills. He was appointed as Regius Professor of Divinity at Oxford to train ministers who would go out from university to announce the word of God throughout the whole kingdom, a position that would enable him to "preach in others."[35] Vermigli lectured, participated in disputations, and preached at Oxford while remaining in close contact with Cranmer who consulted him on liturgical and theological matters. Simler states that Latimer was among Vermigli's English friends; during Lent 1549, while Latimer was delivering his Lenten court sermons and residing with Cranmer, Vermigli returned to London for an extended visit at the Archbishop's palace.[36]

Among the small number of Vermigli's sermons and orations that survive, three deal with scripture and ministry. The first of these, the *Exhortation for Youths to Study Sacred Letters*, was probably delivered early in his teaching at Oxford. Writing in a manner that resembles Erasmus' *Paraclesis*, Vermigli's wisdom aims to cultivate the necessary dispositions for students to learn and speak from scripture. Vermigli's conviction that the character and speech of preachers must be shaped by constant immersion in scripture, the primary means by which God speaks to enact salvation, was consistent with the opinions articulated by Latimer at court.[37]

Vermigli began by complimenting his students for their zeal to study sacred letters, a desire that must be divinely inspired, instilled from heaven, and breathed into their hearts by the power of the Holy Spirit. With the Spirit's power to guide, the study of scripture opens the way to supreme happiness in teaching doctrine and morality that are a "beautiful deposit" (277-78). Vermigli advised that no human orator has ever had so many ornaments, analogies, tropes, coloration, and forms and ways of speaking as the Spirit; thus, no human faculty offers more of an abundance and variety of material as the divine scriptures, "God's sermons" (279).

Addressing the difficulties presented by scripture's obscurity, Vermigli warned against the traps and snares of scholastic commentators in order to call attention to the sources themselves: "Do we give so little credit to the Spirit of

---

[34] King, *English Reformation Literature*, 201-206.

[35] Simler, *Life of Martyr*, 33. For a good summary of Vermigli's life and career see David Steinmetz, *Reformers in the Wings* 2nd ed. (Oxford, 2001), 106-13; *Original Letters*, II.472.

[36] Simler, *Life of Martyr*, 37.

[37] Peter Martyr Vermigli, "Exhortation for Youths to study Sacred Letters," in *Life, Letters, Sermons*, 277-86. Hereafter page numbers will be included in the body of the text.

God, who is the father of orphans and the teachers of infants, that he cannot teach those who are bathed by his Scriptures in heavenly light?" (281). This will require a familiarity with "God's sermons," allowing the Spirit of Christ to make the necessary things of salvation clear, direct, and open. (284).

According to Vermigli, because the superstitious mass has been abolished, devotion to scripture, the sermons by which God is understood and graciously present, are of great profit to whoever treats them with a pure and sincere heart. Such attentiveness will produce speech that fosters pure and sincere worship, capable of striking with the power of thunder and lightening against errors and ungodliness (285). Vermigli concludes with a call to pray that the Word might penetrate hearts to bring forth speech, thoughts, and works worthy of its calling. Recalling the parable of the sower, he prayed that his students might become good soil that brings forth fruit a hundredfold for life everlasting (286).

In his third sermon before Edward, Latimer expressed his considerable admiration for the two Italians, while defending himself in response to accusations of seditious preaching. He referred to Ochino and Vermigli as learned models of excellence whom the king would do well to support for the benefit of the whole realm: "Petrus Martyr and Bernard Ochin, I would the king bestow a thousand pound on that sort" (Works, I.141). Latimer's effusive praise of Ochino and Vermigli provides a clue to understanding his court preaching, since he viewed the two Italians, who traced their roots to the fifteenth-century tradition of prophetic preaching which included Bernadino of Sienna and Girolamo Savaronola, as exemplars for the English clergy.[38] Indeed, in a manner similar to many popular medieval preachers, Latimer's 1549 Lenten sermons were a theatrical display of homiletic wisdom and eloquence, a dramatic enterprise, a lively and absorbing conversation between preacher, scripture, and audience which invited a serious probing of new identity for England.[39]

A second important characteristic of the prophetic tradition which was exemplified by Ochino and Vermigli was the exilic condition they shared with other Continental reformers in Edwardian England. Vermigli corresponded with Bucer shortly after assuming his position at Oxford,

---

[38] For a good description of prophetic preaching in fifteenth-century Italy see Hugh Oliphant Old, *The Reading and Preaching of the Scriptures in the Worship of the Christian Church* (Grand Rapids, 1999), III.545-605.

[39] Owst claims, "Every feature characteristic of this new presentation of plays is familiar to us already in the methods of open-air preaching inaugurated by the friars." *Literature and Pulpit in Medieval England*, 478; Owst, *Preaching in Medieval England*, 313ff. O'Day, "Hugh Latimer: Prophet of the Kingdom", 259-60, compares Latimer's preaching to medieval morality plays to highlight his dramatization of the path to salvation and the need for repentance along the way. See King's discussion of the persuasive and polemical uses of drama during the Edwardian period by Bucer and Ochino and their influence in England. King, *English Reformation Literature*, 201-6, 290-99; Davies, *A Religion of the Word*, 177-97.

Up to this time this subject [the kingdom of Christ] has been one of doubt and
certainty; for many persons have been afraid, that by reason of the unhappy events
in Germany this kingdom would be yet more tardy, and employ new delays fully
taking up the cause of religion . . . There are two things, however, which alarm me
exceedingly [concerning England]. The one is, the most obstinate pertinacity of
the friends of popery. If you knew by what fury, impudence and perverseness they
are actuated, you would be astonished . . . May it please God some time to deliver
his church from this plague! . . . Wherefore I have no doubt that something must
be decided upon [for a change of religion] and I hope it may under good auspices,
and with the favor of Christ; and when this shall be the case, we must also entreat
the Lord that the powers of hell, which are everywhere in arms, may not prevail
against the truth of his word.[40]

Latimer voiced similar sentiments at court, identifying himself as a participant
in the ongoing narrative of a suffering, minority community—Israel—and as a
prophet speaking from the margins of power, and authorized only by the word
of God.[41]

Catharine Davies highlights this exilic identity and argues that during this
time, the Edwardian evangelicals, despite their advancements of reform, were
still more preoccupied with attacking popery and all its manifestations than
with defending their own practices and institutions.[42] Davies describes the early
Edwardian period as a twilight time, when evangelicals struggled within the
tension created by two visions of themselves: the church as a persecuted
minority, and the church as a commonwealth of Christians. Davies shows that a
persistence of persecution may be attributed to Somerset's policy of toleration,
which allowed for the ongoing activity and competition between traditionalists,
radicals, and "carnal gospellers." Thus in a time of rapid social change, and
without a clear consensus, the Edwardian evangelicals perceived themselves as
the "little flock" of Christ against whom all the forces of Satan, the world, and
anti-Christ were aligned. Davies points to this self-identity as enabling the

---

[40] *Original Letters*, II.469-70.
[41] O'Day, "Hugh Latimer: Prophet of the Kingdom," 262, 268; Patrick Collinson, *The
Birthpangs of Protestant England* (New York, 1988), 8-11; "Biblical Rhetoric: the
English nation and national sentiment in the prophetic mode" in ed. C. McEachern
and Debora Shuger, *Religion and Culture in Renaissance England* (Cambridge,
1997), 15-45; Richard Helgerson, *Forms of Nationhood: The Elizabethan Writing of
England* (Chicago, 1992). On reading scripture in a realistic mode see Hans Frei, *The
Eclipse of Biblical Narrative: A Study in Eighteenth and Nineteenth Century
Hermeneutics* (Yale, 1974), 18-37; George Lindbeck, *The Nature of Doctrine*, 113-
24.
[42] Catharine Davies, "'Poor Persecuted Little Flock' or 'Commonwealth Christians':
Edwardian Protestant Concepts of Church" in eds. P. Lake and M. Dowling,
Protestantism and the National Church in Sixteenth Century England (London,
1987), 78-102; Davies, *A Religion of the Word*, 231-33; MacCulloch, *Tudor Church
Militant*, 142.

evangelicals to distance themselves from both church and realm, while remaining sufficiently engaged for delivering their polemic against a variety of spiritual, moral, and social ills. This was a conscious adaptation of the language of anti-popery for defining and criticizing a presumably Christian commonwealth, an age-old theme that was invested with fresh contemporary relevance by evangelical preaching.

According to Davies, the first goal of the evangelicals was to create and to build up a faithful, obedient minority through preaching. Latimer and other evangelical preachers defined themselves in prophetic terms, as citizens of an Israel captivated by idolatry and corruption, conditions which they attacked, armed only with the gospel message, as a means of empowering Christian freedom and discipline. Accordingly, Latimer's court sermons called upon the prince and magistrates to heed the prophetic voice to lead the people in repentance through obedience to the Word, thus fulfilling the nation's covenant with God.[43]

Latimer's choice of Romans 15:4 as his thematic text for the 1549 court sermons reveals this purpose: "Whatsoever things are written aforetime, are written for our learning; that we through patience and comfort of scripture might have hope." Erasmus' *Paraphrase on Romans* 15:3-4 renders the text,

> Therefore, just as Christ lowered himself to our level so that he might gradually raise us to his own height, so it is proper for us to strive to imitate his example in enticing our neighbor to true piety. This example has been portrayed for us in sacred literature as though in a picture, and we should continually have it set before our eyes.[44]

In keeping with the scope of the *Book of Homilies* and the penitential purpose of Lent, Latimer proposed to set before his listeners' eyes a series of pictures for their learning, for their imitation of holy exemplars, and for the transformation of their lives. In treating scripture in this manner, Latimer hoped to engage the imagination of his listeners, tapping into religious sensibilities that were formed over a period of centuries. George Lindbeck writes,

> As the Middle Ages manifest, the Bible classically interpreted can shape communal and personal identities even when most lay folk are illiterate. The laity learned the fundamental outline and episodes of the scriptural drama through

---

[43] Davies, "Poor Persecuted Little Flock," 86-88; idem, *A Religion of the Word*, 197-209; Pettegree, *Reformation and the Culture of Persuasion*, 1-10.

[44] Erasmus, *CWE*: 42. *Paraphrase on The Epistle to the Romans* (Toronto, 1977), 83-84. LB, VII.826-27. Tyndale also considered this text as significant, citing it in the *Preface to the Pentateuch* in 1534, "Then go to and read the stories of the Bible for thy learning and comfort, and see everything practiced before thine eyes, for according to those examples shall it go with thee and all men until the world's end." William Tyndale, *Preface to the Pentateuch*, ed. Gerald Bray, *Documents of the English Reformation*, 37.

liturgy, catechesis, and occasional preaching. That drama defined for them the truly real world, and within it they inscribed their own reality (as the products of the popular imagination from paintings, sculpture, and mystery plays to oaths and proverbs make evident). Nor was this absorption of ordinary life by the Bible simply an imaginative matter . . . it was above all the result of the reality-defining power of a single preeminent text classically interpreted.[45]

Because the scope of Latimer's text was wide-ranging, he began with a disclaimer that he might appear to be lazy, a "truant" content to easily use the Bible for his own pleasure. However, it was the largeness of his chosen text, the sweep of the entire drama of salvation and its particular exemplars of humility and obedience, which prompted him to offer an encomium to the Word, God's Book, above all human words.

> The author thereof is great, that is, God himself, eternal, everlasting, almighty. The scripture, because of him, is also great, eternal, most mighty, and holy. There is no king, emperor, magistrate, and ruler, of what state soever they be, but are bound to obey this God, and to give credence to God's holy word, in directing their steps ordinately according to the same word (Works, I.85).

Latimer proposed to weave together the world of the Bible and the world of Edwardian England, a challenge he described in terms provided by the examples of Moses and Micah, fearless preachers both: "Therefore, let the preacher teach, improve, amend, and instruct in righteousness, with the spiritual sword; fearing no man, though death should ensue" (Works, I.86). Adhering to the rhetorical principle of *decorum*, Latimer made pastoral use of scripture to facilitate its enactment in the lives of listeners. "All things written in God's Book are most certain true and profitable for all men." With this aim, Latimer echoed the words of the *Book of Homilies:*

> Unto a Christian man there can be nothynge either more necessarie or profitable then the knowledge of Holy Scripture: forasmuche as in it is conteyned Gods true Word, settyngefurth his glorie and also mannes duetie. And there is no truth, nor doctrine, necessary for our justificacion and everlastyng salvacion, but that is, or may be, drawn out of that fountain and welle of truth. Therefore, as many as be

---

[45] George Lindbeck, "Scripture, Consensus, and Community" in ed. R.J. Neuhaus, *Biblical Interpretation in Crisis* (Grand Rapids, 1989), 79. See John King's discussion of iconoclasm and iconography in the Edwardian period, but especially his treatment of the role played by biblical images. "The reformers believed that the Bible was a storehouse of precedents concerning diction, genres, and figurative language. Early Protestants approved of the arts as long as they conformed to their ideals of religious truth" (*English Reformation Literature*, 14-19). On Erasmus' dramatic depiction of biblical characters in his *Paraphrases*, see Jacques Chomarat, "Grammar and Rhetoric in the Paraphrases of the Gospels by Erasmus" in *ERSY* 1 (October, 1981), 40-46.

desirous to entre into the right and perfect way unto God must applie their myndes to knowe Holy Scripture, without the which they can neyther sufficiently knowe God and his will, neither their office and duetie.[46]

Latimer sought to be faithful to scripture by accommodating its message to the requirements and capacities of his listeners: "If he preach before a king, let his matter be concerning the office of a king; if he before a bishop, then let him treat of bishoply duties and orders; and so forth in other matters, as time and audience shall require" (Works, I.87). This is a matter of effective homiletic and pastoral strategy—fitting the topics of the sermon to the circumstances and conditions of the audience—which requires practical wisdom and discernment. By depicting the biblical word in this manner, Latimer aimed to effect a dramatic transformation, a change of mind and amendment of life, which he described for Edward,

> Wherefore he [the king] must have a pair of spectacles, which shall have clear sights in them: that is, one is faith; not a seasonable faith, which shall last for a while, but a faith which is continuing in God: the second clear sight is charity, which is fervent towards his Christian brother (Works, I.98).

To understand the scope of Latimer's practical vision—living faith which brings forth the fruit of good works—the court sermons must be read with an eye for his dramatic performances of scripture, observing the parade of biblical images and ideas that move across the remarkably accessible stage of Edward's Court.[47] Latimer's strategy is similar to the description of Reformation rhetoric provided by Peter Matheson: "a carnival procession of importunate and impertinent images, of maskings and unmaskings, of knotty questions and triumphantly simple answers. Like a novel, they enable alternative worlds to be presented."[48]

Carnival processions, however, are often not the most organized of affairs. G.W. Blench characterizes the court sermons as suffering from looseness of structure, of being encumbered with too many digressions.[49] Indeed, a cursory reading of the court sermons gives the impression of ill-organized, repetitious, and prolix discourse. Blench fails to consider the possibility that Latimer's larger purpose of moving his audience to repentance required the sacrifice of form for persuasive force: to elaborate ideas; to evoke emotion; to entice and motivate as well as to inform. When the sermons are considered from the perspective of a theater and stage, rather than a lecture hall, Latimer's repetition of biblical figures, themes, images, and stories clearly enlivens and amplifies

---

[46] *Homilies*, 61.
[47] See MacCulloch's discussion of the significance of the court and its accessibility. MacCulloch, *Tudor Church Militant*, 105-110; McCullough, *Sermons at Court*, 2-7.
[48] Matheson, *The Rhetoric of the Reformation*, 130.
[49] Blench, *Preaching in England*, 92-93.

his judgments to increase their emotional and persuasive impact upon listeners.[50]

Latimer crafted the plot of the 1549 court sermons around four overlapping main passages which knit each part into the whole. This arrangement produces a dramatic quality, a sense of movement that calls the audience to participate in the journey of Lent, to sojourn with Israel from the exodus to the promised, land, to follow Christ with the disciples to cross and resurrection. These four texts constitute the main acts of Latimer's dramatic performance: Deuteronomy 17:14-20, on the duties of a godly king; Luke 18:2-5, the Parable of the Importunate Widow and the Corrupt Judge; I Samuel 8, on Israel's desire for a new king; Luke 5:1-3, on Christ preaching to the crowds from the boat of Simon Peter. Within the larger drama of primary texts, Latimer ranged throughout the whole of scripture, amplifying themes and alluring listeners to see themselves in new ways. His digressions play a prominent part in this movement between text and context, serving as interludes in the flow of the primary narratives that enable him to clarify their practical wisdom for his listeners and to depict its embodiment in their lives.[51]

The first court sermon defends the authority of Edward's supremacy and offers instruction for his nurture in Christian virtue. Latimer addressed Edward's critics, comparing them with the "stiff-necked and wild people of Israel" whose desire was for choosing a king after their own phantasies, rather than receiving one chosen by God: "We will walk without the limits of God's word; we will choose a king at our own pleasure." He criticized England's pride and called its people to Edward's support: "But let us learn to frame our lives after the noble king David who walked after the word of God. Let us follow David, our brother both by nativity and godly religion. Let us pray for his good state that he live long among us." Latimer's summons was even more urgent in light of the imminent wrath of God against an unrepentant England: "Oh what a plague were it, that a strange king, of a strange land, and of a strange religion should reign over us and then plant again all damnation and popery!" (*Works*, I.91-2).[52]

Speaking from the story of the Exodus, Latimer warned that England's failure to honor Edward would lead to a return to the fleshpots of Egypt, and to a life of fear under papal Pharaoh. Edward was England's deliverer,

---

[50] Matheson, *The Rhetoric of the Reformation*, 111-30. See the description of Luther's similar preaching strategy in Robert Kolb, *Luther and the Stories of God: Biblical Narratives as a Foundation for Christian Living* (Grand Rapids, 2012), 29-62.

[51] A digression is a tale or interpolated anecdote, which is inserted to illustrate or amplify a point. Richard A. Lanham, *A Handlist of Rhetorical Terms* (Berkeley, 1991), 54.

[52] The homily, an *Exhortacion to Obedience*, speaks of Edward in this manner: "And praised be God, that we knowe the great excellent benefite of God shewed towards us in this behalfe. God hath sent us his high gifte, our most dere sovereigne lord, King Edward the Sixth" (*Homilies*, 162).

acknowledgment of his supremacy would mean the acceptance of God's gift and ordinance, while rejection of his supremacy would only provoke God's wrath: "Stand ye in the liberty wherewith Christ has set us free!" (Works, I.93).

Latimer's use of such language cannot be easily dismissed as mere propaganda for Edward's regime.[53] Its driving force was the power for a renewed future, the liberation of captives for freedom in a land of abundant blessing. Latimer's appeal was for England to discover its vocation in the story of Israel, and by walking in the way created by the Word.[54] His primary goal was not for producing structural change within the realm, but for seeing the word of God produce a changed people who would render godly service, the fruit of living faith, in their fields of relationships and responsibilities.[55] The second court sermon, then, directs Edward to discover his Christian vocation in Deuteronomy 17: "And when the king is set in the seat of his kingdom, he shall write him out a book, and take a copy of the priests or Levites" (Works, I.112).[56] For depicting an identity appropriate for a king, Latimer drew from I Kings, which is a narrative about David, the boy who became king, and Solomon, the wisest man in Israel. Latimer's discourse played on the childhood of David to emphasize his youthful vulnerability, "as an old man, twice a child." He told the story in a way that also exploited the weakness of old David, "in his childhood," and the ambition of his son Adonias, who connived with Joab, leader of David's army, to make himself king. He applied this description of sinful characters to citizens of England who had refused to acknowledge Edward's authority (Works, I.113-14).

Latimer interpreted David's story in support Edward's kingship, as a revelation of God's intervention which moved David to swear that Solomon, although still a child, would succeed him as king. Thus Solomon was wise, following his father's counsel to learn from God's Book; while Adonias was foolish, driven by ambition that eventually led to his demise. The story is a warning to England's "by-walkers" who circumvented God's purposes through their resistance to Edward's rule.[57]

---

[53] See Matheson's excellent discussion of propaganda that does not dismiss the religious convictions of those who are its creators and communicators; *The Rhetoric of the Reformation*, 27-58. Also, Davies, *A Religion of the Word*, 177-82, 232-33.

[54] Here Latimer echoes the *Second Parte of the Sermon of Declinyng from God*, *Homilies*, 143-44.

[55] O'Day, "Hugh Latimer, Prophet of the Kingdom," 259-60.

[56] On the instruction of Edward see King, *English Reformation Literature*, 174-77; James McConica, *English Humanists and Reformation Politics*, 215-17; W.K. Jordan, *Edward VI*, Vol. II. (London, 1970), 21-25, 400-412. See MacCulloch's recent discussion of Edward's piety in *Tudor Church Militant*, 21-36; Davies, *A Religion of the Word*, 197-99.

[57] On the figures of David and Solomon and their significance for Tudor Kingship, see King, *Tudor Royal Iconography*, 54-95; MacCulloch, *Tudor Church Militant*, 15.

I have ript the matter now to the pill, and have told you have plain-walkers and of by-walkers; and how a king in his childhood is a king, as well as in any other age. Happy is he who can beware by another man's jeopardy. For if we offend not as other do, it is not our own deserts. If we fall not, it is God's preservation. I pray God we may all amend and repent! But we all amend now, I trust (Works, I.115-17).

"Wo to thee o land, where the king is a child," was a favorite text of Edward's critics.[58] Latimer countered, "Blessed is the land where there is a noble king" shifting attention from the king's minority to his virtue. The flourishing of court preaching and its profitability to the realm was proof of England's blessing under Edward, and sufficient for dispelling rumors that the minority kingship was arranged by councillors: "Jesu mercy! . . . I will tell you this, and I speak it even as I think: his Majesty hath more godly wit and understanding, more learning and knowledge at this age, than twenty of his progenitors that I could name, had at any time of their life" (Works, I.118).[59]

Latimer was charged with responsibility for instructing Edward on ordering the realm according to the word of God. He admonished the king to avoid snares set by advisors, "flattering claw-backs" who would tempt him to squander time hawking and hunting, rather than reading God's Book and the *Book of Homilies*. Because conservatives derided the official *Homilies* as "homelies," he advised bishops be required to enforce the *Royal Injunctions* or be deprived their seats on bench. Latimer revealed his contempt for conservative prelates who were resistors to reform, calling for their removal from office: "Make them quondams, all the pack of them" (Works, I.121-22). Repeating the radical proposal he made in the *Sermon of the Plough*, Latimer urged that laymen who displayed sufficient learning in scripture and godliness of life be appointed to replace non-preaching prelates.[60]

---

[58] Spoken by Dr. John Story in parliamentary debate—cited by Chester in *Hugh Latimer*, 179.

[59] On the challenges presented by a minority monarch and the reformers' response, see King, *English Reformation Literature*, 161-67; *Tudor Royal Iconography*, 90-101; see *Letters of Gardiner*, 265-314. For the reformers' counter see Christopher Bradshaw, "David or Josiah? Old Testament Kings as Exemplars in Edwardian Religious Polemic" in ed. Bruce Gordon, *Protestant History and Identity in Sixteenth-Century Europe* (Aldershot, 1996), II.77-90.

[60] MacCulloch considers this incident to be an expression of Latimer's impatience with Cranmer's more cautious advancement of reform, and his advocacy for removing conservative bishops rather than wasting valuable time trying to win them over. MacCulloch, *Tudor Church Militant*, 60-61. "Thus the regime felt the need to work around three hostile constituencies: the Emperor, the majority of the lay political nation and those bishops who were not part of the inner circle." The problem, according to MacCulloch, is that the regime urged radicals like Latimer to move forward in dismantling the old order, while urging everyone else, especially conservatives, to peace and unity. See also Davies, *A Religion of the Word*, 158-68.

The reign of Edward VI tested the loyalty of conservative bishops, since Protestant beliefs had become the official doctrine of the new church. New commissions which were issued to the bishops in 1547 referred to them as "delegates" and declared that they retained authority only with the prince's good pleasure. In addition, the abolition of the procedure of *conge d' elire*, whereby new episcopal incumbents were officially appointed by cathedral chapters, ended the semblance of independent elections; in one stroke the bishops were transformed from ordinaries with their own independent jurisdictional powers into little more than crown civil servants.[61]

The group of committed Protestant bishops on the Edwardian bench numbered no more than ten, and would eventually include Cranmer, Coverdale, Hooper, Ponet, Ridley, and Scory. Most of the remaining bishops were Henrician Catholics, supporters of the royal supremacy who were believers in purgatory and transubstantiation. Their presence was a continuing thorn in the flesh for evangelicals who were anxious to accelerate the pace of change across the realm. Vermigli wrote to Bucer in January 1549, "many things have been determined in our parliament respecting religion, but with such obstinate opposition from certain bishops."[62] In particular, Gardiner and Bonner, the most prominent conservative bishops under Edward, and the only episcopal leaders to protest, were singled out for harassment by the government until they were arrested for opposing reforms, tried, and eventually deprived of their sees. Significantly, Gardiner and Bonner had established themselves as two of Latimer's strongest conservative opponents; they presumably were the primary targets of an outburst in Edward's presence: "Out with them . . . make them quondams, all the pack of them!"[63]

Gardiner was placed in the fleet in September 1547 for refusing to obey the injunctions of the council. He continued to argue from prison against the *Homilies* and *Paraphrases of the New Testament* by Erasmus, which were key instruments for reform at the parish level. In January 1548, the government, at the initiative of Somerset, offered Gardiner a general pardon on the condition that he accept the recently approved act for the reception of the Sacrament in both kinds along with the *Homilies*. After an initial refusal, Gardiner presumably reached an agreement with the council, later returning to this diocese where he began to implement the parliamentary measures passed during his imprisonment. Called before the council in May, Gardiner remained in London under orders. In June 1548, the council requested that he preach before Edward VI in support of the religious changes thus far implemented.[64]

[61] Doran and Durston, *Princes, Pastors, and People*, 127.
[62] *Original Letters*, II.477.
[63] Macek, *The Loyal Opposition*, 1-36; O'Grady, *Henry VIII and the Conforming Catholics*, 127-35; Chester, *Latimer*, 151-61; Elton, *Reform and Reformation*, 339-40.
[64] Macek, *The Loyal Opposition*, 8-9; Redworth, *In Defence of the Church Catholic*,

Gardiner was scheduled to speak on St. Peter's Day, June 29 1548. King comments that date was not mere coincidence but was selected intentionally to make Gardiner the butt of anti-papal criticism.[65] In addition, he was commanded by Somerset to speak of no controversial matters regarding the Sacrament and the Mass while a general ban on preaching was imposed as a means of controlling public debate on the doctrine.[66] In the course of the sermon, which was preached before a large crowd at Whitehall palace, Gardiner alluded plainly to the Sacrament of the Altar, not as a separate sacrifice for sin, but as the sacrificial remembrance of Christ's passion through which Christians were strengthened in their faith when they offer prayers for the dead. He agreed with a number of changes, including the dissolution of the chantries, and supported the law for the reception of the Sacrament under both kinds. Gardiner acknowledged that certain religious rituals, such as preaching and baptism were necessary and must be reformed when abused, but indifferent ceremonies, if abused, may be reformed or abolished. Gardiner's fatal error, however, was his failure to make any reference to the authority of the council during a king's minority, which created even more suspicion as to whether he could be trusted to support not only the law of reform, but also its spirit.[67] He was imprisoned on the basis of a long list of accusations, and remained in the Tower for two-and-a-half years without trial, until he was convicted by a royal commission, declared guilty, and deprived of his bishopric.[68]

Bonner was briefly imprisoned in September 1547 for his opposition to the religious innovations and injunctions of Edward's early reign. He voted against the act of 1547 which allowed for the reception of the Sacrament under both kinds, and expressed traditional views on the sacrament when questioned by Cranmer. In addition, during the discussion in the House of Lords before the adoption of the first prayer book, Bonner protested the heretical treatment of the Sacrament contained therein. From spring of 1549, around the time Latimer was appointed to preach at court, Bonner made known more openly his opposition to Protestant doctrine and practice.[69]

By August 1549, Bonner faced the charge of failure to attend services and was commanded to preach quarterly at Paul's Cross, to participate in certain ceremonies, and to attend the sermons of reforming colleagues. In September, the council ordered Bonner to preach against insurrection and in support of the

272-75; Jordan, *The Young King*, 434-45; Foxe, *Acts and Monuments*, vi.67-178.

[65] King, *English Reformation Literature*, 152.

[66] *Tudor Royal Proclamations*, ed. Hughes and Larking, I, nos. 303, 313.

[67] Redworth, *In Defence of the Church Catholic*, 278-81; Macek, *The Loyal Opposition*, 9-10. Foxe's account includes the drafts of the sermon recorded by Nicholas Udall and John Redman, *Acts and Monuments*, vi. 87-93, 236-9. Winchester was ordered to preach without notes.

[68] Macek, *The Royal Opposition*, 193; Muller, *Stephen Gardiner and the Tudor Reaction*, 187-93; Foxe, *Acts and Monuments*, vi.24-266.

[69] Brigden, *London and the Reformation*, 447; Foxe, *Acts and Monuments*, v.745.

legitimacy of a minor king's power.[70] In addition, Bonner's trial sermon became a pivotal event for Somerset who was struggling to preserve his power on the council. The removal of the prominent conservative bishop of London might win him the allegiance of a powerful section of the city.[71] Bonner failed to preach of Edward's authority and said little against the rebels. Displaying even more defiance than had Gardiner in his St. Peter's Day sermon, Bonner chastised his audience and admonished them to come more often to Holy Communion, and exhorted them to renounce the false beliefs that caused them to deny the Real Presence, the "true and catholic belief."[72] Bonner's sermon stirred the city of London, provoking preachers who railed against traditional religion and the mass. After a series of hearings by a commission of lay members, Bonner was placed in the Marshelsea, deprived of his bishopric and goods, and committed to strict confinement without paper, pen, and fire. John Hooper was appointed to preach at Paul's Cross to provide justification for the trial of the bishop to conservatives and to delight his enemies.[73] However, the denial of Gardiner and Bonner was just the beginning, as the episcopal bench in 1550 witnessed a decisive shift in the balance of forces, which had slowed the pace of reform during the first two years of Edward's reign. Through confrontation with the Edwardians, deaths, and forced retirements, conservatives lost no fewer than seven sees out of a total of twenty-seven, with all but one going to evangelicals.[74]

Following his digression against the conservative bishops, Latimer returned his attention to Edward to offer examples of proud rulers—Pharaoh, Jereboam, and Herod—whose behavior was displeasing to God. He depicted King Solomon as a salutary example of humility, one who studied scripture and prayed for wisdom to govern well. Solomon heard the complaints of two harlots who claimed they had given birth to the same child, a model for Edward and Somerset to hear the complaints of the poor: "Hear then, saith he, the small as well as the great, the poor as well as the rich. Regard no person, fear no man . . . The judgment is God's. Mark this saying thou proud judge. Hell will be full of these judges if they repent not and amend.[75] A benediction concluded the

---

[70] Foxe, v.729-39, 763.
[71] Brigden, *London and the Reformation*, 449.
[72] Brigden, *London and the Reformation*, 449; Foxe, v.784.
[73] Brigden, *London and the Reformation*, 451; Foxe, v.785.
[74] MacCulloch, *Tudor Church Militant*, 96-97.
[75] O'Day, "Hugh Latimer, Prophet of the Kingdom," 269. "Evidence of the rich exploiting the poor dishonours the king, shows the ineffectiveness of his rule according to God's book, shows that he is a 'by-walker' who does not tread the king's highway . . . Much of Latimer's preaching is, therefore, dedicated to exposing the corrupted fruits of the commonwealth, to convincing the king and his council of the fact that they are rotten fruits of a decaying tree and that radical husbandry is required to produce a good harvest." Latimer viewed vocation as a sacred matter to be treated in a sacred way, in the manner set forth in scripture. He deplored the abuse

sermon that bestowed strength for its enactment: "Blessed are they that hear the word of God, and keep it" (Works, I.127-8). The biblical narrative of Israel provided Latimer with prophetic material to announce the arrival of a new world constituted by God's sovereignty over England, God's solidarity with the poor and humble, God's judgment against presumed relations of power and privilege, and God's call to turn from the pride, injustice, sin, and evil of the past.[76]

The sharpness of Latimer's polemic provoked accusations of seditious preaching. He defended himself by identifying with a company of courageous preachers whose names brought to mind recognizable heroes and anti-heroes. "Preachers have two offices: to teach true doctrine and to reprehend, to convince, to confute gainsayers and spurners against the truth." Latimer asked, "Why will anybody gainsay true and sound doctrine?" He answered with a story of faithful exemplars, who, in times of conflict and martyrdom remained steadfast in preaching the Word: Moses against Pharaoh, Jeremiah against false prophets, Elijah against the priests of Baal, John the Baptist against Herod, and most importantly, Christ himself, who opposed Pharisees, scribes, and priests. Finally, there was Paul at Rome and the persecuted preachers of the early church under Nero, Maxentius, and Domitian (Works, I.129-30).[77]

Conspicuous by their absence from this list was the clergy of "the papal mass time," which, in Latimer's view, was characterized by false peace: "There was no true preaching during the time of pardon matters, purgatory matters, and pilgrimage matters, the peace of that time was inspired by the devil. When he hath the religion in possession, he stirreth no sedition, I warrant you" (Works, I.130). Latimer invoked the authority of Christ, the incomparable prophet and preacher, and standard by which all preachers should be judged. There was never more dissension than during the time when Christ preached, "If it be contraried then, will ye think it shall not be contraried now?" Since his preaching was modeled after Christ, Latimer must too be contentious. "This day I must somewhat do the second office: I must be a gainsayer, and I must stop their mouths, convince, repel and confute those that speak slanderously of

---

of vocation.
[76] See the excellent discussion in Davies, *A Religion of the Word*, 140-46, 177-82.
[77] Davies, "Poor Persecuted Little Flock," 84, "The capacity to identify themselves [reformers] against a persecuting power had become an integral part of the self-image of English protestants, and one which they were unwilling to give up even when it no longer really fitted with their objective situation. Such a self-image allowed protestants to distance themselves from a regime whose intentions toward the church and the gospel they might not entirely trust and thus to maintain a crucial pocket of ideological independence in what were otherwise dourly erastian times. Here the political and social instability of the reign, together with the inability of the church to finance a proper preaching ministry came to the protestants' rescue, enabling them to continue to present themselves as the poor persecuted flock of Christ." Idem, *A Religion of the Word*, 231-33.

me" (Works, I.131).

Latimer's hope was that his polemical language would be able to challenge the presumption of traditionalists and shock them into entertaining new possibilities. This playful, yet serious discourse allowed for a controlled release of aggression against his opponents, as the following humorous story demonstrates. A listener who charged Latimer with seditious preaching at court later attended a sermon at Paul's Cross, London. When asked about the latter sermon, Latimer's critic remarked: "Marry, wonderful news; we were there clear absolved, my mule and I had full absolution." Latimer responded to this critic, "Indeed, his mule was wiser than he; for I dare say the mule never slandered the preacher. O what an unhappy choice had this mule, to carry such an ass upon his back!" Such use of ridicule was a handy weapon for undermining false certainties, for clearing the way for alternative solutions, and for exposing incongruities. Latimer concludes: "This mule was wiser than he a great deal. I speak not of worldly wisdom . . . but in wisdom which consisteth in godly matters, and appertaining to our salvation. In this wisdom he is as blind as a beetle" (Works, I.134-35).[78]

In addition, Latimer's identification with a tradition of prophetic preachers lent an all or nothing tone to his discourse. Challenging the authority of centuries-old ideas and practices, he deployed abrasive, destabilizing speech to create room for serious thought of radical change.[79] The fourth court sermon issued a call to conversion by means of the Parable of the Wicked Judge and Importunate Widow from Luke 18. A casual reading of the sermon could lead one to conclude that Latimer was primarily interested in political instead of religious affairs. However, the pastoral aim of his message becomes increasingly clear as the sermon unfolds. At the beginning of the sermon, Latimer affirmed the good use of laws in the realm and the importance of judges, though he acknowledged that some might be wicked. He then launched into a fierce attack against the Anabaptists, "who will have no magistrates and judges on earth," calling upon Edward for an increase of preaching to purify the realm of false religion: "Take away preaching, take away salvation" (Works, I.151-52).[80]

---

[78] Matheson, *The Rhetoric of the Reformation*, 124-25.
[79] Matheson, *The Rhetoric of the Reformation*, 13-14.
[80] On Anabaptist activity in England see I.B. Horst, *The Radical Brethren* (Nieuwkoop, 1972); D.M. Loades, "Anabaptism and English Sectarianism in the mid-sixteenth century" in *Reform and Reformation: England and the Continent*, ed. Derek Baker (Oxford, 1979); idem, *The Oxford Martyrs* (London, 1973), 83-93; Daniel Petty, "Anabaptism and the Edwardian Reformation" (PhD diss. Texas Christian University, 1988). MacCulloch discusses the reformers' management strategies against the radicals under Edward, *Thomas Cranmer*, 145-46, 230-32, 424-76. Davies provides a good discussion of Edwardian magistrates in *A Religion of the Word*, 146-57.

Latimer resumed his discussion of judges to recall the stories of Solomon and Isaiah, godly leaders who contended with bribe-taking officials. These examples prompted him to call England's judges and magistrates to reconsider their eternal destiny, warning that the number of bribe-taking judges in hell exceeded only the number of non-preaching prelates. He asserted the threat of eternal punishment extended to all who presumed to stand in judgment over wicked judges, especially Anabaptists and their sympathizers: "If there be charity, it worketh to believe all things, to hope all; to say the best of magistrates, and not to stand to the defending of a wicked matter" (Works, I.165).

The conclusion of the sermon revealed its evangelical purpose, issuing a summons for all to petition God for assistance. Prayers offered by traditionalist clergy, "lip-labouring, babbling or monkery," must yield to prayer that speaks "to miserable folk who are oppressed, a comfort, a solace, and a remedy." True prayer is possible through Christ, the mediator of God's word to his people, and the mediator of their words to God, "Yea, a poor woman in the belfry hath as good authority to offer up this sacrifice, as hath the bishop with his miter on his head, his rings on his fingers and sandals on his feet." A prayer offered by a humble layperson to the Father for Christ's sake is as acceptable as a prayer offered by any bishop (Works, I.165).[81]

Latimer's use of the parable shifted the focus from human judges to Christ and from politics to religion: "When the Son of man shall come, shall he find faith on earth?" "This faith is not a temporary, political faith; rather it is a constant, permanent faith as durable as God's Word." He concluded by inviting all to embrace the gift of living faith, . . . that is a lady, a duchess, a great woman proceeded by a gentleman-usher, the knowledge of sin. And when received, faith is accompanied by her household, the works of our vocation; to be good to our neighbor and to obey God." This call was voiced in the preaching of Noah to no avail, which brought God's judgment. According to Latimer, its promise was yet to be realized in England, since it "still hangs on the end of the tale, in crediting and assenting to the word, and following of it" (Works, I.168-70).

An important aspect of Latimer's court sermons was his discourse that asserted the significance of preachers and preaching for the promotion of reform. MacCulloch concludes that, Edward's preachers, "told them (devout traditionalists) not so much that the old system did not work, but that it had no right to work; so the devout desperately needed to find a structured alternative and the preachers had it in hand."[82] This conviction was at the heart of Latimer's court sermons—preaching is reform, reform is preaching—if preaching is taken away, salvation will be denied, as well as its fruit: a

[81] See *Of the Misery of All Mankynde, Homilies*, 72-73.
[82] MacCulloch, *Tudor Church Militant*, 115-16.

Christian commonwealth.[83]

Latimer expounded these views while admonishing Edward to avoid the counsel of advisors who attempted to lead him "to by-walk, and to stumble," following traditional precepts rather than scripture. He likened this path to a downward descent on a ladder, *scala coela*, masses said for souls in purgatory, and a practice attacked by the Henrician *Ten Articles*.[84] Recasting this familiar image for his purposes, Latimer depicted the true ladder to heaven as knowledge of and obedience to scripture (Works, I.97). He returned to this image during the second court sermon, inviting his audience to visualize the steps of ascent in Romans 10: The top step, "whosoever calleth upon the name of the Lord shall be saved." The second step, "How shall they call upon him in whom they have not believed?" The third step, "How shall they believe in him, of whom they never heard?" The fourth step, "How shall they hear without a preacher?" The nether end of the ladder is, "How shall they preach except they be sent?" He then inverted this order, beginning at the lowest and proceeding to the highest rung, *a primo ad ultimatum*, to score his most important point: "take away preaching, take away salvation" (Works, I.122-23).[85]

Latimer viewed evangelical preaching as God's instrument of salvation and its promotion as a sign of God's activity and blessing. He feared that failure to hear and obey God's word would result in a second divine visitation of vengeance: "We are yet well; but the house is not clean swept yet, let us receive with all obedience and prayer the Word of God." A sign of the "yet but not yet" condition of the realm was the continuing presence of Anabaptist activity, which Latimer attributed to the negligence of certain bishops, "unpreaching prelates, unreformed." The transformation of the realm required bishops and prelates who will "feed the flock with pure food and example of life" (Works, I.122-23).

Latimer's primary aim was to persuade his audiences to accept the superiority of evangelical faith over traditional religion, to accept preaching over the mass, and to accept the Word as the constituting activity of the church and reforming power of the realm: "I am God's instrument for a time; it is he that must give the increase; and yet preaching is necessary; for take away preaching, and take away salvation." While his model for preaching was the example and pattern of Christ, "the preacher that all preachers ought to follow," it also emphasized Christ's failure and rejection rather than his popularity and success. Christ was learned, wise, and circumspect; yet the Parable of the Sower (Luke 9) demonstrates that only one quarter of his field was fruitful. Latimer surmised that if Christ, the greatest of preacher-ploughmen had such

---

[83] See Davies' discussion of preaching and its significance for the Edwardians, *A Religion of the Word*, 87-93.

[84] See Duffy, *Stripping of the Altars*, 391.

[85] This view epitomizes the message of *A Fruitful Exhortation and Knowledge of Holy Scripture*, Homilies, 61.

luck no more should be expected of preachers in England, "since the people there have stony hearts and thorny hearts." He expressed hope that Edward would promote an outpouring of preaching, since to allow the continued presence of un-preaching prelates would be the equivalent of having no king at all (Works, I.155).[86]

Latimer made his strongest appeal for an increase of evangelical preaching during the sixth court sermon. The sermon, taken from Luke 5, began with a fierce attack against papal authority and a refutation of Reginald Pole's *Pro Ecclesiastical Unitatis Defensione*, "a text that he doth greatly abuse for the supremacy: he racks it he violates it, to serve for the maintenance of the bishop of Rome" (Works, I.198-99).[87]

Latimer contended that Pole, in his interpretation of the gospel story, gave primacy to Peter and neglected Christ.[88] Latimer retold the story to shift the focus from the authority of Peter to the miraculous action of Christ's preaching and the response of the people to his words. Taking Christ's words as his theme, "I was sent to preach the Word of God," Latimer portrayed Christ as the preacher of all preachers, which prompted him to ask, "Is it not a marvelous thing that our unpreaching prelates can read this place, and yet preach no more than they do?" The answer is found in Christ's humility, the source of his passion for preaching. Unpreaching prelates, in stark contrast to the Lord, lack the virtue of humility that is required, since their ambition for worldly honor keeps them in darkness and, most importantly, unwilling to handle the Word of God. Latimer likened them to proud Pharisees and bishops who refused to follow Christ; he contrasted their stubbornness with the common people who came to Christ in flocks and by great numbers. His judgment: "There is more devotion in lay folk, and old wives, these simple folk, the vulgar people, than in the clerks" (Works, I.198-99). Simple faith is the primary requirement for hearing the word of God.[89]

Continuing to speak from within the gospel narrative,[90] Latimer asserted that

---

[86] *Exhortacion concernyng Good Ordre and Obedience to Rulers and Magistrates*, *Homilies*, 161.

[87] Reginald Pole, *Defense of the Unity of the Church*, ed. Joseph G. Dwyer (Westminster, 1965).

[88] An *Homelie of the Miserie of Al Mankynd, and of Condemnacion to Death Everlastyying*, by *Hys Awne Synne* begins with these words: "The Holy Ghost in writing Holy Scripture is in nothinge more diligent then to pulle doune mannes vainglory and pride, whiche, of all vices, is most universally grafted in al mankynd, even from the first infection of our first father Adam" (*Homilies*, 70).

[89] This polemic against traditionalist clergy also contains a hopeful summons to the laity to become hearers and doers of the Word in a Christian commonwealth. See Erasmus, *Paraclesis*, 100. "The journey is simple, it is open to everyone. Only bring a pious and open mind, possessed above all with a pure and simple faith." Cranmer echoes this summons in the preface to the *Book of Homilies.*

[90] The role of Christ as teacher and orator was a central topic for Erasmus, "Jacques

common folk sought Christ like eagles in pursuit of a carcass, "the smell of life to life." The teaching of the scribes and pharisees (traditional religion and its clergy) was inferior by comparison with the preaching of Christ; it stank in the noses of the people because it lacked comfort, consolation, and a remedy for sin. Although the crowds assembled to hear Christ for many reasons, including curiosity and entertainment, he preached the word with sufficient power to effect what it declares: "for we cannot be saved with hearing the word; it is a necessary way to salvation. We cannot be saved without faith, and faith cometh by hearing of the word, *Fides ex auditu*, there must be preachers if we are to be saved" (Works, I.199-200).

Latimer envisaged the word of God proclaimed by faithful prelates, with their words authorized by Christ to effect what is spoken. Christ is God's Word, God's saving activity brought to speech; Christ is the preacher's referent, example, enabler, and goal. Preaching is dependent upon the authority and example of Christ's Incarnation, the divine means for producing personal and social regeneration: "By the Word of the living God, by the word preached and opened, thus cometh our new birth (Works, I.202).[91]

A consequence of traditional religion, however, was a loss of listening to God's word. Citing John Chrysostom, who claimed that people heard Christ in reverence and silence without interrupting the order of his preaching, Latimer viewed his own preaching from a different perspective: "Surely it is an ill misorder that folk shall be walking up and down in the sermon-time as I have seen in this place this Lent; and their shall be such huzzing and buzzing in the preacher's ear, that it maketh him often times to forget his matter" (Works, I.203-4). Evangelical preachers faced the challenge of creating listeners who would acquire the necessary devotion to the word of God for exceeding traditionalist, eucharistic piety experienced during the Mass. Latimer implored that reverence be shown for Edward, Christ's vicar on earth. He called for reverence towards Holy Scripture, the Word spoken through the words of Christ, and towards the sermon, the word of God spoken through the words of Christ's poor preacher (Works, I.204).[92]

Chomarat, "Grammar and Rhetoric in the Paraphrases of the Gospels by Erasmus," 50. "As a man Erasmus' Christ is above all a pedagogue, if preaching is considered as a form of teaching which is addressed to everybody." On the significance of Christ as the transforming speech of God in the thought of Erasmus, see John Wall, *Transformations of the Word*, 41-42.

[91] "The wordes of scripture be called wordes of everlastying life" (*Homilies*, 62). In Latimer's view of preaching, Christ, scripture, and the proclamation of the gospel co-inhere, which reveals similarities to the patristic understanding that Boyle develops at length in her discussion of Erasmus. Boyle, *Erasmus on Language and Method in Theology*, 3-128.

[92] MacCulloch challenges revisionist accounts that point to a lack of sermon listeners as a sign of indifference or even abandonment, choosing rather to call it the result of trauma: *Tudor Church Militant*, 107-108. Boyle writes of Erasmus' work: "Erasmus

Latimer's sermon from Luke 5 challenged traditionalists who held that Christ's seat in Peter's boat was a sign of papal authority. Moreover, Latimer viewed his interpretation as a matter of the plain sense of scripture. To illustrate this point, he told of his ride from Lambeth Palace to Edward's Court, for which he simply boarded the nearest ferry at Westminster. This experience enabled him to deduce that Christ's choice was a matter of authority, since it revealed Christ's supremacy over Peter and provided a lesson on humility for all preachers, including the Bishop of Rome and the College of Cardinals (Works, I.206).

Latimer continued to illustrate the need for more preaching by means of two entertaining stories, or *exempla*.[93] The first was of a bishop on visitation who entered a town where the great clapper of the church bell was broken, so that the bishop could not be rung into town. Apparently, this offended the bishop and he let this be known. After some discussion of the bell and its repair, a bystander who, in Latimer's view displayed much wisdom, pointed to the pulpit and said, "Here is a bell that hath lacked a clapper, this twenty years." Latimer's conclusion: "Ever this office of preaching hath been least regarded, it hath scant had the name of God's service" (Works, I.207).

The second story told of an Episcopal visit Latimer made to a town on holiday, where he expected to find a great crowd gathered to listen. Much to his surprise, he was all alone and waited for an hour and a half for the church to be opened. A member of the parish finally informed him that it was Robin Hood's Day, that its members were busy gathering money for its events. Latimer expressed his dismay at this tale, "I thought my rochet should have been regarded, though I were not, it was fain to give place to Robin Hood's men." He concluded this was, "A weeping matter, a heavy matter, a preacher of God's Word was esteemed less than Robin Hood, a traitor and a thief." He expressed hope that God would prompt an increase of preaching: "We have good hope of better, we have had a good beginning; I beseech God to continue it!" (Works, I.207-208).[94]

---

proclaims Christ as speech distilled from the Father's inmost heart, and Scripture as speech distilled from the most secret recesses of Christ's heart. Christ as the conversation of the Father's heart, gospel as the conversation of Christ's heart, theology as the conversation of the gospel's heart." See *Erasmus on Language and Method in Theology*, 119.

[93] Owst, *Literature and Pulpit in Medieval England*, 149-209; idem, *Preaching in Medieval England*, 60-64. Latimer's use of stories to engage and amuse his listeners, while putting flesh on his points, has many characteristics of the popular medieval preaching described by Owst. Blench considers Latimer's use of *exempla* to be moderate in comparison to the excesses of late medieval preachers, and his frequently are personal reminiscences, giving illuminating examples from his life. Blench, *Preaching in England*, 147-52.

[94] The figure of Robin Hood represents discourse that has run out of control, speech that is undisciplined by scripture. The good beginning to which Latimer refers presumably is the publication of the *Book of Homilies* and the *Injunctions*. See King,

According to Latimer, evangelical proclamation was capable of granting public significance to faith and effecting social regeneration throughout the realm. His application of the story of Christ and Peter was not limited to clergy but also provided a moral vision for lay vocations by emphasizing the necessity of labor and addressing the issues of unemployment and idleness. Christ not only preached the Word to call the common people to discipleship; Christ also commanded his followers to cast their nets, proving that in their labor he gives the increase. As the example and authority for both clerical and lay vocations, Christ lived humbly and blessed human nature, its occupations, and its arts. Christ did the work of his calling as a carpenter, but as a preacher he too did the work of that calling. Faith in Christ is the means of creating a Christian commonwealth in England, and the power of Christ works through the labors of clergy and laity. Latimer admonished Edward to accept his calling and to work for its fulfillment: "To study God's book, to see that there be no unpreaching prelates in this realm, poor bribing judges; to see that all estates; to provide for the poor; to see victuals good cheap" (Works, I.210-15).[95]

The seventh court sermon, which was preached on Good Friday, brought Latimer's appeal for repentance to completion with a call to embrace living faith in Christ that bears fruit through works of charity:

> I have walked this Lent in the broad field of scripture, and used my liberty, and entreated of such matters as I thought meet for my auditory. I have entreated of the duty of kings, of the duty of magistrates and judges, of the duty of prelates; allowing that that is good, and disallowing the contrary . . . I here entreated of many faults, and rebuked many kinds of sins. I intend here today, by God's grace, to shew you the remedy of sin. We be in the place of repentance; now is the time to call for mercy, whilst we be in this world (Works, I.216).

The sermon weaves together commemoration of the suffering of Christ with instruction and exhortation to active discipleship.[96] Latimer explicates the passion as a redemptive event and salutary example, depicting the dramatic victory of Christ over the power and fear of death. The sermon calls listeners to repentance, to a change of mind and amendment of life which is shaped by the humility displayed by Christ in Gesthemane. "This is a notable place, and one of the most especial and chiefest of all that be in the story of the passion of Christ. Here is our remedy: here we must have in consideration all his doings and sayings, for our learning, for our edification, for our comfort and consolation" (Works, I.218).

Focusing on Christ's torment, Latimer stressed the heaviness and

---

English Reformation Literature, 84, 212-13.

[95] O'Day provides a good discussion of Latimer's vision of vocation in a Christian commonwealth. See "Hugh Latimer, Prophet of the Kingdom," 268-69. See Davies' discussion, *A Religion of the Word*, 140-68.

[96] This sermon follows the message of *Against the Feare of Death*, *Homilies*, 147-157.

pensiveness of his heart, the pain of his soul, which was more grievious than the pain of the cross: "The horror and weariness of death is sorer than death itself." In the garden, Christ saw the image of death, experiencing the sense of hell which was brought into the world through the disobedience of sin: Achtophel betrayed David and hung himself; Judas sold Jesus for money and upon beholding death's terrible face at the cross, took his own life; Job suffered great loss and questioned God; David stood against death in the face of Goliath; Jonah cried out to God from the belly of the whale; King Hezekiah did not fear Sennacherub but instead feared death; Peter, James and John saw death in the anguish of Christ; and lastly, "Bilney, little Bilney, that blessed martyr of God," went patiently to his death at the hands of Rome's deadly regime.[97]

Most important, however, was that Christ's suffering did not affect his divinity but only his humanity. Because he did not help himself with his deity he was able to extend help to humanity. "He took upon him our sins: not the work of sin; I mean not so; not to do it, not to commit it; but to purge it, to cleanse it, to bear the stipend of it: and that way he was the great sinner of the world." Christ suffered to purge and cleanse sin, to take and feel human misery, thus signifying that death can be overcome. "We shall indeed overcome it, if we repent, and acknowledge that our Saviour Jesus Christ pacified with his pangs and pains the wrath of the Father; having a love to walk in the ways of God" (Works, I.227-28).[98]

Latimer exhorted his listeners to the imitation of Christ through remembrance that is profitable for everyday: "Let us not follow men, but let us follow Christ, which in his agony resorted to his Father with his prayer. This must be our pattern to work by." Christ was truly human; he took upon himself human weaknesses, the stipend of sin, even trembling at the cross. Yet unlike weak humanity, he referred the matter to the will of God the Father. "Nevertheless, thy will be done, not mine." Latimer concludes, "His fact teacheth us what to do." Christ did not rely on his friends, but prayed to God: "We have to pray ever to God" (Works, I.229-30).

Continuing his discussion, Latimer turned to Christ's descent into hell, adducing two texts from Scripture to support the teaching: "Go ye into the whole world, and preach the gospel," and "God will have all men to be saved." These prove not only the doctrine, but announce its imperative: "Go and preach to Englishmen: I will that Englishmen be saved." Although the suffering and descent of Christ into hell set out God's hatred for sin, this teaching does not derogate anything from the rest of his ministry. "It is whole Christ. What with

[97] See Dunnan's discussion of the importance of Bilney's example for Latimer. Dunnan, *Hugh Latimer: A Reappraisal of his Preaching*, 31-72. Marshall, in "Evangelical conversion," emphasizes the reformers use of "books and burnings" to advance their message (35).
[98] Latimer's exposition is informed by the teaching of the homilies on sin, death, salvation and faith. See *Homilies*, 70-102.

his nativity; what with his circumcision; what with his incarnation and the whole process of his life; with his preaching; what with his ascending, descending; what with his death; it is all Christ that worketh our salvation." Because Christ's whole ministry is the work of salvation, Christians should give thanks for his victory, striving to imitate his faithfulness in every aspect of life: "The life of a Christian man is nothing but a readiness to die and a remembrance of death" (Works, I.235-36).[99]

Latimer's homiletic presentation of the passion was a bold invitation to glad acceptance of the salvation and renewal of faith available through Christ's death and resurrection. "Look where remission of sin is, there is acknowledging of sin also. Faith is a noble duchess, she hath ever her gentleman-usher going before her; the confessing of sins; she hath a train after her, the fruits of good works, the walking in the commandments of God" (Works, I.237-38).

The strong Christocentric focus of Latimer's Good Friday sermon was consistent with the scope of his Lenten call to repentance. It provided the scriptural means for an explication of the narrative of Christ's passion that evokes faith, devotion, and discipline, and inspires personal and public righteousness.[100]

A hopeful vision and expectation of a future yet to be realized pervades Latimer's 1549 court sermons. However, the mood and message of Latimer's lone court appearance in 1550 betrays a change in outlook that may have been precipitated by popular rebellion and a conservative coup which precipitated Somerset's demise.[101] Preaching during his final appearance at Westminster, his *ultimatum vale,* Latimer rebuked a carnival atmosphere which had been created by the intoxicating power of liberation from Rome, calling the Edwardian court to sobriety and moral responsibility.[102]

Latimer's viewed himself as addressing England for its failure to respond to evangelical preaching of the gospel; he repeated his sermon text three times—

---

[99] Latimer's exhortation against the fear of death follows the teaching of the homily bearing that title, *An Exhortacion against the Feare of Deathe* (*Homilies*, 147-57).

[100] See the *Enchiridion* of Erasmus for a depiction of the Christian life in active, militant terms, *CWE 66.* The homily, *Against the Feare of Deathe* concludes with a similar call and exhortation (*Homilies*, 157). See the discussion in Wall, "Godly and Fruitful Lessons," 117.

[101] Guy, *Tudor England*, 205-25; Elton, *Reform and Reformation*, 338-52; Hoak, *King's Council*, 241-55. See Davies, *A Religion of the Word*, on the Edwardians' hope and fear and perceptions of both imminent reform and destruction, 177-82, 200-209.

[102] On the changes that occurred in 1549-50, see the discussion by MacCulloch, *Thomas Cranmer,* 410-500; *Tudor Church Militant,* 119-156: "The year 1549 also represented a deep disappointment and trauma for evangelical clergy who had promoted commonwealth rhetoric as part of reformation, and who clearly felt that popular activism had besmirched the cause." See also Chester, *Hugh Latimer,* 182-84; King, *English Reformation Literature,* 76-121; Dickens, *The English Reformation,* 254-57; Elton, G.R., "Reform and the Commonwealth-men," 234-53; Davies, *A Religion of the Word*, 231-33.

"Take heed and beware of covetousness." To emphasize his theme in the king's mind, Latimer identified himself with the prophet Jonah who delivered God's word in few words to the Ninevites: "There is yet forty days to come, and Nineveh shall be destroyed" (Works, I.239). Moving quickly to the heart of the matter, he asserted that Jonah preached one sermon with few words that had great effect and bore much fruit, while England, with many preachers and many long sermons, had neither repented or been converted. Moreover, the English people continued to criticize their preachers, message, and learning. Remembering his own experience, Latimer complained that preachers who dared to confront sin and to speak sharply were accused of stirring sedition, inciting rebellions, and lacking discretion. Significantly, Latimer claimed these accusations vindicated his preaching. For just as Christ prophesied, "Nineveh shall rise against the Jews at the last day and bear witness against them," so too he must prophesy: "Nineveh shall rise against England, because it will not believe God nor hear his preachers that cry daily unto them, nor amend their lives, and especially their covetousness" (Works, I.240).

Latimer warned that God's wrath was rapidly falling upon England for its sins; that the nation's time was short, its future uncertain, and the time for its repentance was limited to what remains of this life. His theme was chosen from words taken from the Apostle Paul, "covetousness is the root of all evil," and St. Luke, "See and beware of covetousness." He viewed his task as "striking at the root of covetousness with the sword of the Word" rather than, "ticking and toying at the branches and the boughs." This required that he pluck out the roots of evil by standing against the "giants," men of power and wealth who oppressed the poor (Works, I.244-45).

This sermon has attracted much interest from historians because of Latimer's comments on practitioners of enclosure and the rebels who participated in the "stirrings" of 1549: "Covetousness is the root of all evil; rebellion is an evil; ergo, covetousness is the root of rebellion and both parties had covetousness as well the gentlemen and the commons." Those that criticize Latimer as a commonwealth preacher whose sermons were idealistic and ineffective tend to overlook that the topics of enclosure and rebellion occupy little more than two out of forty two pages in the sermon.[103] On the other hand, it is also possible to read Latimer's message as the words of a religious moralist who was out of touch with the social and economic realities of his time. Yet to arrive at this conclusion requires that one dismiss the prophetic nature of his speech, which was shaped by the message and authority of Jonah; the overall scope of his message, which was informed by the *Book of Homilies*; and the purpose of the Lenten season, which was to call the church to repentance, faith, and obedience.[104]

---

[103] See O'Day's excellent discussion, "Hugh Latimer: Prophet of the Kingdom," 259-263; Davies, *A Religion of the Word*, 206-14.

[104] Elton is Latimer's severest critic on this score, "Reform and the Commonwealth-

When viewed in light of Latimer's previous appearances at court the sermon may be read as an extended conversation between Latimer and the Edwardians regarding the "branches and boughs" of sin within the soul of the realm, a condition crying out for root-and-branch reform. Latimer therefore spoke as prophet to summon the realm to an ordering of just relationships within divinely appointed callings, joining moral imperative and attention to detail: "The poorest ploughman is in Christ equal to the greatest prince that is."[105] His identification with the prophet Jonah lent authority to and illumined his purpose of speaking God's judgment against sins of inordinate desire, rebellion, greed, lechery, adultery, whoredom, worldly, immodest women, drunkenness, dicing, and carding (Works, I.245).

Latimer asked his audience to consider, "who is speaking, what is being spoken, to whom is it spoken, and why is it spoken?" so that they might discern the voice of Christ: "Christ speaketh these words at that time, and now he speaketh them by his preacher, who ye ought to believe, and so it all is one" (Works, I.256-57). According to Latimer, the Word incarnate, the Word of scripture, and the Word spoken become one in the act of preaching; Christ speaks to sow good seed; his Word comes from God and contains the power of God (Works, I.256).[106] Adhering to the pattern of Christ's preaching in Luke 12, Latimer hoped to draw listeners into its world to be changed through the process outlined in the *Book of Homilies.*

And in readying of God's Woorde, he moste profiteth not alwaies that is most ready in turnyng of the boke, or in saiyng of it without the boke, but he that is moste turned into it, that is most inspired with the Holy Ghost, moste in his harte

---

men," 23-38.

[105] O'Day writes of Latimer's preaching on these matters: "Latimer preaches against the covetousness of the poor as well of the rich. It is this covetousness, he says, which is the root of rebellion. Latimer, it should be noted, does not advocate or condemn an unequal society: he accepts what exists. He abhors the absence of discipline in England. It is a society in which 'servant' does not respect 'master.' He does seem to say that, if men truly follow their vocations, with their eyes on heaven, extremes of riches and poverty will disappear. For all men will work with God and God will provide the increase. Latimer does not comment further. It is worth observing, however, that this happy state of affairs does not require a negation of monarch or hierarchy. Indeed, it can only exist in a society which acknowledges a hierarchy of vocations. 'Balance' in this commonwealth (in the economic and social spheres) will result from godliness, not from mere economic reform" (276). See also the good discussions in McRae, *God speed the plough*, 45-6; Davies, *A Religion of the Word*, 128-40.

[106] See Erasmus, *Paraclesis*, 104. "In this kind of philosophy, located as it is in the disposition of the mind than in syllogisms, life means more than debate, inspiration is preferable to erudition, transformation is a more important matter than intellectual comprehension." Latimer hoped to purify vision, to change disposition, to inspire virtuous action, to effect a transformation of life by means of his biblical discourse. See Pierre Hadot, *Philosophy as a Way of Life*, 50-61.

and life altered and transformed into that thyng whiche he readeth: he that is daily lesse and lesse proud, lesse irefull, lesse covetous and lesse desirous of worldly and vayne pleasures; he that daily, forsakying his olde vicious life, increaseth in verture, more and more.[107]

---

[107] On the efficacy of the Word to enact what it speaks, see *Homilies*, 62-63. Davies shows the importance of preaching the Word to evoke repentance and hope for the Edwardians, *A Religion of the Word*, 232-33.

Chapter 5

Edwardian Evangelism:
Common Prayer and Preaching

> Most of all he began to set forth his plough, and to till the ground of the Lord, and
> to sow the corn of God's word, behaving himself as a faithful messenger of God's
> word, being afraid of no men; telling all degrees their duties faithfully and truly,
> without respect of persons, as a kind of flattery (Augustine Brehner, describing
> Latimer's preaching under Edward VI).

From late 1550, and until the death of Edward VI in 1553, Latimer was the
most prominent among a company of preachers who ploughed the fields of
England, sowing the seed of the Word to evangelize and edify popular
audiences. Haigh has described these preachers "as remarkable a group of
evangelists as can ever be seen."[1] Indeed, the Edwardian evangelists made
known their presence and their message. For example, MacCulloch cites
correspondence from the imperial ambassador Van der Delft who, so alarmed
by the impact of the Reformation among ordinary people, described how
common folk, encouraged by dramatic preaching, had turned against traditional
religion.[2]

While preaching at court during Lent of 1549-50, Latimer urged Edward to
promote an increase of preaching to advance reform across the realm.[3] Writing
from Oxford, Peter Vermigli also lamented England's shortage of qualified
preachers.

> There is no lack of preachers in London, but throughout the whole kingdom they
> are very rare: wherefore every godly person mourns over and deplores this great

---

[1] Haigh, *English Reformations*, 189. Gregory suggests we see the English Reformation
as a revival as well as a reform, that it aimed to both purge and bring to life the old
faith in a new form appropriate for its future: Jeremy Gregory, "The Making of a
Protestant Nation," 314-20. For a good description of the Edwardians' emphasis on
preaching, see Davies, *A Religion of the Word*, 87-93; Haigh, *English Reformations*,
189-202; Robert Whiting, *Local Responses to the English Reformation*, 167-82;
Christopher Marsh, *Popular Religion in Sixteenth Century England*, 32-42, 52-54,
119-22; Whiting, *The Blind Devotion of the People*, 234-55; Nicholas Tyacke,
"Introduction: re-thinking the 'English Reformation" in *England's Long Reformation
1500-1800*, 4-7.

[2] MacCulloch, *Tudor Church Militant*, 23; McRae, *God Speed the Plough*, 34-35.

[3] *Works*, I.85-281.

calamity of the church. The sheep of divine pasture, the sheep of God's hand, the sheep redeemed by the blood of Christ, are defrauded of their proper nourishment of the divine word; and unless the people be taught, the change of religion will certainly avail them but little.[4]

Moreover, in late 1550 Martin Bucer issued a direct appeal to Edward in *De Regno Christi*, exhorting the king to diligently persuade, both personally and through others gifted by God, that both Parliament and the people should accept "the whole plan for the restoration of the religion of Christ in doctrine as well as in rites and discipline." Echoing Latimer's vision for spiritual and social renewal by means of preaching, Bucer appealed to Edward to send out to all the churches of the realm learned, motivated evangelists,

> . . . To announce assiduously, zealously, and in a timely fashion . . . the good news of the Kingdom. And they should teach from the Gospel, with strength and energy, whatever pertains to the Kingdom of Christ and wherever it is necessary to believe and do for present and future happiness . . . utmost care must be taken that none are sent out except those from whose whole life and manner of devotion it is obvious that they are not in any way seeking their own interests in this office but only those things which pertain to the glory of Christ and the repair of the churches.[5]

Powicke comments on Bucer's plan, "An intensive educational campaign by preachers was more important and would be more effective than a policy of legal discipline."[6] Bucer had given his enthusiastic endorsement to the *Book of Homilies* as a source for teaching Christian doctrine and life and for guarding against inefficient preaching by untrained clergy.[7] He continued, however, to look for improvement in England's pastoral ministry, especially in the office of preaching, a need he described in a letter to John Calvin.

> You may find parishes in which there has not been a sermon for some years. And you are well aware how little can be effected for the restoration of the kingdom of Christ by mere ordinances, and the removal of instruments of superstition . . . And even our friends are so sparing of their sermons, that during the whole season of Lent, which nevertheless they still seem to wish to observe, with the exception of one or two Sundays, they have not once preached to the people, not even on the

---

[4] *Original Letters*, II.485.

[5] Martin Bucer, *De Regno Christi* in *Melancthon and Bucer*, ed. and trans. Wilhelm Pauck, Library of Christian Classics, Vol. XIX (Philadelphia, 1969), 269-70.

[6] F.M. Powicke, *The Reformation in England* (Oxford, 1941), 88; Martin Bucer, *De Regno Christi*, 158-394.

[7] Constantin Hopf, *Martin Bucer and the English Reformation* (Oxford, 1946), 16, 81f.

day of the commemoration of Christ's death or resurrection, or on this day.[8]

It appears that Edward seriously considered heeding the call of Latimer and Bucer, based on evidence provided by his *Discourse on the Reform of Abuses in Church and State.*

> The ecclesiastical [the other part being the temporal] consists in setting forth the word of God, continuing the people in prayer, and the discipline. The setting forth of the word of God consists in good discreet doctrine and example of the preachers and spiritual officers. For as the good husbandman makes his ground good and plentiful, so does the true preacher with doctrine and example print and engrave in the peoples' mind the word of God, that they at length become plentiful.[9]

The Edwardians demonstrated their commitment to the advancement of reform by means of preaching in December 1551, when a royal decision turned the Court chaplains, including Latimer, Hooper, and Lever, into itinerant preachers.[10] Of "six chaplains ordinary," only two were to remain at court, while four were to be absent preaching in the outer provinces of the realm.[11] Of significant in this turn of events was that Latimer's preaching career was brought to completion *ad populum*, far removed from the familiar scenes of his well-known homiletic performances at the preaching station of St. Paul's Cross, the Tudor Court, the Convocation of clergy, and the pulpits of Cambridge University. Indeed, while preaching at Grimsthorpe in Lincolnshire, Latimer confirmed his personal inclination for this task.

> I have a manner of teaching which is very tedious to them that be learned. I am wont ever to repeat those things which I have said before, which are nothing pleasant to the learned; but it is no matter, I care not for them; I seek more the profit of these who be ignorant, than to please learned men (Works, I.341).

The purpose of this chapter is to shed new light on Latimer's popular sermons, and on their profitability for increasing our understanding of his contributions to preaching and the advancement of reform during the reign of Edward VI.[12]

---

[8] *Original Letters,* II.546-7; David Steinmetz, *Reformers in the Wings: from Geiler von Kaysersberg to Theodore Beza* 2nd ed. (Oxford, 2001), 91-92. On Bucer's role as a mediator see Matheson, *The Rhetoric of the Reformation,* 224-30.

[9] *The Chronicles and Political Papers of King Edward VI,* ed. W.K. Jordan (Ithaca, 1966), 159-60. Edward wrote these words in 1551. On Edward's expression of his theological views, see Diarmaid McCulloch, *The Boy King: Edward VI and the Protestant Reformation* (New York, 1999), 30-42; David Loades, *John Dudley, Duke of Northumberland* (Oxford, 1996), 190-202.

[10] McCullough, *Sermons at Court,* 58; *Chronicles and Political Papers,* 101.

[11] John Hayward, *The Life and Raigne of King Edward the Sixth,* ed. Barret L. Beer (Kent, 1993), 150.

[12] The sermons I will discuss are contained in *The Works of Hugh Latimer,* 2 Vols. ed. Rev. George Corrie, M.A., Parker Society (Cambridge, 1968 reprint). Hereafter,

This discussion shows that Latimer's plain, vernacular sermons were the fulfillment of his practice of the preaching life, the homiletic exercise of pastoral wisdom for the implementation of the vision announced in the *Sermon of the Plough*. Latimer's popular preaching wove together elements and emphases of both, the old and the new, the known and the unknown, in religion, devotion, and life to create common ground for the gospel, a middle way between the extreme positions held by traditionalists and radicals. This strategy enabled his discourse to engage or overlap with much that was familiar to his audiences, thus softening the impact of religious change. Although Latimer aimed to reach a wide audience, he preached for commitment deeper than mere outward conformity, selectively employing his polemical language to remove obstacles that prevented listeners from receiving his consensus forming message.

David Steinmetz has written of the reforming perspective and purpose of Latimer's generation, the first among sixteenth-century Protestants.

> What set the Protestant message off from the medieval tradition was not the uniqueness of its questions or the newness of its sources. What set it off was the angle of vision from which these traditional sources were read and evaluated. The Christian past was not so much rejected by the Protestant reformers as refashioned in the light of a different and competing vision of its development and continuing significance.[13]

For Edwardian England, the refashioning of a new church and polity was shaped by the implementation of Cranmer's liturgical reforms.[14] The work of

---

references will be given in the body of the text. Of Latimer's 40 extant sermons, 25 are included in this collection of popular sermons that were preached at several different locations in the diocese of Lincoln between late 1550, and possibly as late as the beginning of 1553. Latimer's is the only extant sermon collection from this period of intense evangelistic efforts by Edwardian preachers. These sermons were organized by the editor according to the liturgical calendar, so that the entire collection is located within the seasons of Ordinary Time, Advent, Christmas, and Epiphany. My exposition treats selected sermons in their order of liturgical (and editorial) arrangement. See Chester's detailed discussion of the dating of the sermons. Chester, *Hugh Latimer*, 182-94.

[13] David Steinmetz, "The Intellectual Appeal of the Reformation" in *Theology Today*, 57.4 (2001), 460-61.

[14] "There was probably no other single aspect of the Reformation in England which touched more directly and fundamentally the consciousness, or lack of it, of ordinary clergy and laity, than did the reform of rituals and liturgy," Judith Maltby, *Prayer Book and People in Elizabethan and early Stuart England* (Cambridge, 1998), 4. See the conclusions drawn by Sharon Arnoult, "Spiritual and Sacred Publique Actions: The Book of Common Prayer and the Understanding of Worship in the Elizabethan and Jacobean Church of England" in *Religion and the English People 1500-1640: New Voices, New Perspectives*, ed. Eric Josef Carlson, Sixteenth Century Essays and Studies Vol. 45 (1998), 25-48.

John Wall has clarified the role of common worship for the Edwardian commonwealth and helps to locate Latimer's popular sermons against the background of Cranmer's larger program. Wall persuasively argues that the distinctive marks of the Edwardian Church, the *Ecclesia Anglicana*, included its recovery of the Bible in the vernacular as a living text addressed to English folk; its creation of a vernacular discipline of common prayer as the appropriate context for reading and preaching scripture. By placing the prayer book, basic Christian texts, and liturgical events, at the center of religious discourse, Cranmer sought the transformation of England into a Christian commonwealth through participation in Christ and active love of neighbor as citizenship in the Kingdom of God.[15] The theological significance of liturgical reform was affirmed in the preface to the 1549 *Book of Common Prayer*.

> There was never anything by the wit of man so well devised or so sure established, which in continuance of time hath not been corrupted, as among other things, it may plainly appear by the common prayers in the Church, commonly called Divine Service. The first and original ground whereof if a man would search out by the ancient Fathers, he shall find that the same was not ordained but of a good purpose and for a great advancement of godliness. For they so ordered the matter that the whole Bible (or the greatest part thereof) should be read over once every year; intending thereby that the clergy, and especially such as were ministers in the congregation, should be stirred up to godliness themselves, and be more able to exhort others by wholesome doctrine, and to confute them that were adversaries to the truth; and further that the people (by daily reading of Holy Scripture in the Church) might continually profit more and more in the knowledge of God and be more inflamed with the love of his true religion.[16]

The practical wisdom of Cranmer's program is confirmed by Christopher Marsh, who challenges the emphasis of revisionist scholarship on the inescapable hold of late medieval Christianity over the English church; and that Protestantism held little appeal for ordinary people.[17] Marsh argues that the

---

[15] Wall, *Transformations of the Word*, 11-15.

[16] *Documents of the English Reformation*, ed. G. Bray, 273. MacCulloch uses the term reformed Catholic to describe the position of Cranmer, which also could apply to Latimer: "for they [the reformers] sought to build up the Catholic Church on the same foundations of Bible, creeds, and the great councils of the early Church . . . Cranmer was guiding the Church of England to a renewed Catholicity through thickets of wicked deceit which must be avoided at all costs; on the one hand, papistry, and on the other Anabaptism, both equally 'sects' in his eyes" (*Thomas Cranmer*, 617). Paul Avis, *Anglicanism and the Christian Church* (Oxford, 1988) "Particular (i.e., national) churches are catholic when they profess and teach the faith and religion of Christ according to the scripture and apostolic doctrine" (35).

[17] Marsh, *Popular Religion in Sixteenth-Century England*, 195-216. See the essay by Eric Josef Carlson, "New Research on Religion in Tudor and Early Stuart England" in *Religion and the English People 1500-1640: New Voices, New Perspectives*, 3. "If

radical distinction between the old and the new did not predominate in the way
that revisionists tend to portray in asserting that key Protestant doctrines were
too demanding and dangerously divisive; that an emphasis on the printed
vernacular Bible was misplaced in a largely illiterate society; that godly
attempts to reform popular practices inspired contempt. Marsh notes that not all
English Reformers were cast in the mold of John Hooper, who adopted radical,
uncompromising strategies.[18] For example, in composing the *Book of Common
Prayer*, Cranmer retained certain ceremonies and traditions (including
vestments) insisting, "Lest the people not having yet learned Christ, should be
deterred by too extensive innovation from embracing his religion." He therefore
designed the practices of the prayer book to be a middle path between "those
addicted to the old customs and those so new-fangled that they would innovate
all things."[19]

My discussion treats Latimer's popular sermons against the background of
Cranmer's more gradualist liturgical and pastoral strategy that aimed to convert
the nation from traditional religion into evangelical faith and life. This
relationship is reflected in the content and arrangement of Latimer's sermons,
according to scripture lessons for the liturgical year prescribed by the 1549
Book of Common Prayer, with each one being a textual and rhetorical
expression of the Edwardian message of the gospel, rendering a persuasive
vision of England reformed and reunited.[20]

An additional element in the Edwardians' construction of a Christian
commonwealth was the use of English as the medium for its liturgical life. Wall
concludes, "Thus the translation of the Bible into English and the
transformation of diverse Latin rites into a life of common prayer in the
vernacular through a single use for all English folk became vehicles for

---

the English Reformation is seen as sort of a dialectical process in which a synthesis
was shaped over time, things start to make sense."

[18] Marsh, *Popular Religion*, 197-20; Gregory Jeremy, "The Making of a Protestant
Nation," 314-33.

[19] Marsh, *Popular Religion*, 206-207; Frank Senn, "The Reform of the Mass" in *The
Catholicity of the Reformation*, eds. Carl Bratten and Robert W. Jenson (Grand
Rapids, 1996), 47-50. On Cranmer's moderating position, Senn states: "It seemed,
however, that no one was satisfied with the prayer book." For a detailed account of
Cranmer's struggle over acceptance of the prayer book with Hooper on one hand and
Gardiner on the other, and his attempt to secure the cooperation of both, see
MacCulloch, *Thomas Cranmer*, 454-93.

[20] Of Cranmer's liturgical reforms, Collinson writes: "No other Protestant liturgy kept
more closely in touch with the pre-Reformation past . . . Cranmer made the Protestant
religion, even, we might say, Protestantism, a cradle to the grave thing, a matter of
lifelong habit," Patrick Collinson, *The Birthpangs of Protestant England: Religious
and Cultural Change in the Sixteenth and Seventeenth Centuries* (Oxford, 1988), 23.
Latimer's sermons are based on scripture lessons prescribed by the liturgical calendar
in *The Two Liturgies*, 41-75.

realizing that new sense of God's actions in the present life of the nation."[21] In 1549 Cranmer declared this theological purpose for a new book of common prayers.

> And moreover, whereas St. Paul would have such language spoken to the people in the Church as they might understand and have profit by hearing the same, the service in this Church of England these many years hath been read in Latin to the people, which they understand not, so that they have heard with their ears only and their heart, spirit and mind have not been edified thereby.[22]

King remarks, "Gone forever was the supremacy of the medieval mass, which had been celebrated out of the sight of the people in a language they could not understand." This union of common prayer through common language promoted a communal dialogue between a speaking, summoning God and a listening, responsive people; thus biblically mediated colloquy, godly conversation, replaced the medieval distinction between priest and people.[23] The 1552 *Act of Uniformity*, in announcing the implementation of a revised *Book of Common Prayer*, refers to its "very godly order . . . to be used in the mother tongue within the Church of England . . . very comfortable to all good people desiring to live in Christian conversation . . . by common prayers, due using of the sacraments and frequent preaching of the Word of God with the devotion of its hearers."[24]

Blench has shown that Latimer was the outstanding exemplar of the colloquial style among Edwardian preachers.[25] His plain style of preaching, in imitation of Bible English, is speech accommodated to facilitate conversation and conversion of the broadest possible audience—universal and catholic—thus granting his sermons a flavor that has prompted historians to describe him as a "typically medieval preacher."[26] Indeed, Latimer's popularizing style, marked by its picturesque imagery, earthy diction, and figures of speech, enabled him to communicate through direct, concrete, unadorned, passionate language, displaying obvious continuities with the best of patristic and

[21] Wall, *Transformations of the Word*, 47.
[22] *Documents of the English Reformation*, 273.
[23] King, *English Reformation Literature*, 135-36.
[24] *Documents of the English Reformation*, 281.
[25] Blench, *Preaching in England*, 142-53; Darby, *Hugh Latimer, A Biography*, 201-55; Tulloch, *Luther and Other Leaders of the Reformation*, 339-51; Demaus, *Hugh Latimer*, 468-71; Charles Symth, *The Art of Preaching in the Church of England: 747-1939*, (London, 1940), 107.
[26] Smyth, *The Art of Preaching in the Church of England*, 107; Horton Davies, *Worship and Theology in England: From Cranmer to Hooker*, "Latimer was a people's preacher, not a preacher's preacher" (I.248). See Owst's description of medieval popular preaching, *Preaching in Medieval England*, 253-333.

medieval preaching *ad populum*.[27] H.O. Taylor describes Latimer's use of language.

> He drew his convictions from the Scriptures as spontaneously as he drew the illustrations of them from the world around him. His sermons reflected and absorbed the habits, the demands, the hardships, the very implements and incidents of English life, all straight from the preacher to his audience. Here indeed was an English Gospeller whose thoughts and phrases seemed to echo Wyclif: "right prelating is busy labouring, and not lording" might have been Wyclif's or Latimer's.[28]

The issue of language and style in popular preaching was not simply a matter of social concern, but reflected theological and moral issues that were bound up with the reformation of church and society in England. Latimer had announced the need for a decisive change in this matter in the *Sermon of the Plough*: "The people must have meat that must be familiar and continual and daily given unto them to feed upon." The Bible, then, is the book of the people, and through its regulated use they are to become a people of the book. A challenge faced by the Edwardian preachers, however, was being able to bridge the gap between "high and low," the need for cultivating a capacity to open new lines of communication that would include both learned piety and lay devotion. This required the discovery of plain, fitting speech that held to scripture's message for the enactment of lively faith, sacred rhetoric that would be capable of engaging diverse audiences by means of language sufficiently persuasive for overcoming habits of passivity and resistance to the Edwardian revival. As Cranmer wrote in the preface to the *Great Bible*,

> Here may all manner of persons, men, women, young, old, learned, unlearned, rich, poor, priests, laymen, lords, ladies, officers, tenants, and mean men, virgins, wives, widows, lawyers, merchants, artificers, husbandmen, and all manner of persons, of what estate or condition soever they be, may in THIS BOOK learn all things, that they ought to believe, what they ought to do, and what they should not do, as well concerning Almighty God, as also concerning themselves, and all other.[29]

Compounding this challenge was the fact that enthusiasm for the tradition of medieval popular preaching, reaching back to the middle and latter half of the fourteenth-century, had diminished. It was the mendicant orders, the itinerant friars, who preached abroad in towns, villages, churchyards, cemeteries, cathedrals, larger town churches, and in their own churches, which were the

---

[27] See Shuger, *Sacred Rhetoric*, 243-44: "In England, the vernacular sacred rhetorics tend to carry on the medieval passionate plain style under Protestant auspices."

[28] H.O. Taylor, *Thought and Expression in the Sixteenth Century* (New York, 1925), 125.

[29] *Documents of the English Reformation*, 238-39.

principal theaters for homiletic performance. With the waning of the friars' enthusiasm and effectiveness, which, ironically, was brought about in part by their extraordinary successes and popularity, came behavior that tended towards the bizarre in the desire for the novel and new when preaching to audiences that were already excessively stimulated by such tactics.[30] More importantly, the fear of heresy, especially Lollardy, produced legislative precautions in the early decades of the fifteenth century.[31] At the parish level, a combination of inadequate training and resources was often seasoned with a healthy dose of caution which limited the preaching of many to occasional expositions of sanctioned Christian essentials: the *Pater Noster*, the seven short petitions, the *Ave Maria*, the *Articles of Faith*, the *Commandments*, the *Seven Sacraments*, the deeds of mercy, the virtues and vices, the pains of hell, the three elements of penance, and the general sentence of excommunication. As Duffy explains this minimalist approach: "It will be evident that preaching is not given a high priority . . . At any rate, everyone expected that the average parish priest was ill-equipped for preaching; most parish priests concentrated on two functions . . . the priest as confessor and as 'plebis doctor,' since these were held to be intimately related."[32]

Peter Heath concludes that even the best parochial pre-reformation sermons, guided by approved collections such as Myrc's *Festial* or the *Speculum Sacerdotale*, were hampered by, "their stale hackneyed structure, their derivative and ossified mode of interpretation, their singular absence of any personal insights into, or any direct contemplation of the scripture." Heath characterizes the typical parish preacher as "uninspired and uninspiring," incapable of offering a clear, competent declaration of personal conviction.[33]

---

[30] David Knowles, *The Religious Orders in England: The End of the Middle Ages* (Cambridge, 1959), II.151-53; Owst, *Literature and Pulpit in Medieval England*, 210-86; Owst, *Preaching in England*, 93-155, 244-313; Smyth, *The Art of Preaching in the Church of England*, 87-89; A.G. Little, *Studies in English Franciscan History* (Manchester, 1917), 123-57; John Moorman, *A History of the Franciscan Order* (Oxford, 1968), 518-21. On popular preaching in the Patristic period, especially by Augustine and Chrysostom, see Hugh Old, *The Reading and Preaching of the Scriptures in the Worship of the Christian Church* (Grand Rapids,1998), II.171-222, 344-98. On Augustine's popular preaching see Van der Meer, *Augustine the Pastor*, 417-19.

[31] For the fear of negative influence on preaching by Lollardy and church leaders' attempts to control heresy in the late Middle Ages see H. Leith Spencer, *English Preaching in the Late Middle Ages* (Oxford, 1993), 47-163; Owst, *Preaching in Medieval England*, 132-45. Owst shows that the Reformation complaint against "non-preaching prelates" was not new. Its purpose was rhetorical, not to be quantified, but by perception based upon prophetic insight.

[32] Duffy, *The Stripping of the Altars*, 55-58.

[33] Peter Heath, *English Parish Clergy on the Eve of the Reformation* (Toronto, 1969), 93-103; John A.F. Thomson, *The Early Church and Society, 1485-1529*, 315-18; Marshall, *The Catholic Priesthood and the English Reformation*, 86-107; Spencer,

Latimer was exceptionally qualified to address the challenge of preaching on the ground level in England. Although he was trained and formed by the learned piety of late medieval Cambridge his roots were in Leicestershire, where he was raised as the son of a yeoman. The potential effectiveness of Latimer as a common preacher was enhanced by his plain manner of speaking that de-professionalized and popularized the basic teaching of the Edwardian church, enabling him to engage listeners in a way uncommon for bishops and high-ranking ecclesiastical or university officials. This kind of vernacular preaching by a learned preacher was potentially subversive, since its appeal presented an alternative to what was typically expected within the late medieval church, an expectation caricatured by Erasmus in *The Praise of Folly*.[34]

> Tell me now, is there any comedian or pitchman you would rather see than these men when they orate in these sermons, imitating quite absurdedly but still very amusingly what the rhetoricians have handed down about the way to make a speech? Good lord! How they gesticulate, how fittingly they vary the tone of their voice, how they croon, how they strut, continually changing their facial expressions, drowning out everything with their shouts! And the mysterious secret of this oratorical artistry is passed down personally from one friar to another.

To gain a better understanding of Latimer's popular sermons, it is necessary to locate him within the context of the Augustinian renaissance promoted by Erasmus, and which was marked by a return to sacred rhetoric, modeled on the plain style of scripture and appropriate to its sacred subject.[35] Erich Auerbach has traced the roots of the *Sermo Humilis* to the Fathers, with Augustine as its most outstanding proponent in defending and practicing the lowliness of the biblical writers.[36] *Humilis* is related to humus, or the soil, which literally means low-lying, and of small stature. This alludes to the ploughman-preacher who embodies the humility of the incarnation in speech and life, a voluntary humiliation displayed among the lowest social classes, among the materially

English Preaching in the Late Middle Ages, 208-209; Wabuda, *Preaching During the English Reformation*, 34-36; Davies, *A Religion of the Word*, 87-108.

[34] Desiderius Erasmus, *The Praise of Folly*, trans. and ed. Clarence H. Miller (New Haven, 1979), 101. See also Blench, *Preaching in England*, 113-41; Owst, *Literature and Pulpit in Medieval England*, 210-86; Janet L. Mueller, *The Native Tongue and the Word: Developments in English Prose Style 1380-1580* (Chicago, 1984) 164-72. Mueller shows that aureation and authority were joined in Latinity to grant late medieval clergy power over the laity. Preaching and writing in the vernacular gave the Reformers the advantage of immediate, personal, oral communication. Their scripturalism, based on the imitation of the Bible, and their modest use of rhetoric, as derived from and subordinated to scripture's message, gave preaching a freshness and directness that was not typical of late medieval learned clergy; see the discussion by King, *English Reformation Literature*, 122-44.

[35] Shuger, *Sacred Rhetoric*, 151-218.

[36] Erich Auerbach, *Literary Language and Its Public In Late Antiquity and In the Middle Ages*, trans. Ralph Manheim (New York, 1965), 31-66.

and spiritually poor, and which reflects the whole character, or manner, of Christ's acts and teachings.[37]

The purpose of Christ's humility, the *ethos* of scripture, which is shared by the preacher and embodied in the sermon, is to make the message of the truth of the Word available to all, without intimidating or repelling the unlearned. In popular preaching, then, the lowly, earthy style incarnate in Christ and embodied in scripture evinces a humility that overcomes barriers, evoking a world of the divine accommodating itself to the lowly in the plain, humble Word and in the manner of preachers who exemplify its character.[38]

This "catholic" use of scripture, which sought to return the word of God to the body of Christians as a whole—especially common folk—had been enthusiastically endorsed by Erasmus in the *Paraclesis.*

> The journey is simple, and it is ready for anyone. Only bring a pious and open mind, possessed above all with a pure and simple faith . . . This doctrine in an equal degree accommodates itself to all, lowers itself to the little ones, adjusts itself to their measure, nourishing them with milk, bearing, fostering, sustaining them, doing everything until we grow into Christ. Again, not only does it serve the lowliest, but it also is an object of wonder to those at the top . . . It is a small affair to the little ones and more than the highest affair to the great. It casts aside no age, no sex, no fortune or position in life.[39]

Humility is the most necessary virtue for producing competent speaking, hearing, and doing of the message incarnate in scripture, the embodiment, or enactment, of the Bible, as prescribed in the *Book of Homilies.*

> Read it [Holy Scripture] humbly, with a meke and a lowly harte, to thinet you maie glorifie God, and not your self, with the knowledge of it; and reade it not without daily praiying to God that he would directe your readyng to good effecte; and take upon you to expounde it no further than you can plainly understande it. For, as St. Augustine saieth, the knowledge of Holy Scripture is a great, large, and high palace, but the door is verie lowe so the the high and arrogant man cannot runne in, but he must stoupe lowe and humble hym self that shall entre into it

---

[37] See King's treatment of Robert Crowley's 1550 edition of *Piers Plowman*, *English Reformation Literature*, 319-39. In terms of being radical, as in the "root" of the matter, the popular sermons may be more radical in activity if not in tone, simply because they are the actual implementation of the vision articulated in earlier sermons.

[38] Auerbach, *Literary Language*, 39-47. See the excellent discussion by Peter Auski, *Christian Plain Style: The Evolution of a Spiritual Ideal* (Montreal, 1995) 13-67, 232-66. The Franciscans also offered a style of *sermo humilis* preaching that utilized narrative, emotion and the commonplace, focusing on the humanity of Christ in his incarnation and his passion. Peter Hawkins, *Dante's Testaments*, 23. On Franciscan preaching see Old, *The Reading and Preaching of the Scripture: The Medieval Period* (Grand Rapids, 1998), III.342-48.

[39] Erasmus, *Paraclesis*, 100.

(Readying of Holy Scripture, 65).

For the Edwardian church, worship did not seek to lift its participants to a spiritual realm or higher world, a purpose the reformers pejoratively ascribed to the medieval mass. Rather, the evangelicals' use of the Bible in common prayer and preaching sought to make common places such as Grimsthorpe and Stamford theaters of divine revelation, scenes of vivid, dramatic performances of scripture representing the divine-human paradox of the incarnation, the "high within the low," thus transforming ordinary parishes into holy places for speaking and hearing the Word, for celebrating Holy Communion, and for offering public obedience to God.[40] Although we have no record of why Latimer was sent to this region, Lincoln was his home diocese, his place of birth and childhood, and where he returned to receive holy orders for the priesthood in 1524.[41] It will be necessary to provide an overview of its landscape before discussing Latimer's performance of sowing the Word among its people.

In making the transition from preaching at court to preaching among the commons, Latimer would need to accommodate his message for a diocese that had been led from 1521-47 by John Longland, who was one of England's most conservative bishops and a vigorous heresy hunter. Margaret Bowker comments in her study of Lincoln and Longland's tenure as bishop.

> But it looks as though for Lancanshire, York, Chichester, and the vast area of the diocese of Lincoln the picture is different-not one of Protestant triumph; nor of an inevitable event, nor even of bishops profligate with land and conspicuously lacking in responsibility, but of a hard fight for the consciences of Englishmen, fought not on the battlefields of Europe, but in many hearts and minds in the length and breadth of England.[42]

Longland was a well-known and respected theologian, humanist scholar, and preacher, although his pulpit ministry seems to have been limited to the court, the clergy, and the monasteries. Bowker concludes that at the time of Longland's death in 1547, he left a diocese with priests and laity as conservative as he was which is attested by his swiftness in prosecuting the Lollards of Buckinghamshire and the academic Lutherans of Oxford (of which he was chancellor). In addition, Longland grasped the importance of preaching as an instrument for teaching and shaping faith and loyalty, carefully controlling the pulpits of Lincoln through his scrutiny of ordinands and the use of his own patronage. After the break with Rome, non-conforming priests were unlikely to get either pulpit or parish at his hands. Bowker notes that Longland

---

[40] Shuger, *Sacred Rhetoric*, 204-23; Wall, *Transformations of the Word*, 48-49.

[41] Chester, *Hugh Latimer*, 1-28.

[42] Margaret Bowker, *The Henrician Reformation: the Diocese of Lincoln under John Longland 1521-1547* (Cambridge, 1981), 156.

used his control of diocesan policy to serve the conservative cause, just as Cranmer or Cromwell used policy to serve reformist causes. However, Longland was not completely opposed to reform, but only reform that fell outside the boundaries of his own traditionalist leanings.[43]

The vast size of the diocese inevitably fostered a certain amount of diversity within Longland's administration. The southern counties, nearer to London and the universities, were more accepting of change in the mid-1530s than was Lincolnshire, where the 1536 risings opposed legislation by the Reformation Parliament and the issuing of the *Ten Articles*, which dated from the Convocation of July 1536. Coincidentally, when Latimer preached at Paul's Cross in 1536 to address the threat posed by the Pilgrimage of Grace, included among those rebels were clergy, commons, monastics, and a limited number of gentry who marched in protest to Lincoln Cathedral, voicing their outrage over religious innovations.[44]

There was also a radical, non-conformist underside to Longland's conservative rule, a stream of heterodox activity reaching back to Oldcastle's Rebellion in 1413, near the region of Leicester. Recent studies reveal that Lollard activity did not cease after Oldcastle's failure. Episcopal records indicate that Lollards were pursued and tried in the diocese of Lincoln well into the Henrician period, culminating in Longland's attack on Buckinghamshire Lollards in 1521, when according to Foxe, nearly 350 persons were accused, leading to six executions and about fifty abjurations. Their heretical activity was similar to Lollardy; disbelief in transubstantiation, use of the English Bible, rude expressions towards church bells, saints, images, pilgrimage, purgatory, and papal authority.[45]

In addition to a long history of Lollard presence, during the early Edwardian period the diocese of Lincoln was a site of radical stirrings that were commonly believed to be the activity of Anabaptists, radicals who openly expressed dissatisfaction with the slow pace of reform as administered by the crown. Horst argues for the possibility that Lollards who were not absorbed into the mainstream of Edwardian religion could have continued their non-conformist ways by joining England's newest forms of radical religion. He concludes that Anabaptists were known to be active in Lincolnshire during the latter

---

[43] Bowker, *The Henrician Reformation: the Diocese of Lincoln under John Longland*, 157-85.

[44] Bowker, *The Henrician Reformation*, 139-55; Gerald A.J. Hadgett, *History of Lincolnshire: Tudor Lincolnshire* (Lincolnshire, 1975), IV.24-40; J.F.H. Hill, *Tudor and Stuart England* (Cambridge, 1956), 8-41; D.M. Owen, *Church and Society in Medieval Lincolnshire: History of Lincolnshire* (Lincolnshire, 1971), V.7-126.

[45] Bowker, *The Henrician Reformation*, 175-85; Malcolm Lambert, *Medieval Heresy: Popular Movements from the Gregorian Reform to the Reformation* (London, 1992), 262-66, 280-83; J.A.F. Thomson, *Later Lollards*, 224-29.

Edwardian years; their radicalism presumably creating both a threat and an embarrassment for the Edwardians.[46]

The assignment to Lincolnshire also allowed Latimer to spend time with friends and family in the countryside. He preached at Stamford in 1550, not far from his old home at Thurcaston, and at Leicester itself, spending time with the Glovers of Baxterly in nearby Warwickshire, a place where he resided for a time during his years of exile from 1539-47. Most frequently, Latimer was a houseguest of the duchess of Suffolk at Grimsthorpe where he enjoyed the patronage of Katherine Brandon at her principal residence outside London. Indeed, the dedication of the 1562 edition of Latimer's sermons to Katherine reflects her devotion to the evangelical cause, and particularly, to Latimer's evangelistic preaching. Chester has shown that Latimer probably delivered the majority of his popular sermons at or nearby the residence of Katherine Brandon, thus providing him with an unknown number of sympathetic listeners and an evangelical base for his preaching mission in Lincolnshire.[47] We may surmise that while planted in Lincolnshire, Latimer addressed audiences whose members represented a variety of religious views, loyalties, hopes, and desires within a region that, in its majority, remained contested.[48]

In addition to confronting the challenges presented by diverse religious conditions, Latimer's preaching in Lincolnshire occurred in a region that was humbled by its economic and social conditions, circumstances brought about by the widespread financial instability, unemployment, and inflation that afflicted Edward's England. In the late 1540s, conditions in Lincolnshire were so severe that a number of parishes were combined in order to sustain a priestly ministry and essential religious activities.[49] Latimer's frequent references to human misery, affliction, and poverty in its spiritual and moral expressions should not be seen as more than rhetorical flourishes, as expressions of the Edwardian social gospel being announced and implemented in this depressed region.

The first of Latimer's popular sermons was preached at Stamford in the fall of 1550; its theme was derived from the gospel of the day: "Give that is Caesar's to Caesar, and that is God's to God." The sermon was informed by the vision embodied in the *Book of Homilies*: the creation of a Christian

---

[46] Horst, *The Radical Brethren*, 34-5, 65-66, 97-137. Horst views Lincolnshire to have been a region affected by "liberal protestantism" during the Edwardian period, becoming a center of Anabaptist activity that supplanted Lollardy as the norm for English non-conformity; see the good discussion of the evangelicals perception of Anabaptism in Davies, *A Religion of the Word*, 67-86, "If such radicals had not existed, it would have been necessary to invent them, and that, to a great extent was what protestants did" (80).

[47] Chester, *Hugh Latimer*, 184-88.

[48] Hadgett, *Tudor Linconshire*, 168-88.

[49] Hadgett, *Tudor Linconshire*, 129-30, J.W.F. Hill, *Tudor and Stuart Lincoln*, 8. Hill refers to the isolation and ignorance of Lincolnshire as "the most brute and beastly in the realm."

commonwealth through the preaching of the Word under the authority of the royal supremacy. The message of the sermon is essentially a replication of the *Sermon of the Plough*, adapted to enfold Lincolnshire into its vision. Latimer's aim was to persuade his listeners: to respond to the arrival of a new future that was articulated by his evangelical preaching; to believe that the Edwardian Reformation offered fresh possibilities for the common life of the realm, participating in this new arrangement and receiving its temporal and spiritual benefits.

The sermon theme was derived from Matthew 23, calling attention to the suspicious character of the Pharisees: "Thus went the Pharisees, and took a counsel. Luke hath *observantes*, mocking, spying, looking, testing, watching; like subtle crafty, and sleighty fellows" (Works, I.287). Playing on the word *observantes*, Latimer identified Franciscan Observants, the most orthodox and zealous of the religious orders, with Christ's opponents. His aim was to draw listeners from the hold of traditional religion and to dispose them favorably towards his message.[50] This move set the tone for the sermon, elevating the importance of its discourse and preparing his audience for the possibility of imminent change.

Latimer's evangelization of Stamford was conducted within the framework of liturgical practices prescribed by the Edwardian reforms. The purpose of his preaching was to mediate an encounter between Christ and the people: "For whose words should we delight to hear and to learn, but the words and doctrine of our Saviour Christ? And that I may at this time so declare them, as may be for God's glory, edifying you, and my discharge, I pray you all to help me with your prayers." Accordingly, he bid his audience to offer prayers for the universal church; for the preservation of Edward VI, sole head of the church; for Edward's council; for the souls of the departed; for themselves; for the grace to trust Christ and his death, and to die in that faith; and lastly, to say the Lord's Prayer (Works, I.283-84).[51]

Matthew's Gospel provided homiletic material—a parable told by Christ about a king who gave a wedding feast for his son—for Latimer's response to

---

[50] On the Observants, see David Knowles, *The Religious Orders in England, The Tudor Age*, 206-11. Knowles describes the English Observants as the most Catholic in temper, with the strongest Roman sympathies, upholding papal authority and condemning Henry's divorce. See also, Rex, "The Friars in the English Reformation," 54-59; A.G. Little, *Studies in English Franciscan History* (Manchester, 1917), 123-57. Little describes the favorable reputation enjoyed by the Observants because of their commitment to reform and simplicity. On the history of the Friars Minor in the diocese of Lincoln, especially during the episcopate of Grosseteste in the thirteenth-century, see Mary E. O'Carroll, SND, *A Thirteenth-Century Preacher's Handbook* (Toronto, 1997), 17-20.

[51] *Documents of the English Reformation*, "The Form of Bidding the Common Prayers," 257; see the discussion of the Edwardians' strategy in Davies, *A Religion of the Word*, 13-66.

his conservative critics who questioned the effectiveness of the *Book of Homilies* and evangelical preaching. Alluding to the king's messengers and his guests who failed to respond to the royal invitation, Latimer declared: "The preachers called good and bad. They can do no more at all; God is he that must bring it in; God must open the hearts." According to Latimer, biblical imagery confirms this truth: preaching is like a fisher's net, it catches good and bad fish, drawing all to shore; preaching draws multitudes, but not all practice what is preached even though they bear the name Christian. Moreover, all preachers in England are not truthful; some are card-gospellers, some are pot-gospellers, some are dice-gospellers; even the apostles included a devil—Judas—among their number (Works, I.285-86).

Latimer advised that preachers cannot control the responsiveness of their listeners, since their primary task is to call the wicked back to God, a charge that, "nippeth, pincheth, toucheth the quick . . . if you do not your office, if you feed not the people and warn them, you shall be damned for it." These comments echo the official homily, *On The Readying of Holye Scripture*, which affirmed the efficacy of God's Word through its reading and appropriation: "They [the wordes of Holy Scripture] have power to converte through God's promise and thei be effectual through God's assistance; and beying received in a faithfull harte, thei have ever an heavenly spiritual woorkying in them" (Homilies, 62). Latimer announced that God is the source of homiletic persuasion; therefore curates who teach the words and wisdom of God warrant the confidence of their people, especially those patrons who may grant their livings.[52]

> But this office of preaching is it that God hath ordained as St. Paul saith: it pleaseth God by foolish preaching to save creditors, those that believe, by foolishness of preaching, or foolish preaching, it maketh no matter; it is most godly wisdom, and the preaching office is the office of salvation, and the only means that God hath appointed to salvation (Works, I.286).

The acceptance of preaching as the office of salvation required radical change of mind for a people accustomed to traditional practices.[53] In defense of this change, Latimer returned to the story of Christ: "Oh these flatterers! No greater mischief in the commonwealth, than these flatterers! But who would have discovered this but our Saviour Jesus Christ? . . . "Hypocrites, hypocrites, hypocrites! One in heart, another in mouth, fair in pretense, but full of mischief and malicious hatred within he saw" (Works, I.290-91). Identifying with the

---

[52] Bowker shows that during the later years of Longland's episcopate, patronage was increasingly taken over by the laity, *The Henrician Reformation*, 159.
[53] Marshall, *The Catholic Priesthood and the English Reformation*, 138. "For Protestants, the priest was essentially a preacher of God's Word, and a minister of his sacraments; they denied the priest had the power to offer Christ in the sacrifice of the mass." See the previous discussions in chapters 1-3.

scriptural words of Paul and those of Christ,[54] Latimer declared his willingness to suffer for the sake of his message.[55] "The highest promotion that God can bring his unto this life is, to suffer for his truth. And it is the greatest setting forth of his word; it is God's seed. And one suffering for the truth turneth more than a thousand sermons."

Illustrating this point, Latimer imaginatively recreated an event from an earlier time in his life, during the reign of Henry VIII when he [Latimer] was examined by a council of bishops and charged with preaching heresy. He described the room where he stood, with a chimney behind him. As his interlocutors worked to entrap him in a manner similar to those who spied on Christ, he received wisdom from the chimney, from a hidden one appointed to provide his answers: "But God, which always hath given me answer, helped me, or else I could never have escaped; and delivered me from their hands." Latimer drew a lesson from this experience to encourage confidence in God's word and providential care, calling his listeners to return to godliness: "with thy soul, thy faith, thy hope, thy obedient mind" (Works, I.294-95).[56] This is the pattern of faith and good works set forth in the homily, *Of the True and Lively Faithe*,

> Thys is the true, lively, and unfayned Christian faith, and is not in the mouthe and outward profession onlely, but it liveth and stirreth inwardly in the hart. This faythe is not without hope and truste in God, nor without love for God and of our neyghbors, nor without the feare of God, nor without the desyre to heare God's Worde, and to folowe the same in eschewying evill and doying gladly all good workes (Homilies, 92).

The second half of the sermon, the *Residue of the Gospel*, was delivered in the afternoon. Latimer reviewed his text and moved to his theme: "Give Caesar what is Caesar's, and to God that is due God . . . Give to your Caesar, to your king, to our most noble King Edward, our Caesar." Latimer considered this to be a command of God, comparable in authority to the Ten Commandments: "I cannot say much of Lincolnshire, for I know it not. But I dare say, if Lincolnshire be as other places I know, this text condemneth a great many of Lincolnshire, and driveth them down to hell for breaking of this commandment" (Works, I.296).

---

[54] On assuming a biblical identity and language, see John A. Alford, "The Scriptural Self" in ed. Bernard S. Levy, *The Bible in the Middle Ages* (Binghamton, 1992), 1-21.

[55] Resner calls this apologetic *ethos* "the preacher's personal testimony to God's redemptive activity in the world as the preacher has been privileged to see it or experience it." Its purpose is to persuade through identification rather than argument. It is especially important when the preacher must initially establish credibility with an audience. Andre Resner, *Preacher and Cross: Person and Message in Theology and Rhetoric* (Grand Rapids, 1999), 171.

[56] Chester, *Hugh Latimer*, 71-72.

As was the case in the morning sermon, Latimer alerted listeners to reposition themselves, to alter their expectations, to prepare themselves to be challenged and for the necessity to be changed.[57] Addressing the objections to Edward's reforms, Latimer invoked the example of Christ who, by keeping to his vocation, did not meddle in Caesar's affairs. Latimer reasoned that if Christ did not determine an amount that should be rendered to Caesar the king's treasurer should have authority for the maintenance of the commonwealth.

Latimer's brief apology in defense of the king and Parliament offered assurance that it is God who judges unjust rulers and vindicates those who suffer obediently. Moreover, such confidence warrants payment of one's duties for the common good as commanded by royal injunction, "that substance previously bestowed upon pardons, pilgrimage, trentals, decking of images, offering of candles, giving to friars, and upon other blind devotions . . . ought at this time to be offered to help the poor and the needy, knowing that to relieve the poor is a true worshipping of God" (Works, I.300-301).[58]

According to Latimer, scripture itself provides examples of worship through the payments of tithes and money by the people of Israel, "to church-ministries, the promotion of the clergy, poor widows, fatherless children, and the maintenance of poor scholars." Since the time of the New Testament the ministry of salvation and preachers had received a sufficient living in spite of negligent curates: "Some will say, our curate is naught, an ass-head; a dodipole, a lack-latin, and can do nothing. Shall I pay him my tithes, that doth us no good?" Complaints of this nature should be directed to the bishop, to the council, and, to God: "Pray, Pray. Prayer is the remedy that never faileth" (Works, I.303-304).

Latimer blamed such confusion on the abundance of resources lavished upon monasteries, chantries, masses, gild images, copes, torches, tapers, and "a hundred things more." Bringing clarity to these matters, he announced that a new time had arrived through the preaching of the word and the implementation of Edwardian reforms. God's desire was for the hearts of his people through daily obedience, through offering loyalty to the king and assistance to the poor and needy.

---

[57] Resner, in *Preacher and Cross*, calls this polemical *ethos*, "If the hearers are scandalized in some way by the preacher, then an appropriate defense can reposition the hearers so that they can hear again the true scandal with the surperimposed scandal of the preacher removed altogether" (166). Resner argues that situations of attack and polemic always raise the stakes for all involved. In Lincolnshire, Latimer was attempting to raise the stakes of the conflict from the merely political to the theological, thus placing the Edwardian Reformation within a religious framework created by his preaching of the gospel. For a discussion of conditions that created the need for apologetic polemic sufficient to overcome the scandal of the government's political policies, see MacCulloch, *Tudor Church Militant*, 52-6, 154-56.

[58] *Documents of the English Reformation*, 255; Dickens, *The English Reformation*, 256-86.

While he acknowledged that changes in traditional devotional practices might prompt some to ask, "What is become of our forefathers?" Latimer assurance his listeners that God would indeed care for his elect, citing the stories of Moses, Elijah, and the young men in the fiery furnace. This raised yet another question: "What need we preachers then?" Preaching is the ordinary means by which God intends to save all. Returning to the words of Christ, "Give Caesar what is Caesar's," Latimer exhorted his audience to be loyal to God and to Edward. If Caesar was a pagan, and Christians still paid duties to him, then English folk should gladly pay their duties to Edward, who is a Christian, godly, and virtuous king (Works, I.306-307). This was the call issued in the homily, *On Good Order and Obedience to Rulers and Magistrates.*

> And praise be to God, that we knowe the great excellent benefite of God shewed towards us in this behalfe. God hath sente us his high gifte, our most dere sovereigne lord, King Edward the Sixt, with godly, wise, and honorable counsail, with other superiors and inferiors in a beutifull ordre. Wherefore, let us subjectes do our bounden duties, geving harte thankes to God and praiying for the preservacion of this godly ordre. Let us obey from the bottome of our hartes al their godly procedynges, lawes, statutes, proclamacions, and injunctions, with al godly orders (Homilies,162).

Latimer's two-part sermon at Stamford is significant for understanding his preaching to the commons in Lincolnshire. At a crossroads of that region, he introduced himself and his message to promote the conversion of a contested diocese known for its resistance to religious change. His sermons invited the commons into new possibilities offered by the Edwardian Reformation, rendering an alternative vision of the realm for their acceptance and participation.[59]

During his ministry in Lincolnshire, Latimer provided extensive teaching on the *Pater Noster*, utilizing a familiar form of popular devotion for introducing new possibilities to the realm under the rule of Edward.[60] The Lord's Prayer was a traditional piece of late medieval *pastoralia*, catechetical instruction that formed the "irreducible core" of a more elaborate educational program formulated at Archbishop Pecham's provincial Council of Lambeth in 1281: *Ignorantia Sacerdotum.* Duffy states that Pecham's scheme, which was to be expounded in the vernacular to parishioners four times a year, was intended to provide a comprehensive guide to Christian belief and practice structured

---

[59] Davies provides a good discussion of the Edwardians' hope and fear in their desire to advance the reform, Davies, *A Religion of the Word*, 177-90.

[60] Wayne Meeks comments on how scripture moves a community to social embodiment, that "the proper context and aim of interpretation are not merely ideas or attitudes, but ethos and practice." Meeks, "A Hermeneutics of Social Embodiment" in *Harvard Theological Review* 79 (1986), 184-85. See Davies, *A Religion of the Word*, on the Edwardians' aim for an increase in the participation of the English people in godly commonwealth.

around the Creed, Ten Commandments, the dual precepts of love, the seven works of mercy, the seven virtues, the seven vices, and the seven sacraments. This catechetical program was linked to the obligations imposed on the laity in 1215 by the Fourth Lateran Council; that of annual confession to parish priests. Duffy concludes that the abundance of surviving catechetical and penitential material for clerical use points to the high priority given to such pastoral activity.[61]

The English Reformers retained the Lord's Prayer in a place of prominence. Edward's 1547 injunctions required that on every holy day ministers openly and plainly recite in English the Lord's Prayer, the Creed, and the Ten Commandments for the learning of the people. In addition, at the time of annual confession during Lent, the ministers were to examine the people on their knowledge, in English, of these essentials.[62] Latimer was accustomed to teaching the Lord's Prayer as a guide for Christian faith and practice. In 1536, while serving as Bishop of Worcester, he issued injunctions for his diocese to implement reforms instituted by Thomas Cromwell that stressed the regular use of the Bible and the *Pater Noster* in English by the laity (Works, II.243). Latimer continued to attribute a place of importance to the Lord's Prayer during the Edwardian period.

> Marvel not that I use at the sermon's end to make prayer, for I do it not of singularity; but when I am at home, and in the country where I go, sometime when the poor people come and ask me, I appose them myself, or cause my servant to appose them of the Lord's Prayer . . . Therefore that all that cannot say it may learn, I use before the sermon and after to say it. Wherefore now I beseech you, let us say together: 'Our Father, which art'. . . (Works, I.307-308).

The Duchess of Suffolk's servants were the audience for Latimer's practical exposition which is divided according to the prayer's seven petitions into a series that occupies one hundred and twenty pages of his extant works.[63] In keeping with his popular style, his exposition includes much repetition, and is delivered by means of direct speech utilizing concrete, vivid imagery that communicates his personal conviction and wisdom. Latimer's introductory remarks established the significance of his subject matter, its worthiness of his listeners' attention, and his competence for its handling and use. Because the Lord's Prayer was given by Christ, "a most perfect schoolmaster," it contains great and wonderful things that should be handled by a learned man: "This prayer is the sum and abridgment of all other prayers . . . yea whatsoever

---

[61] Duffy, *The Stripping of the Altars*, 53-55; Marshall, *The Catholic Priesthood and the English Reformation*, 101-103; Spencer, *English Preaching in the Late Middle Ages*, 199-208.

[62] *Documents of the English Reformation*, 249.

[63] The sermons can be found in *Works*, I. 326-446. Chester considers them to be the most interesting part of Latimer's Lincolnshire ministry (*Hugh Latimer*, 191).

mankind hath need of in soul and body is contained in this prayer" (Works, I.326-27). Erasmus had emphasized the importance of scripture as a medium for conversation between Christ and the church.

If we desire to learn, why is another author more pleasing than Christ himself? If we seek a model for life, why does another example take precedence for us over that of Christ himself? . . . And He, since He promised to be with us all days, even unto the consummation of the world, stands forth especially in this literature, in which He lives for us even at this time, breathes and speaks. I should say almost more effectively than when he dwelt among men.[64]

Latimer intended that the Lord's Prayer not be mindlessly repeated as an act of private devotion, but rather, that it be spoken as performative speech, a public declaration of faith by its people, and defined by its Teacher.[65]

This prayer hath two parts; it hath a preface, which some call a salutation or a loving entrance; secondarily, the prayer itself. The entrance is this: *Cum oratis, dicte*, Pater Noster, *qui es in coelis*; "When ye pray, say, Our Father, which art in heaven." As who should say, "You Christian people, you that bear the name Christians, must pray so" (Works, I.327).

Because Christ is the original teacher of the prayer, he is the schoolmaster and orator embodying fully its wisdom and eloquence. Latimer viewed himself as Christ's auditor, one appointed to teach the words of the prayer for the transformation of Christ's people[66] (Works, I.327). Speaking plainly, Latimer

---

[64] Erasmus, *Paraclesis*, 101. "Erasmus' textual portraiture of Christ is not one falsely adapted to humanist interest in pedagogy; rather, he adopted pedagogy as the excellent vocation because it was the role which God himself had assumed, teaching in flesh and voice the lessons of wisdom," Boyle, *Erasmus on Language and Method in Theology*, 26.

[65] Latimer taught both the language and the grammar (logic) of the Lord's Prayer. See Paul L. Holmer, *The Grammar of Faith* (San Francisco, 1978), 17-23. "If theology is like a grammar, and certainly it is, then it follows that learning theology is not an end in itself . . . be it the creeds, the words of scripture, the words of Jesus, we must note that like grammar and logic, their aim is not that we repeat the words. Theology must be absorbed, and when it is, the hearer is supposed to be godly."

[66] Latimer's allusion to the humanists' reform agenda is obvious. I take his identification of Christ as the perfect schoolmaster to mean that Christ possesses authority to instruct and to persuade by means of his speech, the embodiment of divine wisdom and eloquence in his life, perfectly joining and fulfilling two practices that were at the core of Christian humanism in England. See McConica, *English Humanists and Reformation Politics*; Ronald G. Witt, "The Humanist Movement" in ed. Thomas Brady, Heiko Oberman, James Tracy, *Handbook of European History 1400-1600: Late Middle Ages, Renaissance, and Reformation* (Grand Rapids, 1995), 110-12. This is an example of rhetorical theology. See Marjorie O'Rourke Boyle, "Rhetorical Theology: Charity Seeking Charity" in ed. Walter Jost and Wendy Olmstead, *Rhetorical Invention and Religious Inquiry: New Perspectives* (Yale, 1999), 89-90. "Rhetoric seeks an act of the will, assent, and secures its religious end

enfolded his listeners into its common language and life, weaving together biblical exposition and moral instruction to engender personal and public righteousness.

The first petition, "Our Father, who art in heaven," possesses meaning for those who utter its words according to the example and authority of Christ: "He is the eldest Son; he is the Son of God by nature, we be his sons by adoption through his goodness; therefore, he biddeth us to call him our Father, to be had in fresh memory and great reputation." This Christological focus established the basis for pastoral admonition.

> Therefore when you say this prayer, you must consider what you say: for it is better once said deliberately and with understanding, than a thousand times without understanding . . . for their matter lieth not in much saying, but in well saying . . . so, if it be said to the honor of God, then it hath its effect, and we shall have our petitions. For God is true to his promises: and our Saviour, knowing him to be well affect towards us, commandeth us therefore to call him Father (Works, I.328).

The second lecture discusses "hallowed be thy name," joining the holiness of God's name with the practical holiness of those who pray for its realization, which is the fruit of hearing and obeying the word of God. Latimer envisaged the hallowing of God's name in a diversity of vocations across the realm: "preachers, magistrates, teachers, universities, masters, servants, laborers, husbands, and wives" (Works, I.341-53).

The third talk, "Thy Kingdom Come," stressed the importance of preaching for announcing the arrival of the kingdom, the centrality of the Word in all human affairs. Latimer warned of false preachers, ambitious, covetous persons who turned from godliness to serve the devil's reign. Because the authority of God's kingdom was openly contested in England, Latimer portrayed its citizens as actors engaged in a dramatic struggle with the devil, suffering, and affliction: "The blood of Christians is, as it were, the seed of the fruit of the gospel. For when one is hanged here, and another yonder, then God goeth a sowing of his seed . . . And happy is he to whom it is given to suffer for God's Holy Word's sake." Only faith, which is sent down from heaven, is able to preserve Christian people from the devil and prepare them for God's coming reign (Works, I.354-66).

The discussion of the fourth petition, "Thy will be done," insists upon the political dimension of the Lord's Prayer, public righteousness, and God's help in keeping his holy laws and commandments: "But I fear me, there be many which say this prayer, and yet cannot tell what they say; or at the least their

---

in conversion . . . A particular efficacy of rhetoric towards this transformation defines it as the language of the Spirit that Christ spoke . . . The [humanist] program was the transformation of speech into act, oratory into flesh, just as Speech had become incarnate."

hearts are contrary disposed unto it." Latimer referred to the rebels who participated in the 1549 uprisings at Norfolk and Devonshire: "They said it with their lips only, but not with their hearts. Almighty God has revealed his will in calling magistrates, how he will have them to be honoured and obeyed." The only exception pertains when laws are made against God and his word, "Then I ought to obey God more than man," which is a refusal to obey on the basis of conscience.[67] Rebellion is forbidden, however, since suffering is the mark of obedience and signifies that all matters have been committed to God (Works, I.368-71).

A relevant issue for an audience of servants and common laborers was the sin of sloth, which was viewed as the work of the devil among those who will not labor: "Therefore let us pray to God to do his will, and we will have all things necessary to soul and body." Drunkards, lecherers, whoremongers, liars, swearers, and the Norfolk and Devonshire rebels are the devil's servants. Whoever prays "thy will be done" expresses a desire to obey God from the bottom of one's heart. Examples of obedience illustrate this point: Susanna, a godly woman; Lady Judith; Queen Esther; the Apostle Peter; Joab, David's captain; St. John the Baptist, hearty knight and excellent preacher; King David; the Prophet Elijah. Salutary lives from the past provide inspiration for change in the present: "We have need to say with St. Augustine: 'Lord, do then with me what thou commandeth and thou command what thou wilt'" (Works, I.371-86).[68]

Latimer's exposition of the Lord's Prayer represents a common form of instruction for both priests and people of the late medieval church. The purpose of Latimer's exposition, however, was to challenge normal expectations, while summoning listeners to pursue their Christian vocation in obedience to the words of Christ: "Finally, when we will be preserved from all temptations, that they shall not have victory over us, nor that the devil shall not devour us, we may say: 'Our Father' " . . . (Works, I.445-6). The vocation of the church militant is both a gift and demand; the social embodiment of living faith is realized in personal and public righteousness. Latimer invited the commons to take up a way of life that would be characterized by humility rather than pride, by godly struggle rather than worldly comfort. He invited them into the world of the gospel rendered by the word of Christ.

---

[67] This primary allegiance to God, higher than even loyalty to kings and rulers, is acclaimed in the homily, *An Exhortacion to Obedience*, 167; see the discussion in Davies, *A Religion of the Word*, 158-68.

[68] Duffy shows that honoring and imitating the saints as examples of holy living was only one of a number of ways the late medieval church offered devotion to them. By comparison, Latimer's examples are almost exclusively taken from scripture and offered as examples in their weakness and strength, as paradigmatic examples of faithful obedience with whom, even the most humble of listeners may identify. See Duffy, *Stripping of the Altars*, 160-71.

The teaching of the late medieval church required active participation in a complex system of liturgical and devotional practices within particular spheres of social relations: family, guild, and parish. Latimer's sermon at Grimsthorpe on St. Simon and St. Jude's Day located the virtue of charity within a larger framework, reinterpreting a topic which was at the heart of the Christian life and a requirement for salvation.[69] The Gospel, John 15:12, "This I command you that you love one another," enabled Latimer to paint a vivid picture of the world created by Christian love—divine charity—flowing from simple faith in Christ.[70] "For there are many things that pertain to a Christian man, and yet all these things are contained in this one thing, that is love; he lappeth all things up in love" (Works, I.448).

The sermon portrays two opposing forms of love warring over England's soul. Latimer identified charity with Christ, as Christ's cognizance and livery, and its antithesis as the devil's livery, hatred, malice, and discord. He surmised that, in England, there were more servants of the devil than of Christ, and that carnal love was more abundant than godly love: "I speak not of carnal love, which is beastly love, wherewith the whoremonger loveth his whore; but this charitable love is so necessary, that when a man hath her, without all other things it will suffice" (Works, I.448).

Latimer's exposition of I Corinthians 13 provided the interpretive framework for his reading of John 15: "For right faith is not without love; for love cometh and floweth from faith. Love is a child of faith; for no man can love except he believe; so that they have two several offices, they themselves being inseparable." He illustrates right ordering of faith and love in Christ.

> Like as I cannot say, the mayor of Stamford must make me a pair of shoes, because he is a greater man than the shoemaker is; for the mayor, though he be the greater man, yet it is not his office to make shoes; so, though love be greater, yet it is not her office to save. This much I thought good to say against those who fight against the truth (Works, I.448-52).

Latimer's exposition describes a pattern of social relationships constituted by Christ's love as the foundation of a Christian social order. Christian love is fulfilled in neighbor love, a social reality glorious in scope, embracing but also extending beyond private affection, personal devotion, kinship, parish, and guild.[71] The words of Christ, spoken in John 15, invite to a world created by divine charity which is sustained through faith in Christ and obedience to God's

---

[69] Marshall, *Catholic Priesthood*, 177-91; Davies, *A Religion of the Word*, 18-66, 127-40.

[70] On the significance of charity in late medieval religion and its institutional life, see Duffy, *The Stripping of the Altars*, 126-54; R.N. Swanson, *Church and Society in Late Medieval* England, 299-308; John Bossy, *Christianity in the West 1400-1700* (Oxford, 1985) 140-52.

[71] See Duffy's description of the exclusive circles of charity formed by guilds and chantries in English parishes, *The Stripping of the Altars*, 148-54.

commands. Latimer's application of this teaching addresses the need for restitution from wrong doing and stealing from one's neighbor. "Sirs, I will tell you, except restitution be made, look for no salvation . . . They love not the livery of Christ, nor his cognizance, which is love" (Works, I.453).[72]

In presenting a way of seeing the virtue of charity, Latimer announced that Christ, in giving the law, also promised to give the Holy Spirit for its obedience. "They (the commandments), be heavy on our flesh, if it should not be qualified through the Spirit of God" (Works, I.453-4). His exhortation echoed the message of the homily, *Of The True and Lively Faithe,* "And as Christ undoubtedly affirmeth that true faythe bringeth furth good workes, so doth he say likewyse of charite: Whosoever hath my commaundmentes and keepeth them, that is he that loveth me" (Homilies, 99). Moreover, Latimer's reinterpretation of charity was consistent with the scope of the homily, *Of Christian Love and Charitie*: "You have heard a plaine and fruitful descripcion of charitie and how profitable and necessarie a thing charitie is, how charitie extendeth it self both to God and man, friend and foe, and that by the doctrine and example of Christ" (Homilies, 123).

An additionally important element for Latimer's popular preaching was his use of scriptural metaphors for engaging imaginations and moving hearts to accept the means of salvation set forth in the *Book of Common Prayer*. He appropriates a central topic from medieval pastoral instruction -the eucharist— in a delightful sermon from Matthew 12:1-2, "The kingdom of heaven is like a certain king, which married his son, & c" (Works, I.455).

Latimer announced that both the preaching and hearing of the Word are dependent on the activity of the Triune God who evokes living faith. The Spirit enables the Word to accomplish effectively its divine purpose, generating faith and obedience in response to the voice of the living God.[73] He thus bid his audience,

> To call upon God in the name of Christ to give unto us the Holy Ghost—unto me, that I may speak the Word of God, and teach you to understand the same; that you may hear it fruitfully, to the edification of your souls; so that you may be edified through it, and your lives amended and reformed; and that his honour and glory may increase daily amongst us (Works, I.455-56).

---

[72] Marshall shows that the priestly role of confessor would often include arbitration for the return of stolen goods and restitution as a condition for absolution (*The Catholic Priesthood*, 19).

[73] On the sacramental use of scripture within the context of prayer book worship, see the discussion in Wall, *Transformations of the Word*, 44-50. Wall quotes Cranmer, "By which manner of speech it is not meant that Christ is corporately present in the voice or sound of the speaker (which sound perisheth as soon the words be spoken), but this speech meaneth that he worketh with his word, *using the voice of the speaker, as his instrument to work by; as he useth also his sacrament, whereby he worketh, and therefore is said to be present in them*" (italics mine).

Latimer introduced the king, the marriage or feast-maker, as the Triune God, the Father, the Son, and the Holy Ghost "who decked the Son with manhood, taking human flesh of the virgin Mary." Who is the bridegroom, and who should be his spouse? Latimer declared, "Marry, that was our Saviour Jesus Christ and his church and congregation." God has desired that the whole world come since the beginning, even though the most part have refused despite the sending of many callers. Yet God the Father has prepared a feast which is the body and blood of his own natural son, a gift of divine generosity, of feasting beyond compare, "when the Father will have his Son, the bridegroom, to be eaten and his blood to be drunk in the feast with his bride, the congregation" (Works, I.457-58).

Latimer lamented that many curates and ministers neglected the holy meal, since its purpose was "to help our imperfectedness, to help our memory." Yet it is available to all,

> So whosoever eateth the mystical bread, and drinketh the mystical wine worthily, according to the ordinance of Christ, he receiveth surely the very body and blood of Christ spiritually, as it shall be most comfortable unto his soul . . . Whosoever believeth in Christ, putteth his hope, trust, and confidence in him, he eateth and drinketh him: for the spiritual eating is the right eating unto everlasting life[74] (Works, I.459-60).

The main dish is the body and blood of Christ "powdered" with side dishes: the remission of sins, the gift of the Holy Ghost, the merits of Christ. The Word spoken in the sermon and the supper is of grace, comfort, and consolation: "And though he be the author of the Word, yet he will have men to be called through his ministers to the Word." Preachers should be heard gladly, for God speaks through their words, offering the remission of sins (Works, I.461-62).[75]

God has promised Christ as the main portion, tasting of sauces that season great dishes and delicate fare: "Marry, the cross, affliction, tribulation, persecution, and all manner of miseries; for, like sauces make lusty the stomach to receive meat, so affliction stirreth up in us a desire to Christ." While affliction stirs the spiritual appetite, health and comfortable living will curb its desire. Thus only the sturdy, lofty, and proud remain "saucy fellows." The

---

[74] Interestingly, although this is Latimer's only extensive treatment of the eucharist its purpose is clearly pastoral and practical. For a good discussion on the development of eucharistic theology during this period see Basil Hall, "Cranmer, the Eucharist and the Foreign Divines in the Reign of Edward VI" in ed. Paul Ayris and David Selwyn, *Thomas Cranmer: Churchman and Scholar* (Woodbridge, 1993), 217-61.

[75] This is an expression of the theology of the Word, the liturgical performance of scripture that undergirds the worship of the Edwardian Church. Wall asserts, "Together, sermon, biblical readings, and liturgical texts interpret the present in light of the promise of future fulfillment of meaning that the past events read about in the Bible and the present events enacted in Prayer Book use come to share in the present," *Transformations of the Word*, 56.

sauciness of Christians must be well powdered with signs of surrender to God, affliction, tribulation, and calamities. Most important is the "sour sauce and sharp sauce" of humility, which pulls down the stomach but lifts up the heart (Works, I.464-65). Latimer extended a final invitation to the feast's completion, *bellaria*, sweet and delicate things prepared for those who feed upon the Son and taste his sauces (Works, I.468-69).

According to Latimer, the marriage feast was prepared in paradise; the Lamb of God who takes away the sins of the world. In spite of God's abundant generosity, many appointed callers have not been heeded; John the Baptist was beheaded, Christ crucified, the apostles killed, and true preachers in England continue to suffer: "Faith cometh by hearing, it is God's instrument by which he worketh faith in our hearts, we are born anew not of mortal seed, but of immortal, by the Word of God. It pleaseth God to save the believers through the foolishness of preaching." As a ploughman, Latimer sowed the seed of the Word in anticipation of everlasting joy.[76]

The sermon was an imaginative enactment of the pastoral invitation from the *Communion Order* in the *Book of Common Prayer*.

> Dearly beloved, forasmuch as our duty is to render to Almighty God our heavenly Father most hearty thanks, for that he hath given our Saviour Jesus Christ, not only to die for us, but also to be our spiritual food and sustenance, as it is declared unto us, as well by God's Word as by the holy Sacraments of his blessed body and blood, the which being so comfortable a thing to them which receive it worthily, and so dangerous to them that will presume to receive it unworthily.[77]

The celebration of All Saints provided Latimer with another opportunity to speak by means of the familiar for presenting the new in the world of Edwardian religion. The gospel for the day was Matthew 5, the Beatitudes of Christ in the Sermon on the Mount. Latimer appropriated the medieval practice of pilgrimage, which had enjoyed great popularity in the diocese of Lincoln, as the organizing image for his exposition. Duffy's description of late medieval Catholic devotion underscores the significance of pilgrimage and the spiritual identity it bestowed on its participants.

---

[76] The significance and the strangeness of Latimer's invitation comes to light in Duffy's survey of late medieval worship, since sermons and lay reception of Holy Communion occurred infrequently. See *The Stripping of the Altars*, 53-123. In response to the numerous holy days observed by the late medieval church and their social effects, Edward's *Injunctions* declared, "Also, like as the people be commonly occupied on the workday, with bodily labour for their bodily sustenance, so was the holy day at the first beginning godly instituted and ordained, that the people on that day should give themselves wholly to God," *Documents of the English Reformation*, 254. On the increase of holy days in the late medieval period, see Duffy, *Stripping of the Altars*, 42-43.

[77] *The Two Liturgies*, 271; Davies, *A Religion of the Word*, 127-28.

> The primary purpose of pilgrimage had always been to seek the holy, concretely embodied in a sacred place, a relic, or a specially privileged image . . . Late medieval men and women were also well aware of the symbolic value of pilgrimage as a ritual enactment and consecration of their whole lives, helping them to interpret them as a journey towards the sacred.[78]

Latimer had been critic of pilgrimages since the early 1530s. In 1533, he wrote to complain of country people passing by his home at Kington, "who come by flocks out of the west country to many images." When his preaching created a stir in Bristol, he struck at "pylgremages, worshypping of seyntes, worshyppyng off images, off purgatory."[79] In 1536, Bishop John Longland complained to Cromwell that two of Latimer's preachers, from the diocese of Worcester, had ventured into Lincoln to deliver their reformist message: "Lincolnshire much grudgeth for their attacks against purgatory, pilgrimages, and oblations to the saints."[80] By 1547, the stream of criticism against pilgrimages was taken into and officially proclaimed as a part of Edward's *Royal Injunctions*, furthering the injunctions issued by Cromwell in 1538. The second injunction condemned wandering to pilgrimages, and Injunction 28 ordered the removal of relics, images, pictures, and paintings that were, "monuments of feigned miracles, pilgrimage, idolatry, and superstitions."[81]

These reforms were contested by loyal traditionalists in Lincolnshire, led by their conservative bishop, John Longland, until his death in 1547. In 1536, during the Pilgrimage of Grace, both laity and clergy in Lincolnshire protested in support of these deeply rooted devotional practices.[82] Latimer tapped into these familiar roots for his All Saints sermon, reconfiguring the practice of pilgrimage in light of the Beatitudes, presenting it as the means and goal of the Christian life which was taught and perfected by Christ. After dismissing the "papal pilgrimage of time's past" and declaring he would not speak of such

---

[78] Duffy, *The Stripping of the Altars*, 191. Duffy set his discussion of pilgrimage within his treatment of the Saints, 155-206; Margaret Aston, *Faith and Fire: Popular and Unpopular Religion, 1350-1600* (London, 1993), 2. "Popular belief attached itself to the concrete and the seen, not because the faith of the people was materialistic, but because for them matter was an expression of spiritual forces. Holiness was real because one could see its effects." For a survey of medieval piety and its practices, see Carlos Eire, *War Against the Idols: The Reformation of Worship from Erasmus to Calvin"* (Cambridge, 1986), 8-46. For a satirical view of the spiritual, social, and financial aspects of pilgrimage see Erasmus, *CWE* 40: *A Pilgrimage of Religion's Sake*, ed. Craig R. Thompson (Toronto, 1977).

[79] For Latimer's views on pilgrimage and the saints given to an examining committee of bishops, see *Works*, II.231-33.

[80] Duffy, *The Stripping of the Altars*, 189, 389.

[81] *Documents of the English Reformation*, 251.

[82] Bowker, *The Henrician Reformation*, 139-41; D.M. Owen, *Church and Society in Medieval Lincolnshire*, 125-27; Hadgett, *Tudor Lincolnshire*, 24-40; Duffy, *Stripping of the Altars*, 194-95.

"fooleries," he spoke of a pilgrimage taught by Christ himself, "whosoever will come to the eternal felicity must go that pilgrimage; else he shall never attain thereunto" (Works, I.474-75).

To soften the impact of this new teaching, Latimer invited the commons to be part of the crowds in Matthew's Gospel, "to hear the eternal Son of God, who teacheth us this pilgrimage, of what God the Father saith, 'this is my beloved son, in whom I am well pleased; hear him.'" He called them to join an eschatological pilgrimage enacted by the words and life of Christ, a journey "extending for eight miles and lasting eight days." Serving as their guide, Latimer explicated each blessing that had been spoken by Christ, unfolding the meaning of a sermon "so incredible, unbelievable, for if Christ has not spoken it, who should believe it" (Works, I.476).

On this pilgrimage with Christ, the first mile is poverty, which is a blessing when it is undertaken with a faithful heart; both the rich and the poor in the realm must trust in God. The second mile is that those who weep and mourn in this world are blessed; pilgrims must suffer miseries so at the end they will have everlasting comfort. The third mile is meekness, the avoidance of private and public wrongdoing, since the task of public vengeance is laid upon magistrates. The fourth mile is to desire the meat and drink of righteousness, which is offered to those who suffer wrong and still hunger and thirst for justice.

The fifth mile, "Blessed are the merciful, for they shall obtain mercy," requires that acts of charity be extended to neighbors, attending to their needs and admonishing them in their errors. The sixth mile, "Blessed be the clean of heart, for they shall see God," produces the fruit of speaking God's Word and lively faith that believes it to be true. Purity leads to the vision of God, by faith in this life, and face to face in eternal felicity. The seventh mile is to become "peace-makers, rather than peace-breakers," a way of life characterizing the children of God. This is peace "according to Jesus Christ, God's holy word; else it were better war than peace." It is to be distinguished from the false peace promised by rebels who resisted the Edwardian reforms. The final mile of a Christian's pilgrimage is to be demanded of one's faith, to suffer persecution for righteousness' sake, but without forsaking the truth. Although difficulty in doing one's duty may not bring happiness in the present, it is certain to win God's reward in the future (Works, I.476-88).

The announcement of eternal reward brought Latimer's pilgrimage to its final destination. Because the kingdom of God is merited by Christ, faith in him is required for receiving the gift of eternal life: "For all that, every man shall be rewarded for his good works in everlasting life, but not with everlasting life." The promise of eternal life and the prospect of divine judgment informed Latimer's final exhortation, which is to remember the Christian's pilgrimage, to follow Christ, and to receive his blessings to obtain the promise of everlasting life (Works, I.488-89).

Latimer's All Saints sermon illumines his strategy for preaching to popular audiences in Lincolnshire. While the sermon explicates the new world of the kingdom and its Beatitudes, it is framed in terms of the familiar practice of pilgrimage. And while its theme is built around a popular form of piety, the journey to familiar holy places is transfigured by the eschatological blessings spoken by Christ. The homily, *Against the Feare of Deathe*, calls every Christian to join this pilgrimage,

> . . . consydering the manifuld sicknesses, troubles and sorrowes of this present lyfe, the daungers of this perilous pilgrimage, and the greate encombrance whiche oure spirite hath by thys synful fleshe and frayle body subject to deathe; considerynge the manifolde sorrowes and daungerous deceiptes of this world on every side, the intollerable pride, covetousness and lechery in tyme of prosperitie, whiche cease not to withdrawe and plucke us from God oure savioure Christ (Homilies,152).

In addition, the *Collect for All Saints* petitions,

> Almighty God, which hast knit together thy elect in one communion and fellowship, in the mystical body of thy Son Christ our Lord: grant us grace so to follow thy holy saints in all virtues, and godly living, that we may come to these inspeakable joys, which thou hast prepared for them that unfeignedly love thee: Through Jesus Christ, our Lord. Amen (Introits, Collects, Epistles, and Gospels, 75).

The Church of England under Edward VI envisaged itself as a worshiping community in continuity with the church of Christ, Peter, James, John, Paul, and all the saints. It was a gathering where scripture was encountered as an instrument of the Word, whose force and implications were brought to bear on thought and action in the present. While Latimer accommodated his preaching to specific circumstances in Lincolnshire, he spoke within the context of belief articulated by the official *Homilies* and *Book of Common Prayer*. The Edwardian Reformers, in their efforts to create a Christian commonwealth by means of common prayer and preaching, were challenged with the task of articulating a compelling, unifying vision of faith and life that would be clearly distinguishable from both traditionalist and radical teachings.[83]

---

[83] Davies, *A Religion of the Word*, 231-33.

Chapter 6

Sowing the Seed of the Gospel in Lincolnshire

Christ our Saviour is the chief preacher, and the chief sower . . . all that preach his word are sowers (Latimer, preaching from the Parable of the Sower).

Recent scholarship has called attention to the youthfulness of the English Reformation, its exuberance, excitement, and its hope of new possibilities. As MacCulloch notes, "Symbolic of this excitement, but also of the dangers attached to it, was the idea of liberty, and the attendant fear of disregard of God's law and social chaos." Traditionalists attacked the Edwardians' message for promoting "lewd liberty" as a threat to established sacred institutions.[1] The challenge for the Reformers was to complete the work of uncompromising reformation, while not provoking desperate violence from the large part of the nation at all social levels that held no sympathy for their aims. After the stirrings of 1549, contributing to Somerset's political demise, the Edwardians decided that action was needed that would bring matters under control.[2] Ironically, that which allowed the evangelicals to proceed under Edward also hindered them. The Reformers, non-conformists themselves in relation to the old Church of Rome, relied upon and benefited greatly from these increased freedoms. Other groups however, more radical and anxious for faster and more far-reaching reforms, also utilized them to their advantage.[3] This created a dilemma for the gospel of liberty that was sounded by all the reformations of Europe, and which posed a particularly difficult question for the regime of Edward VI. In its claim to be England's faithful but dissenting remnant, it placed itself at odds with the very church structures that remained in place from late medieval Catholicism, and on which it depended in part for rebuilding a Christian commonwealth.[4]

---

[1] MacCulloch, *Tudor Church Militant*, 126-27.
[2] On conservative resistance to the reform see Duffy, *The Stripping of The Altars*, 448-78; Christopher Haigh, *English Reformations: Religion, Politics, and Society under the Tudors* (Oxford, 1993), 168-201; A.G. Dickens, *The English Reformation*, 2nd. ed. (University Park, 1988), 232-45; King, *Tudor Reformation Literature*, 76-90; Diarmaid MacCulloch, *Thomas Cranmer*, 351-454.
[3] MacCulloch, *Tudor Church Militant*, 140-43.
[4] See the excellent discussion in Davies, *A Religion of the Word*, passim.

MacCulloch argues that part of the popular excitement of the Edwardian Reformation was the independent thought it generated.[5] For example, John Hooper, after returning to England in 1549 lectured daily to large crowds at Paul's Cross London. He wrote to Bullinger in June of that year to express not only concern about conservative resistance to his teaching, but to describe the horrifying presence of radicalism and its heterodox ideas at the very center of England's Reformation.

> I myself, too, as my slender abilities will allow me, having compassion upon the ignorance of my brethren, read a public lecture twice in the day to so numerous an audience; that the church cannot contain them. The anabaptists flock to this place, and give me such trouble with their opinions respecting the incarnation of the Lord; for they deny altogether that Christ was born of the Virgin Mary according to the flesh . . . How dangerously our England is afflicted by heresies of this kind, God only knows; I am unable indeed from sorrow of heart to express to your piety.[6]

Radicalism was the inevitable result of an *ethos* of open religious debate, and it terrified the mainstream reformers.[7] Cranmer felt that such people were worse than papists since they betrayed the cause and prevented conservatives from seeing the light. While evangelicals and conservatives each desired the elimination of the other's cause, they agreed on many of the essentials of Christianity, with both sides assuming the nation was entrusted to them for care and guidance on the way to eternal life. The Edwardians' success, however, soon left them alone in the struggle against non-conformity, and as the Reformation progressed radicalism was increasingly perceived as the primary threat to authority and stability.[8]

Radical religion was already well known in England in the form of Lollardy, but manifested itself in a new way during the1530s, presumably influenced by events unfolding at Muenster. While there is evidence that continental radicals made contact with Lollards in England, such groups were diverse and did not represent a unified movement. The term "Anabaptist" came to be used quite freely in England during the reign of Edward, identifying radical non-conformists representing a rather diffuse collection of idiosyncratic individuals, groups, and beliefs that were perceived by the majority as serious threats to religious and social order. "Anabaptist" thus served as a convenient label for use in religious polemic against all dissenters, non-conformists, and advocates for reforms more radical than the official program being advanced under the

---

[5] MacCulloch, *Tudor Church Militant*, 116.
[6] *Original Letters*, I.65.
[7] King, *English Reformation Literature*, 76-78.
[8] Diarmaid MacCulloch, *The Later Reformation in England, 1547-1603* 2nd ed. (London, 2001), 14, 129.

royal supremacy.[9]

The years 1549-50 were a time of considerable turmoil in the realm of England. In addition to traditionalist criticism, a growing presence of radical religion amplified the Edwardians' insecurities and embarrassment.[10] This made it necessary for the evangelicals to distance themselves from Anabaptist opinions, lest they be identified with them either by conservative clergy or the large but yet to be persuaded segment of the English polity. A traditionalist like Gardiner, who was suspicious of any changes in religion, especially if the teaching of new doctrine was accompanied by disturbances, was quick to utilize the troubles of Lutheranism for his argument against further reform under Edward.

> Do the German examples move us not at all? Those men, hitherto unconquered, now unwilling and reluctant, have been overthrown by that foolish sophism [i.e. justification by faith alone], which they could maintain neither by pen nor sword. But the force of that sophism drove Luther, for the sake of defending his consistency, to pervert the mysteries of the sacraments and fall away to the insane assertion of necessity. When he halted at the Sacrament of the Eucharist, there rose up not a few who assailed the timidity of the man because he did not dare to follow out the full force of that proposition to the end; viz., that he utterly abolish the Eucharist also, which cannot stand with that doctrine . . .[11]

MacCulloch observes that it must have seemed to the English people that the radicals sought to capsize a boat that evangelicals and conservatives were already rocking. As Hooper wrote to Bullinger in late 1549 after the removal of Somerset as Lord Protector,

> Although our vessel is dangerously tossed about on all sides, yet God in his providence holds the helm, and raises up more favourers of his word in his majesty's councils, who with activity and courage defend the cause of Christ.[12]

And Thomas Lever of Oxford may have spoken for many evangelicals when he

---

[9]   On Anabaptist activity in England I am following I.B. Horst, *The Radical Brethren* (Nieuwkoop, 1972); D.M. Loades, "Anabaptism and English sectarianism in the mid-sixteenth century" in ed. Derek Baker, *Reform and Reformation: England and The Continent* (Oxford, 1979); Loades, *The Oxford Martyrs* (London, 1970), 83-93; Daniel Petty, "Anabaptism and the Edwardian Reformation" (PhD diss., Texas Christian University, 1988), chapter 1; Davies, *A Religion of the Word*, 67-86. For the purpose of this essay, I use the terms Anabaptists or Radicals to refer to non-conformists who desired that reform extend beyond the limits defined by the crown.

[10]   For a narrative description of the Edwardians' management strategies against radical threats, see MacCulloch, *Thomas Cranmer*, 145-46, 230-32, 424-76; Davies writes, "If such radicals had not existed, it would have been necessary to invent them, and that, to a great extent was what protestants did" (*A Religion of the Word*, 80).

[11]   Muller, *Stephen Gardiner and the Tudor Reaction*, 335.

[12]   *Original Letters*, I.71.

complained of assaults from "superstitious papists, carnal gospellers, and seditious rebels."[13]

Interestingly, one of the most progressive of the Edwardians who was vehement in his attacks against the threat of radicalism was John Hooper, who was also quick to express openly his disappointment with the 1549 *Book of Common Prayer*.

> The public celebration of our Lord's Supper is very far from the order and institution of our Lord . . . They still retain vestments and the candles before the altars. And that popery may not be lost; the mass priests although they are compelled to discontinue the use of Latin language, yet most carefully observe the same tone and manner of chanting which they have been accustomed in the papacy.

This expression of dissatisfaction was soon followed by another: "I am so much offended with that book, and that not without abundant reason, that if it not be corrected, I can neither nor will continue with the church in the administration of the Lord's Supper."[14] Hooper's views on reform presumably were not in agreement with the vision of Cranmer, who continued to hope that England would assume a leading role in creating an international Protestant consensus.[15] But all this depended on how fast and how far the government and church were prepared to take their reforms. Hooper, whom the Zurichers hailed as the "future Zwingli of England," was anxious to push for reform in England as uncompromising as in Switzerland, removing all vestiges of popery and searching out all radical threats against the godly ordering of the commonwealth. As John Burcher informed Bullinger, "Hooper is striving to effect an entire purification of the church from the very foundation."[16]

Hooper's primary ally for complete reform was John a Lasco, a strong but independent admirer of Bullinger and the Zurich civic churches. Writing later of his troubles during the Vestment controversy, Hooper would praise a Lasco, "Master a Lasco alone, of all the foreigners who have any influence, stood on my side."[17] A Lasco was a former archdeacon of Krakow who had been living in Emden as superintendent of the reformed churches of Friesland. He also had extensive dealings with Anabaptists, including Menno Simons, who he engaged in a debate over Christology.[18] A Lasco and Hooper first met in Zurich where

[13] Thomas Lever, *Sermons* , ed. E. Arber (Westminster,1895), 117. Latimer and Hooper were joined in the campaign against the Radicals by Knox, Cranmer, Hutchinson, Ridley, Lever, Rogers, Coverdale and Taylor, among the best-known Edwardian preachers. See Horst, *The English Brethren*, 123-45.
[14] *Original Letters*, I.78-85.
[15] See Cranmer's correspondence with Calvin and Melanchthon, *Original Letters*, I.21-26.
[16] *Original Letters*, II.674.
[17] *Original Letters*, I.95.
[18] Andrew Pettegree, *Foreign Protestant Communities in Sixteenth-Century London*,

the latter lived in exile after the passage of the Henrician *Six Articles of Religion*. In 1548, after the imposition of the Interim by Charles V, a Lasco was invited with other leading Protestants to participate in Cranmer's internationalism, a plan, "that was to have the assistance of learned men, who, having compared their opinions together with us, may do away with all doctrinal controversies, and build up an entire system of true doctrine."[19]

Immigrating to London in 1550, a Lasco threw himself into the affairs of the large number of foreigners living and worshiping in London, a "strangers" community whose number Ochino once estimated at five thousand.[20] On June 28, 1550 the Austin Friars granted the use of their old London Church to the Strangers, giving official ecclesiastical status to the growing number of refugees, primarily Dutch, but including Germans, Italians, and French. Edward VI noted in his journal at the time of the grant to the Strangers that it was for "avoiding all sects of Anabaptists and such like" and, "in view of the duty of a Christian prince to relieve fugitives from papal tyranny."[21] But it was also out of a need to discipline radicalism that the generous grant was made. As Micronius described the situation to Bullinger, "It is indeed a matter of the first importance that the word of God be preached in German, to guard against the heresies which are introduced to our countrymen . . . Arians, Marcionists, Libertines, Danists, and the like monstrosities, in great numbers." [22]

A Lasco was confirmed as superintendent and named the first minister of the church, which was altogether exempted from the jurisdiction of the English bishops. In addition to a Lasco, preachers were appointed to the ministry of the Word, elders ordained to assist with doctrine and morals, and deacons elected to assist with the poor and exiled.[23] John Utenhovius reported to Bullinger in April, 1551, "The word, however, is proclaimed in all its purity . . . by our friend Micronius, who preaches in a popular manner, like the clergy at Zurich . . . introducing nothing that is forced or trifling, and which does not tend to entire edification."[24]

Bolstered by the Strangers' presence in London, Hooper pushed for further reform in the Church of England. As Court preacher during Lent, 1550 Hooper seized the opportunity to make wholesale criticisms of the clerical vestments retained by the *Book of Common Prayer* and the oath to the saints prescribed by the *Ordinal*, claiming the vestments were, "rather the habit and vesture of Aaron and the gentiles, then of ministers of Christ."[25] Although Cranmer

(Oxford, 1986), 23-75; MacCulloch, *Thomas Cranmer*, 445-85; Dickens, *The English Reformation*, 256-83.

[19] *Original Letters*, I.17.
[20] *Original Letters*, I.336.
[21] Cited in MacCulloch, *Thomas Cranmer*, 478.
[22] *Original Letters*, II.560.
[23] *Original Letters*, II.571.
[24] *Original Letters*, II.587.
[25] John Hooper, *Early Writings*, ed. S. Carr (Cambridge, 1843), 478-79. For a detailed

brought a charge against Hooper in Star Chamber for such remarks, the latter emerged triumphant and soon found him self nominated for the diocese of Gloucester.[26]

Cranmer then joined forces with Ridley, Bishop of London, to block Hooper's consecration, fearing that the pursuit of his goal for religious change might spur popular social and political protest to link up with radicalism throughout London.[27] Hooper, however, laid down the conditions for his acceptance of the office; he would not be called "rabbi," there would be no formal address as "my lord," no shaving of his long beard, no episcopal white rochet and black chimere, and no anointing at his consecration.[28] In addition to this religious debate, important political considerations filled the air; the evangelicals had continued to negotiate with Gardiner to determine whether he could be persuaded to conformity in exchange for his rehabilitation. A concession to Hooper would swing the pendulum towards change and remove any incentive for a key conservative bishop to conform. Vermigli observed to Bullinger that the circumstance had "turned out most acceptable to the papists, inasmuch that they now see us quarreling with each other."[29] So Ridley, grasping the threat to ecclesiastical authority posed by Hooper's refusal on the basis of individual conscience, exclaimed, "What followeth then other things, then to receive the Anabaptist's opinion and to be baptized now? O wicked folly and blind ignorance!"[30]

Ridley might have been particularly sensitive, since Hooper's zealous appeal to the Strangers as a radically purified Protestant alternative threatened his goal to establish official doctrine and authority and to bring "godly unity" to his divided diocese. Hooper and a Lasco shared a common cause against "popish bishops" such as Ridley: the establishment of a total root-and-branch reformed church that would renounce all vestiges of papal idolatry.[31] Yet for moderates such as Cranmer and Ridley whose intention was to build a broad evangelical consensus between the extremes of traditionalism and radicalism, such claims must have smacked of "Anabaptism." As Vermigli reminded Bullinger of conditions in England, "All things cannot be done in a moment, and there must be labour and time for this misshapen embryo to attain its proper symmetry and shape."[32] Hooper eventually surrendered in February 1551; he was consecrated by Edward as Bishop of Gloucester, an office he filled with a high degree of

---

account of the Vestment controversy see J.H. Primus, *The Vestments Controversy* (Kampen, 1960).
[26] MacCulloch, *Thomas Cranmer*, 472.
[27] MacCulloch, *Thomas Cranmer*, 474-75.
[28] *Original Letters*, I.87,187.
[29] *Original Letters*, II.486.
[30] *The Works of Bishop Ridley*, ed. H. Christmas (Cambridge, 1851).
[31] Brigden, *London and the Reformation*, 464-65.
[32] *Original Letters*, II.488.

integrity and evangelical fervor.[33]

The vestment conflict was a defining moment for the Edwardian Reformation, securing the farthest boundaries of religious matters for the realm. The questions of order, of obedience to authority, of continuity and tradition for the church, of authorization of rites and ceremonies without scriptural warrant, of graduated progress with a maximum degree of popular consent were all answered in the affirmative. Significantly, the controversy occurred against the background of increasing Anabaptist activity and the terror it inspired among the evangelicals. Not surprisingly, Hooper proved to be one of the Edwardians' most useful preachers in the campaign against radicals; he was directed by the king to participate in the campaign against them in Essex and Kent.[34]

After the vestment conflict had passed, Peter Martyr Vermigli explained his views to Hooper. Martyr's perspective was in fundamental agreement with the stance taken by Cranmer and Ridley, and it also meshed with Latimer's evangelistic strategy in Lincolnshire.

> For if we first allow the Gospel to grow and send down deep roots, perhaps we can persuade people in a better and easier way to remove these external garments . . . But now when a change in the necessary points of religion is being introduced (and with such great difficulty) if we preach that things indifferent are ungodly, the hearts of practically all the people will be alienated from us so that they will no longer present themselves as attentive and patient listeners to solid teaching and the sermons they need.[35]

Indeed, Latimer was no stranger to the presence of Anabaptism, having been appointed in 1538, 1548, and 1551 to the King's Commission to examine the heretical doctrines held by radicals in the realm. He also challenged radical influence while preaching in Lincolnshire, the site of conservative uprisings in 1536, and again, radical stirrings in 1549 that protested against the slow pace and limited reach of Edward's reforms.[36] Significantly, in refuting the Anabaptists' opinions at Lincolnshire, Latimer preached from Ephesians 6, the sermon text he used in 1536 against the Pilgrimage of Grace (*Works*, I.490).

Latimer began with an brief exposition of a theme common to late medieval piety, describing the Christian life as a pilgrimage characterized by struggles, hardships, and spiritual warfare: "You that be Christians, that be baptized in his name, that look to be saved through Christ, I command you to be strong; ye

---

[33] Steinmetz, *Reformers in the Wings*, 104.

[34] *Original Letters*, I. 86-87.

[35] *Peter Martyr Vermigli: Life, Letters and Sermons*, trans. and ed., John Patrick Donnelly, S.J., The Peter Martyr Library (Kirksville, 1999), V.103-104.

[36] The date and place of the Lincolnshire sermons are actually unknown. Chester suggests late 1550, which would fit the theme of this sermon following the Western rebellions of 1549. See Chester, *Hugh Latimer* 185-89; DeMaus, *Hugh Latimer: A Biography* 460-72; Davies, *A Religion of the Word*, 209-13; McRae, *God speed the plough*, 48-49.

may not be weaklings; for ye must fight hard" (Works, I.491).[37] Because the devil is the primary enemy in spiritual warfare, Christian soldiers must fight against him with Christ's help and power: "We have not fight with flesh and blood." A variety of ideas on this topic was presumably circulating among the commons, which prompted Latimer's attack against Anabaptist opinion in favor of pacifism as, "deceived, foolish, and mistaken," and for confusing private vengeance with public discipline.

> The anabaptists make very much ado here, intending to prove by these words of St. Paul that no Christian may fight or go to warfare; neither may there be any magistrates, say they, which should shed blood and punish the wicked for this wickedness. But these fool fellows are deceived in their own wits, for St. Paul's mind is clean contrary unto their sayings. Therefore, as I said before, the anabaptists cannot prove by that scripture that there shall be no magistrates or battles (Works, I.495-96).

The Anabaptists' most grievous sin was their refusal to accept the common vocation to serve the king and fight the devil. Latimer hurled words of judgment from the prophet Jeremiah at them: "Cursed be he that keepeth his sword from blood-shedding!" This contention was based on two key points: that the radicals' teaching on pacifism was grounded in a false reading of scripture; that it endangered the order and security of the commonwealth. While he acknowledged that the radicals' false opinions might be attributed to ignorance, Latimer blamed non-preaching traditionalist clergy for allowing such heresies to take root and flourish (Works, II.497).

Turning to the *Homilies* to correct the radicals' falsehood, defending doctrine and right order, Latimer called upon Christian soldiers to fight with the two swords of God: the sword of the preacher and the sword of the magistrate. Of these two, the sword of the preacher is privileged with the highest place, with authority to strike even kings and emperors for their transgressions (Works, I.505-507). Alluding to the stirrings in England, Latimer warned, "Subjects may not of their own private authority take the sword, or rebel against the king; for when they rebel, they serve the devil (Works, I.496). This call to resist the temptation to rebellion was voiced in the homily, *An Exhortacion to Obedience.*

> Let us all therefore, feare the moste detestable vice of rebellion, ever knowyng and remembring the he that resisteth common aucthoritie resisteth God and his

---

[37] "The world-view they [magical prayers] enshrined, in which humanity was beleaguered by hostile troops of devils seeking the destruction of body and soul, and to which the appropriate and guaranteed antidote was the incantatory or manual invocation of the cross or names of Christ, is not a construct of the folk imagination" (Duffy, *Stripping of the Altars*, 279). See 266-80 for his discussion of lay piety. The theme of Christian soldiers being called to spiritual warfare was made popular in Tudor England by Erasmus' *Enchridion militis Christiani. CWE* 66.xxiii.

ordinaunce, as it may be proved by many other more places of scripture. And here let us take hede that we understand not these or suche other like places whiche so streightly commaunde obedience to superiors, and so streightly punisheth rebellion and disobedience to the same to be meant in an condicion of the pretensed power of the Bishop of Rome (Homilies, 168).

Latimer's sermon against radical religion in Lincolnshire had particular affinity with his polemic against the Pilgrimage of Grace in 1536. Although the two sermons were delivered approximately fifteen years apart and under different circumstances, Latimer's purpose remained constant: to advance reform by means of the authority of scripture under the rule of a Christian prince.[38] His respective attacks against "Papists" and "Anabaptists" represented the reverse side of a persuasive appeal to embrace the providential gift of Henrician and Edwardian reforms; the rhetorical purpose of his polemic was to break new ground for the gospel without interference from either traditional or radical religion.[39]

These important polemical skirmishes notwithstanding, Latimer's larger evangelistic aim was constructive, to create a renewed Christian identity and vocation among English folk through the preaching of the word of God.[40] He articulated this purpose in a sermon for St. Andrew's Day, when the Gospel was Matthew 9, the call of Christ to Simon Peter and Andrew: "Follow me, and I will make you fishers of men, and they straightway left their nets and followed him" (Works, II.23). Latimer drew a distinction between the general vocation of fishing and the special vocation of apostles, between catching fish with nets and catching people with preaching. He described the difficulties associated with fishing and hunting to portray the contrast between the

---

[38] On the exercise of practical wisdom see Stephen E. Fowl and L. Gregory Jones, *Reading in Communion: Scripture and Ethics in Christian Life* (Grand Rapids, 1991), 29-50; Alasdair Macintyre, *After Virtue: A Study in Moral Theory* (Notre Dame, 1984), 185-225; Joseph Dunne, *Back to the Rough Ground: Practical Judgment and the Lure of Technique* (Notre Dame, 1993).

[39] See Davies discussion of the Edwardians, radical religion, and preaching, *A Religion of the Word*, 80-93.

[40] O'Day writes of Latimer's preaching, "The sermons were about vocation . . . in the commonwealth designed by God, he has called individuals to be Christians with occupations in the commonwealth. So Peter, Andrew, James and John were 'fishers' by general vocation. God has also called to individual 'special' vocations . . . Disqualifications for such a special vocation are ambition and covetousness . . . The commonwealth will, therefore, be modelled upon that of Israel in the Old and New Testaments. And its existence will be proved by its fruits" ("Hugh Latimer: Prophet of the Kingdom," 270-71. See 271-76 for further discussion). See also Davies, *A Religion of the Word*, 1-13, 118-46. Latimer does not refer to the teaching of Luther on this topic, an omission that may be due to the fact that Luther's name had been associated with heresy during the latter Henrician period, and presumably would continue to have negative connotations in a conservative region such as Lincolnshire. On Luther's teaching, see David C. Steinmetz, *Luther in Context*, 15-21, 112-26.

demanding vocations of the laity and the relative comfort of prelates, curates, and vicars who would not cast their nets to preach God's word (Works, II.24).

According to Latimer, Christ displayed great care in calling Peter, Andrew, James, and John, first to follow him, then to preach the gospel, an example that should be followed in the selection of preachers and officers in England. Religious offices should be filled in response to God's calling rather than human ambition, since a Christian commonwealth must be constructed with humility, wisdom, and fear of God, especially among those called to preach the word. However, too many preachers desire to feed themselves rather than feeding their people: "And so likewise all patrons that have to give benefices, they should take heed and beware of such fellows, which seek for benefices, which come before they be called" (Works, II.26).

Biblical examples demonstrate the wisdom of God's calling action and human response: John the Baptist was called to preach; Joseph was called to rule over Egypt; Moses was called to be captain of Israel; King Saul was called to rule Israel; David, shepherd boy who was called to become king; Jonah was called to be a prophet. While each of these was chosen by God through trials, tribulations, and unassuming beginnings, they shared a common call without promoting themselves: "These be ensamples now, which should make us afraid, if we had any fear of God in our hearts, to promote ourselves." Moreover, Peter, Andrew, James, John, and St. Paul were exemplary, since they were content to labor in their calling, for which God aided and assisted them: "I pray God to give us such hearts, that we may be content to live in our calling, and not to gape further" (Works, II.28-34).

Latimer's explication of the gospel story outlined two categories—general and special callings—emphasizing God's action and human response. He announced that every person should discover his or her vocation, even a faculty such as fishing. Although some posses special callings such as the clergy, justices, and magistrates, Christ's call is addressed to each person in a particular place in life: "Everyman hath his vocation: as these men here were fishers, so every man hath his faculty wherein he was brought up; but and if there come a special vocation, then we must leave the vocation which we have had before" (Works, II.37).[41]

Because all have been called and judged by God, preachers must hold all accountable before God: "For the preacher when he reproveth sin, he slandereth not the guiltless, but he seeketh only the amendment of the guilty. There is a

---

[41] "For Latimer the calling to salvation is implicit. For him the general vocation is not the calling to be a Christian, which all of the elect receive; but the calling to a trade or occupation according to one's estate. For him it is the special vocation which only a few receive, for which they must set aside their general vocation . . . There is then, in Latimer's thought, a strong suggestion of a hierarchy of callings: the general calling and the special callings to particular and important roles in the commonwealth," O'Day, "Hugh Latimer: Prophet of the Kingdom," 272-73. On the need for social discipline see Davies, *A Religion of the Word*, 210-15.

common saying, that when a horse is rubbed on the gall, he will kick; when a man casteth a stone among dogs, he that is hit will cry; so it is with fellows too." Latimer's final blessing was for all to remain busy in this life and to find God's pleasure and enjoyment in the life to come (Works, II.41-43).

In preaching from the gospel story about Christ, Peter, and the fishermen, Latimer utilized a familiar form of medieval sermons—*ad status*—for summoning his listeners to take up their respective vocations in light of the call of Christ. [42] This vision was articulated in the homily, *An Exhortacion concernyng Good Ordre and Obedience to Rulers and Magistrates*

> Every degre of people, in their vocacion, callyng and office, hath appoynted to them their dutie and ordre. Some are in high degre, some in lowe, some knynges and princes, some inferiors and subjectes, preistes and laimen, masters and servauntes, fathers and chyldren, husbandes and wifes, riche and poore; and every one have nede of other; so that in all thinges is to be lauded and praysed the goodly ordre of God, without the whiche, no house, no citie, no common wealthe can continue and endure (Homilies, 161).

In his discussion of worship in the late medieval church, Duffy writes: "Any study of late medieval religion must begin with the liturgy, for within that great seasonal cycle of fast and festival, of ritual observance and symbolic gesture, lay Christians found the paradigms and stories which shaped their perception of the world and their place in it." [43] Highlighting this liturgical cycle were the supreme feasts of Christmas, Easter, Pentecost, and also Trinity Sunday, Corpus Christi, and All Saints.

Latimer preached three popular sermons, respectively, on Christmas Day, St. Stephen's Day, and St. John the Evangelist's Day, with each being derived from the narrative of Christ's birth in the *Gospel according to St. Luke* (Works, II.84-128). His various uses of the birth narrative display an imaginative depiction of the biblical drama to evoke Christian faith and obedience among his listeners. [44] The Christmas sermons reveal not only things of importance that

---

[42] On the familiar practice of medieval sermons *ad status*, see Owst, *Preaching in Medieval England*, 264-65; idem, *Literature and Pulpit in Medieval England*, 548-70. O'Day argues that Latimer's model for the shape of a commonwealth is not the medieval tradition but the Bible ("Hugh Latimer: Prophet of the Kingdom," 260-61).

[43] Duffy, *Stripping of the Altars*, 11. See Duffy's summary of medieval plays and drama, 63-68. See Owst on sermons and drama, especially on the nativity, *Literature and Pulpit in Medieval England*, 480-501.

[44] I am indebted to Richard Lischer's work on Luther's use of biblical narrative for illumining similarities in Latimer's practice. See Lischer, "Luther and Comtemporary Preaching: Narrative and Anthropology" in *Scottish Journal of Theology* 36 (1988), 487-504. "The movement of the sacred into the mundane is perceived by faith. Memory and faith permit the kind of narrative preaching in which the sacred story of God's mercy and the not-so-sacred jumble of contemporary events are understood in terms of one another" (497). See also the excellent study of Luther's use of narrative in *Robert Kolb, Luther and the Stories of God: Biblical Narratives as a Foundation*

Latimer believed about the Bible, they also demonstrate something of what he did with it, adapting its words to Lincolnshire audiences, just as Christ, the Word become flesh, accommodated himself for the redemption of humanity.[45]

Arranging the Christmas Day sermon to follow the plot of the birth narrative, Latimer wove together proclamation of Christ and a call to receive him. He announced that great comfort and gladness were available through Christ's coming; the Savior born in Bethlehem was now proclaimed in Lincolnshire. Just as angels sang praises to God for sending his Son; so too, praise, song, and joy are those gospel notes produced by the unspeakable goodness of Almighty God the Father (Works, II.84-85). From the high note of heavenly praise, Latimer moved to the mundane world of his listeners. Because the angels did their business and returned to heaven, so too, must servants be about their masters' business without loitering or lewdness. Angels are present whenever and wherever the gospel is preached, defending hearers of the Word, even those among the commons of Lincolnshire[46] (Works, II.85-86).

The shepherds played a significant role in Latimer's sermons as examples of God's love for lowly servants, those who received the glad tidings before kings and rulers of the earth.[47] And their response to the news was salutary, since they exercised charity and exhorted one another to follow the word of God without thievery, wickedness, or lewdness in their behavior. They serve as exemplars for all who desire to seek Christ, to obey God's commandments, and to serve the commonwealth. They even left their flocks, risking themselves and their possessions, placing their lives in adventure. As Latimer announced, "Here is verified that saying of our Saviour Christ, whoever shall lose his life shall find it" (Works, II.87-89).

---

for *Christian Living* (Grand Rapids, 2012). See Davies' discussion of social obedience, *A Religion of the Word*, 215-18.

[45] George Lindbeck writes: "A theological way of making the same point is to say that the Bible exists for the sake of the church . . . The purpose of the Old and New Testaments is the formation of peoples, which live in accordance with God's commands and promises and embody his will for the world. Thus Christians use the Bible's stories, images, categories and concepts to interpret all that is," Lindbeck, "Atonement and the Hermeneutics of Social Embodiment" in *Pro Ecclesia*, V.2 (January, 1996), 150-52.

[46] This way of illuminating the close connection between the world of the biblical story and the world of the listeners' experience was utilized in patristic exegesis and homilies. A good summary is provided by Lawrence T. Martin, "The Two Worlds in Bede's Homilies" in ed. Thomas Amos, Eugene Green, Beverly Mayne Kienzle, *Ore Domini: Preacher and Word in the Middle Ages* (Kalamazo, 1989), 29-36; Lischer, "Luther and Preaching." 497. The identification between the biblical story and the present was so intimate that "Reformation developments may be said to re-embody or re-enact the ancient drama."

[47] Latimer presents the shepherds in a favorable light in spite of his previous defense of ploughmen against the practice of enclosure.

The faith of the shepherds was strong enough to overcome even the offense of Christ's poverty. They believed in Christ, were despised with Christ, and will also receive everlasting life from Christ. Moreover, they manifested their faith by telling their neighbors what they had seen and speaking to many who would not believe. Latimer surmised there were in England many gospellers, those who loved to talk but would neither believe nor receive the benefits of Christ (Works, II.90-91).

On the other hand, Mary, the mother of Christ, did not preach, boast, or act hastily. Even though she was tempted and tried, assisted only by poor shepherds, she continued to trust the word and promise of God. Latimer observed, "All things work for the best to them that love God." Even more important, however, is that the poor shepherds reveal the impartiality of God, who is no respecter of either: the wise or the mighty and who delights in the weak and lowly of spirit. God hides his divine mysteries from popes, cardinals, bishops, and the learned, but extends them to humble listeners in Lincolnshire: "Let us go to Bethlehem, that is, to Christ, with an earnest mind and hearty zeal to hear the word of God and to follow it indeed." Since the shepherds were neither monks nor members of the religious, they returned to their occupations, signifying that every member of the realm is called to follow an occupation acceptable to God (Works, II.93-94).

A brief anecdote, or *exemplum*, concludes the sermon. St. Anthony once visited a cobbler in Alexandria. The cobbler, a poor, simple man, was a person of great piety and prayer, honesty and faithfulness, and kind in all his dealings. He taught his wife and children to love and to fear God, as did he. Latimer assured his audience: "You see how God loveth those that follow their vocation and live uprightly, without any falsehood in their dealing."

Latimer's preaching of the nativity of Christ aimed to transform his listeners' perceptions of the world and their role within it. Speaking from the perspective provided by his reading of the gospel narrative, he repeated its joyful announcement to Lincolnshire, calling its citizens to imitate the obedience of the shepherds, to acquire the enduring trust of Mary, and to remain faithful in their respective vocations. The homily, *A Fruitful Exhortation to the Readying and Knowledge of Holy Scripture* declares,

> And moreover, the effecte and verture of God's Worde is to illumine the ignorant and to geve more light unto theim that faithefully and dilligently reade it, to comfort their hartes, and to incorage theim to performe that whiche God is commaunded. It teacheth pacience in all adversitie; in prosperitie, humblenes; what honour is due unto God, what mercie and charitie to our neighbor (Homilies, 63).

Latimer returned to the story of Christ's nativity on St. Stephen's Day, taking as his theme, "And it fortuned that while they were there, her time was come that she should be delivered" (Works, II.96). The obedience of Mary and Joseph served to highlight their role in the divinely arranged circumstances surrounding Christ's birth. Describing their long journey to Bethlehem, Latimer observed that in their poverty they traveled on foot, with no "jolly gear," while displaying a spirit of obedience, which serves as a lesson to all (Works, II.97).

Although Latimer's sermon on Christmas Day focused on the faithful obedience of the shepherds, his St. Stephen's Day sermon was devoted to the importance of receiving Christ: "Well, she was great with child, and was now come to Bethlehem. A wonderful thing to consider the works of God." Latimer emphasized the humility and poverty Christ demonstrated in taking away sins, in overcoming evil, in defeating the devil, and in inspiring hope for the glory of his promised coming (Works, II.97-99).[48] He affirmed the divine and human natures of Christ to refute the erroneous opinions of those who claimed that Christ was not truly human, that he did not suffer the pains of the cross. Latimer concluded by acclaiming Christ as God's Son, not by adoption, but God himself who alone is worthy to be called upon, rather than the saints.[49]

St. Stephen, moreover, provides an example of faith in Christ through his prayer, his devotion, but especially in his death, when he cried out, "Lord Jesus take thou my spirit!" He was stoned because of his obedience; he was killed because he rebuked the wicked priests and bishops who brought false witness against him. All Christians who offer true worship that imitates St. Stephen will also forsake the world and be willing to suffer for the word of God: "God grant us that we may say with a good faith, from the bottom of our hearts, 'Lord Jesus, receive our spirits'" (Works, II.99-100).

Shifting the focus from Stephen to the person of Christ, Latimer emphasized the moral and social significance of welcoming him. He touched upon the two natures of Christ, the sinful nature of humanity, the need for salvation, and the power of Christ over sin and death. Christ's birth into poverty provides a salutary example for lowly Christians who seek comfort in their misery. Moreover, the city of Bethlehem demonstrates how the word of God is easily ignored and despised, since only a few in that place knew of Christ's birth, just as a few in England are able to hear the voice of Christ speaking through his preachers (Works, II.102-107).

---

[48] For an excellent study of the pastoral use of doctrine see Ellen T. Charry, *By The Renewing of Your Minds: The Pastoral Function of Christian Doctrine* (Oxford, 1997), 18, "Christian doctrines function pastorally when a theologian unearths the divine pedagogy in order to engage the listener or reader in considering that life with the Triune God facilitates dignity and excellence." Latimer consistently uses the doctrine of the incarnation in this pastoral manner, but it is especially pronounced in the sermons on the birth of Christ, enabling him to engage his audience by means of familiar Christological images and themes in late medieval piety. See Marsh, *Popular Religion*, 199-200. See Erasmus, *Enchridion*, for an example of late medieval piety that was strongly christocentric in its representation.

[49] On the role of the saints in late medieval piety see Duffy, *Stripping of the Altars*, 155-200; Eire, *War Against the Idols*, 28-45.

Mary and Joseph exemplified humble obedience in receiving Christ, accepting their circumstances, and caring for the babe: "Who fetched water to wash the child after it was born into the world, and who made a fire? It was Joseph." According to Latimer, the simplicity of the story reveals the oneness of humanity with the lowly Son of God, an honor that exceeds the dignity of the angels. A closing *exemplum* brought this truth to life. According to Latimer, the devil once went into a church while the priest was saying mass. At that place in the creed, *et homo factus est*, the devil looked about, and seeing none in the church kneeling or bowing, declared, "What! Will you not reverence him for this great benefit, which he hath done unto you? I tell you if he had taken upon him our nature, as he hath taken upon him yours, we would more reverence him than ye do." Latimer appealed for his listeners' grateful reception of Christ, "that he might deliver us from our sins and wickedness" (Works, II.108-109).

For the sermon on St. John the Evangelist's Day, Latimer focused on the journey of Mary and Joseph to Bethlehem, interpreting it as an act of obedience to God. The story emphasizes the duties of subjects, the commands of God, and the bearing of the common burdens of the realm. Latimer exhorted listeners to practice glad obedience with neither inward nor outward rebellion, offering heartfelt gratitude for the incarnation of the God the Son. All Christians who have received the benefits of Christ's humble birth are to take up his cross in the hardships that have befallen Lincolnshire: "To bear the common burthen is not an increase, but a diminishing and hurt; for their have been many burthens in England, as the burthens of the fall of money. Therefore that it is not as you say; for I know that some have lost as much, that they can never recover the same again so long as I live" (Works, II.111-12). This subject of the incarnation, the vocation of the Son of God, turned Latimer's attention to the notorious Anabaptist, Joan of Kent.

> Further, I told you that our Saviour Christ was framed and formed of poorest flesh: and he became the natural Son of Mary. I told you, the last time of Joan of Kent, which was in this foolish opinion, that she should say our saviour was not very man, and had not received flesh of his mother Mary; and yet she could show no reason why she should believe so. Her opinion was this, as I told you before. The Son of God, she said, penetrated through her, as light through glass, taking no substance of her (Works, II.114).

The case of Joan of Kent (Boocher, Bochier, Boucher, etc.) the most famous heretic of Edward's short reign, exemplifies the threat of radical religion to the Edwardian commonwealth.[50] Joan, who actively spread her opinions since the reign of Henry VIII, was a woman of considerable social standing, an uncompromising character, having sufficient knowledge of the Bible to dispute

---

[50] For details on Joan see Horst, *Radical Brethren*, 108-111; MacCulloch, *Thomas Cranmer*, 424-26; Petty, "Anabaptists and the Edwardian Reformation," 156-84.

intelligently with theologians. She was examined at Paul's Cross in April 1549 before Cranmer, several bishops, members of the Privy Council, and the only Anabaptist leader to abjure. She was condemned to death as heretic on 29 April, and after a delay of over a year, she was burnt at Smithfield in May 1550. The charge brought against her in 1549 stated her views as follows: "That you believe that the word was made fleshe in the virgin's belly, but that Christ took fleshe of the virgyn you believe not; because the flesh of the virgyn being the outward many synfully gotten, and bourne in syn, but the worde by the consent of the inward many of the virgin made flesh."[51]

This view of the incarnation was similar to an Anabaptist opinion reported by John Hooper in a letter to Bullinger of June 1549, "for they deny altogether that Christ was born of the Virgin Mary according to the flesh." Joan was fervent indeed in her faith and went to the stake publicly scorning her executioners. At the time of her trial she claimed that a thousand in London were of her sect, a boast sure to cause anxiety among the leading reformers. The particular heresy for which Joan of Kent was condemned and yet steadfastly retained was the Anabaptist teaching on the incarnation, the "Celestial Flesh."

The Celestial Flesh of Christ was a fairly common teaching of the Radical Reformation, although not held by all. It was based on distinctive, usually non-Chalcedonian christologies, with a corresponding sanctifying, or deifying, view of salvation. Given the turmoil and confusion in Tudor England, which was provoked by the break from Rome and breakdown of authority, it is not difficult to imagine how such ideas could develop, especially among groups with mystical, spiritualist, and perfectionist tendencies. The Celestial Flesh was basically a revival of Gnostic and Monophysite christologies that attempted to account for the sinlessness of Christ and his incapability of sinning. Various views of the Celestial Christ were held by Melchior Hoffman, Caspar Schwenkfeld, Clement Ziegler, Obbe Phillips, David Joris, Dirk Phillips, and Menno Simons. There were ample opportunities for this teaching to be brought to England and spread throughout the social order.[52]

Latimer appealed to the creed and scripture to disprove Joan's teaching: "But our creed teacheth us contrariwise; for we say, 'Born of the Virgin Mary,' so this foolish woman denied the common creed and said that our Saviour had a phantastical body; which is most untrue, as it appeareth in the epistle to the Hebrews where St. Paul plainly saith that Christ was made of a woman, that he took flesh from the woman." This common Christian teaching was embodied in

---

[51] *Concilia Magna Britanniae et Hiberniae* ed. David Wilkins (London, 1773), IV.35.
[52] On the Celestial Flesh I follow the discussion by George Williams, *The Radical Reformation*, 3rd. ed. (Kirksville, 1992), 487-500; For two views on its development see J.N.D. Kelly, *Early Christian Doctrines* (San Francisco, 1978), 331-34; Jaroslav Pelikan, *The Christian Tradition: The Growth of Medieval Theology: 600-1300* (Chicago, 1978), III.229-41.

the humble obedience of Mary and Joseph who, without lodging, took all things in good faith, content in their poverty and miseries. The Anabaptists' refusal to adhere to this teaching was a serious threat to the common life of the realm. In contrast to the radicals' arrogance, Christ, Mary, and Joseph are exemplary models of citizenship in a Christian commonwealth. On the other hand, proud Anabaptists, hypocritical monks and friars, glorious prelates, and stubborn bishops, are the enemies of this commonwealth (Works, II.119-20). The *Book of Homilies* declares,

> And also we rede that the hole virgyn Mary, mother to our Saviour Christ, and Joseph, who was taken for his father, at the emperors commaundemente went to the citie of David, named Bethlehem, to be taxed emong other and to declare their obedience to the magistrates for Gods ordinaunces sake. And here let us not forget the blessed virgin Maries obedience, for although she was highly in Gods favor and Christes naturall mother, and was also great with chylde that same time, and so nigh her travaile that she was delivered in her journey, yet she gladly, without any excuse or grudgyng, for concience sake did take that cold and foule winter journey, beying in the meane ceason so poore that she lay in the stable, and there she was delivered of Christ (Homilies, 168-69).[53]

With his Christmas sermons, Latimer hoped to turn his listeners to see that a new order was being introduced by the Edwardians. The narrative of Christ's nativity was Latimer's primary means of illuminating England's common life according to the teaching of scripture and the creed. His earthy re-telling of the story enabled listeners to identify with its humble characters while inviting them to participate in its world.[54]

The threat posed by the evangelicals to traditional religion was no more evident than its interpretation of the institution of marriage and the new possibilities it extended to clergy and laity alike; if ordination was no longer a sacrament; then clerical celibacy was no longer a requirement. Moreover, if marriage was no longer a sacrament, then it was not indissoluble and the institution of divorce became a possibility. For this reason the 1547 homily, *Against Whoredome and Adultery*, acknowledged the harmful practice of private divorces.[55]

What was new, however, requiring the attention of the evangelical establishment, was the possibility of men and women seeking divorces on the basis of religious and spiritual incompatibility. A good example was the case of Anne Askew, who, near the end of Henry's reign, was tortured and burnt at the stake.[56] Anne had walked out on a marriage with an unsatisfactory and

---

[53] The homily, *On Goode Works*, warns against sects, pride, hypocrisy, and willful poverty.
[54] Lischer, "Luther's Preaching," 494-96.
[55] MacCulloch, *Tudor Church Militant*, 129.
[56] Haigh, *English Reformations*, 165-66; Dickens, *English Reformation*, 194, 218-19.

religiously incompatible husband. Her actions were canonized by evangelicals from John Bale onwards, justified because she was married to a papist, an enemy to God's word.[57] Coincidentally, Askew resided in Lincolnshire, where Latimer, in his preaching to the commons, turned to John 2:1-12: "And upon the third day there was a marriage in Cana, a city of Galilee, and Mary the mother of Jesus was there." The sermon provides a scriptural affirmation of Christian marriage which demonstrates the evangelicals' commitment to its sanctity.

Because Christ's miracle of changing water to wine confirms his authority for all preachers of his word, Latimer began by announcing, "This is a comfortable place for all married folks; for it here appeareth that marriage is a most honorable and acceptable thing in the sight of God." The sermon describes the institution of marriage; its promises, its challenges, its ordination by God and its perversion by sin. Husbands and wives are to trust God's word, to pray for God's Spirit, and to live together after God's commandments. This is a calling which pertains even to priests, even though contrary to traditionalist teaching: "But here ye may see it is the very ordinance of God, and is commendeth by Christ himself: for he cometh into it, and with his presence he sanctifieth it." According to Latimer, because Christ adorns each marriage with his presence, he is to be welcomed as a permanent guest by husband and wife (Works, II.160-62). The *Form of the Solemnization of Matrimony* in the *Book of Common Prayer* begins with the following announcement,

> Dearly beloved friends, we are gathered together here in the sight of God, and in the face of his congregation, to join together this man and this woman in holy matrimony, which is an honorable estate instituted by God in paradise, in the time of man's innocence; signifying unto us the mystical union that is betwixt Christ and his Church: which holy estate Christ adorned and beautifed with his presence, and first miracle that he wrought, in Cana of Galilee.[58]

The action of Mary, the mother of Christ, provides an important moral lesson to all. Because her desire was to provoke Christ to do a new thing, her actions were in vain and constituted sin, a reminder that even the saints of God are sinners. They are saved because God is merciful and forgives whoever hears and believes his word. In their weakness, even the saints turn to Christ for help, just as Mary turned to Christ when no wine was left at the feast.

Mary's submission to Christ teaches another lesson: Christ was free from the authority of his human mother because he was a preacher, a common person

---

[57] MacCulloch, *Tudor Church Militant*, 130; *The Examinations of Anne Askew* ed. Elaine V. Beilin (Oxford, 1996), xv-xxxi; Susan Wabuda, "Sanctified by the believing spouse: women, men and the marital yoke in the early Reformation" in ed. Peter Marshall and Alec Ryrie, *The Beginnings of English Protestantism* (Cambridge, 2002), 122-24.

[58] *The Two Liturgies*, 127.

serving in a common ministry. In addition, Mary's obedience is salutary for all young men who have been placed in the priesthood by their families. According to Latimer, they are bound to obedience if a decision for the priesthood does not require disobedience to God, at which time they must speak as Christ spoke to Mary, "Woman, what have I to do with thee?"[59]

The six water pots in the wedding household signify the gifts of the Spirit whose presence in marriage can turn sour water into sweet wine: "It is the Spirit of God, sent by Christ, who will work in conflicts and calamities, anguish and misery, to make what is bitter, sweet, to bring hope in desperation." Christ performed the miracle to evoke faith in his power to fulfill his promises. Latimer therefore concludes, "Marriage is a school-house, where you shall have occasion of patience, and occasion of love" (Works, II.165-66).

Although Latimer denied the traditional view of marriage as a sacrament of the Church, his assurance of Christ's miraculous power indwelling husband and wife through the presence of the Spirit, granted a "sacramental" dimension to the vocation of Christian matrimony. Moreover, his exposition of the Gospel displayed pastoral sensitivity in accommodating his message to conservative critics in Lincolnshire. In voicing the evangelical establishment's commitment to the sanctity of marriage—for both the clergy and laity—he supported his message with Christ's authority.[60] As the homily, *Against Whoredom, and Adultery* declares,

> And here are all degrees to be monyshed, whether they be maryed or unmaryed, to love chastitie and clennes of lyfe. For the maryed are bounde by the lawe of God so purely to love one an other that neyther of them seke any straunge love. The man must cleve only to hys wyfe, and the wyfe agayne onely to her husband; they must so delight one in an others companye that none of them covit any other (Homilies, 185).

In his preaching Latimer repeatedly turned to biblical narratives to produce sermons that were clear, simple, and lively depictions of the identity and activity of Christ. An example of his narrative preaching is a sermon from Matthew 8:1-3, the story of Christ cleansing a leper. After noting the universal appeal and application of this text, Latimer cited the words of St. Paul, "Whatsoever is written, is written for our instruction . . . Therefore if we will consider and ponder this story well, we shall find much matter in it to our great comfort and edifying" (Works, II.168). The sermon depicts the actions of

---

[59] This would have been of particular importance to young men who were pressured by ambitious parents or families to enter the priesthood in order to gain access to its benefices and career path. See Marshall, *The Catholic Priesthood and the English Reformation*, 112.

[60] The Edwardian position on clerical marriage is set forth in the *Act to Take Away All Positive Laws Against the Marriage of Priests*, *Documents of the English Reformation*, 279-80.

Christ as the revelatory enactment of salvation that produces living faith.[61]

Latimer noted that the preaching of Christ prompted a variety of responses. Those who initially expressed their love turned against him; dissuaded by their opponents, "the bishops." This was a warning for his listeners in Lincolnshire: "to never forsake God and his Word, to even suffer death for it." Latimer's aim, therefore, was to position his audience to hear the words of Jesus as a call for entering the world of evangelical faith (Works, II.169).

He commended the faith of the leper, the "lazar man," as a reminder of Christ: "So let us come to him, for he is the Saviour of mankind." He praised the leper for turning to Christ in seeking the salvation of his body and soul, an act of great benefit for both doctors of divinity and simple folk.[62] The leper's faith moved him to fall upon his knees in reverence for Christ, an outpouring of humility and gratitude challenging even the proud and strong. Although the leper was an outcast according to the Law, he still ran to Christ before any other: "Even his faith, he believed that Christ was able to help him, and therefore according to his faith, it happened to him" (Works, II.168-69).

To enable his listeners to grasp the significance of this story, Latimer offered a simple explanation of his use of the Bible in preaching. The gospel reports do not simply recount historical events from the past; they have been written for the instruction and edification of listeners in the present. Such stories place "eternal things" before the eyes of the imagination that are to be grasped inwardly and enacted publicly. The story of the leper is relevant for all, since whoever hears his story is a leper—in body or in soul—in need of the healing which is offered through faith in Christ. Latimer adds that this insight may also be applied to the story of Sodom and Gommorah, which is a call to avoid sin and wickedness and for living in an upright and godly manner. This perception is also applicable to the story of Abraham, who is an example of living faith that justifies, without which God will punish the unfaithful (Works, II.171-72).[63]

---

[61] For Latimer, the biblical narrative is not important because it provides a homiletic plot for sermons nor because preaching should consist of telling stories. Rather, narrative is important because it provides the vehicle through which the gospels render the person and actions of Christ. Latimer is interested in the character, the identity of Christ, be grasped by his listeners through living faith. See the discussion of biblical narrative and preaching that draws on the work of Hans Frei in Charles L. Campbell, *Preaching Jesus: New Directions For Homiletics in Hans Frei's Postliberal Theology* (Grand Rapids, 1997), 3-28, 117-40. See also Shuger, *Sacred Rhetoric*, 138-39. Shuger states that biblical narrative (and other rhetorical figures of thought) gives invisible truth a concrete, local habitation, turning the heart toward spiritual reality, fulfilling the need for the sensible and corporeal.

[62] This is presumably an echo of Erasmus' *Paraclesis*, "If anyone exemplifies this doctrine [the philosophy of Christ] in his life, he is in fact a great doctor," 102.

[63] Campbell follows Frei in his discussion of the narrative logic that informs preaching from biblical stories. The focus is on the movement of the narrative, dramatic reenactment that is centered on the character of God or Christ that is rendered by

According to Latimer, the leper was a persuasive example of lively faith in Christ who has promised to be with his followers always, even in his resurrection. Such lively faith calls upon Christ, without need for beads or popish prayers, in seeking God's will: "The ordinary way to get faith is through hearing the Word of God; for the Word of God is of such power, that it entereth and presseth the heart of man that heareth it earnestly" (Works, II.173-74).

Latimer's assurance of faith that comes by the miracle of hearing raised the question of the efficacy of the Word; how may listeners know that their names are written in the book of life? He offered three notes to remember: the first is knowledge of sin, the feeling of one's wretchedness; the second is faith in Christ; that God will deliver through his Son; the third is a sturdy desire to repent and to obey God's commandments. These three notes offer faith's simplicity which brings certainty in the book of life; whoever stands with the leper may say: "Lord if thou wilt." Moreover, Christ reached out to the leper— flesh to flesh—to signifying the mediating role of his body, "eaten and drunken for salvation." These are the means of grace which were prescribed by the *Book of Common Prayer*: Faith in Christ is strengthened through the Word, spoken in the sermon, and enacted in the Supper (Works, II.175-76).[64]

Latimer notes that Christ sent the leper to the temple for a priest to witness his healing. The man was not his own judge, and this was no occasion for carnal liberty. His case confirms the moral soundness of evangelical preaching, which does not disregard God's Law. In addition, Christ did not send the man to confess his sins nor to seek absolution, which proves Christ did not support auricular confession.[65] His action towards the leper was pastoral: "And those which find themselves grieved in conscience might go to a learned man, and thus fetch of him comfort of the word of God." Most important, however, is that the narrative renders the character of Christ to call forth living faith, so that a union of the leper's faith and Christ's love demonstrates the basis of earnest prayer, "the art above all arts."

This lengthy sermon sheds important light on Latimer's homiletic use of figural interpretation and its pastoral implications, since his task was to win

---

means of its exposition and application, Campbell, *Preaching Jesus*, 196-211. Shuger shows that in Renaissance rhetorics the dramatic language of scripture was viewed analogically, as participating in the sacramental world view of the Middle Ages, thus becoming rhetorical figures that reflect the structures of existence and thereby have reality-shaping power. See Shuger, *Sacred Rhetoric*, 211-13. See O'Malley, *Praise and Blame*, for the use of *epideictic* rhetoric, creating pictures in the mind that are *deliberative*, or persuasive. 63-65.

[64] In *The Catholic Priesthood*, Marshall shows that only the priest in the pre-Reformation church could "touch Christ" by handling the Eucharist (45-47).

[65] On the role of the medieval priest's role as confessor and the English Reformers' response see Marshall, *The Catholic Priesthood*, 5-10, 30-34. See the *Order of Communion* in the 1549 *Book of Common Prayer*, which allowed for private confession for a communicant with a troubled conscience, *The Two Liturgies*, 82.

assent for the new order of faith and obedience set forth in the *Book of Homilies* and *Book of Common Prayer*. This required that he demonstrate the superiority of "lively faith" to traditional religion in its truthfulness, its practice, and in its moral and social effects. Latimer's proof was in his performance, the dramatic enactment of the biblical story in which text, exposition, and application were united to evoke what was proclaimed.[66] As Erasmus affirmed in the *Paraclesis*, "these writings [holy scripture] bring you the living image of His holy mind and the speaking, healing, dying, rising, Christ Himself, and thus they render Him so fully present that you would see less if you gazed upon Him with your very eyes."[67]

Latimer's artful use of biblical narratives, the portrayal of scripture's characters and their conditions, prepared his listeners for receiving Christ's words and presence in their midst.[68] It was a commonplace of medieval preachers that popular audiences loved stories. The preaching friars transformed the use of homiletic illustrations, fables, and *exempla* into an art form, which became, in its excessive use, a victim of its own success.[69] In the thirteenth century, Humbert of Romans had instructed the preachers of the Dominican Order that sermons should utilize vivid, concrete imagery to grasp the imaginations of common folk, suggesting that scripture itself contains the best source of such characters and stories.[70] Although Latimer's use of vivid imagery, his knack for story telling, and his fondness for the timely, personal anecdote have been recognized,[71] his theological and pastoral use of scripture's narratives and their characters has been overlooked.[72] He repeatedly invited

---

[66] Marshall, *The Catholic Priesthood*, 86-87, "In their [the Reformers] eyes, the paramount priestly duty was rather the preaching of the Word of God, the instruction and encouragement of the laypeople in the faith which alone could save them . . . Indeed, this conviction could be expressed in ways that might make a preaching ministry seem just as much a channel of salvation as a sacramental priesthood.". . . "Nowhere in pre-Reformation England was the distinction between layman and priest more marked than in the theory and practice of auricular confession." See Ryrie, "The problem of allegiance," 107-110. See the discussion of the reformers reading habits in James Simpson, *Burning to Read: English Fundamentalists and its Reformation Opponents* (Cambridge and London, 2007), 4-6.

[67] Erasmus, *Paraclesis*, 108.

[68] See Shuger on the dramatic treatment of scripture that makes the supernatural seem present or "evident," thus making such speech theologically and personally engaging and persuasive, *Sacred Rhetoric*, 219-20.

[69] Owst, *Literature and Pulpit in Medieval England*, 149-209; Smyth, *The Art of Preaching in the Church of England*, 17-39; A.G. Little, *Studies in English Franciscan History*, 123-57.

[70] Humbert of Romans, *Treatise on the Formation of Preachers*, ed. Simon Tugwell, O.P., 373-76.

[71] Blench, *Preaching in England*, 142-52.

[72] This is the Christian grand style as described by Shuger in *Sacred Rhetoric*, 218: "Stress on the visual produces a stylistic ideal at once dramatic and metaphorical." According to Shuger, passion is not only expressed through the inward emotion of

audiences to imagine themselves within the world of the Bible, within its stories and among its actors, and to see their lives in light of the surprising drama unfolding in their hearing.[73] For Latimer, scripture was not simply a source to be mined for material to illustrate or to embellish sermons; since all of scripture serves to disclose the character and activity of the God who commands and saves, offering paradigmatic and persuasive patterns of faith and obedience to be received and enacted by hearing the Word.

A sermon from Matthew 8 highlights the excellence of Latimer's narrative preaching, beginning with his introduction of its purpose:

> Here in the gospel we have a notable story, and a wonderful miracle, which our Saviour did, being with his disciples upon the sea; which story is written for our doctrine and instruction that we may comfort ourselves withal, when we are in like trouble in the tempests of this world. For we learn here many good things, if we consider the story itself, and the circumstances thereof.

Latimer's telling of the story incorporated his listeners into its drama. His words transformed the boat into a sign of Christ and his Church, thereby bridging the gap between the world of the Gospel and the world of Lincolnshire, "all those who are in the church of Christ shall be saved and preserved by him" (Works, II.181-82). The disciples exemplify Christian faith and life; first, in their presumption and conceit; second, in their feebleness and weakness when they ran to Christ to be saved. Most important is Christ, the enactment of God's salvation with them, since he is both human and divine. As God, he possesses authority to reform the wind and waters according to his word. But as man, he slept, was tired and weary, he ate, drank and wept; he tasted human affliction, miseries, and troubles, but was without sin. The promise of scripture is trustworthy: "Our Savior will have compassion over us; he will be more inclined to help and assist us with his Holy Spirit" (Works, II.183).

Latimer's artful use of the gospel story invited the commons to Christ as salvation. As the homily, *Of the Salvacion of All Mankynde* declares,

> This faythe the Holy Scripture teacheth; this is the strong rock and foundacion of Christian religion; this doctryne advaunceth and setteth furthe the true glory of Christ, and suppresseth the vayne glory of man; this whosoever denieth, is not to

---

the preacher, but also through vividness, drama, and figures of thought (244-45).

[73] Here I follow the work of Hans Frei, *The Eclipse of Biblical Narrative: A Study in Eighteenth and Nineteenth Century Hermeneutics* (New Haven, 1974), 13-27. Frei's interpretation of "realistic narrative" was influenced by Erich Auerbach, *Mimesis: The Representation of Reality in Western Literature* trans. Willard Trask (Princeton, 1953), 1-15. See Shuger's interpretation of Renaissance preaching rhetorics and their emphasis on the role of imagination; the clarifying, affective power of biblical drama, metaphor, image, narrative, and figure, when expressed with vivid immediacy, Shuger, *Sacred Rhetoric*, 218-45.

be reputed for a true Christian man, not for a setter furth of Christes glory, but for an adversarye of Christe and his Gospell, and for a setter furth of mennes vainglory (Works, II.185.)

Latimer's preaching in Lincolnshire was a means for advancing the vision he had articulated through the *Sermon of the Plough*. In a sermon to the commons from Matthew 13: 24-30, the *Parable of the Sower*, he revisited the theme of God's ploughman.[74] Introducing the sermon, Latimer gave a simple lesson to explain how parables compare two things outwardly unlike. He cited Christ's parable, which compares the word of God to a sower. Just as seed is sown in the earth, so is the word of God sown in the hearts of those who receive it from the sower (Works, II.188-89).

According to Latimer, those who sleep are slothful bishops, prelates, curates, and ministers who, in their neglect of preaching allow the devil to sow his seed, filling hearts with his desires. On the other hand, it is the disciples, in their curiosity towards Christ's teaching, who demonstrated a desire for God's word. Latimer saw himself as a ploughman, calling his listeners to imitate the example of the disciples. Lincolnshire was a field where Christ was sowing his word, and the devil his tares; but it was also a place where the judgment of Christ was drawing near: "You must understand that there are but two places appointed by Almighty God for all mankind; this is, heaven and hell" (Works, II.190).

Latimer concludes that God freely scatters his seed, sows in abundance, and advances his kingdom through the preaching of the word.

> For all are, and must be, justified by the justification of Christ our Saviour; and so we must be justified, and not through our own well-doings, but our justice standeth in this, that our unrighteousness is forgiven us through the righteousness of Christ; for if we believe in him, then we are made righteous. For he fulfilled the Law, and afterward granted the same to be ours, if we believe that his fulfilling is our fulfilling: for St. Paul saith, 'He hath not spared his own Son, but hath given him for us; and how then may it be, but we should give all things to him?' Therefore it must needs follow, that when he gave us his only Son, he gave us also his righteousness, and his fulfilling of the Law . . . Therefore be not proud, and be humble and low, trust not too much in yourselves; but put your only trust in Christ our Saviour (Works, II.194).

Resuming the theme of sowing on the following Sunday, "Behold, there went out a sower to sow," Latimer continued speaking of Christ as the sower, the chief preacher, and all that preach as sowers of his word. Even though Christ sowed and tilled the ground, his preaching brought forth little fruit; his seed fell on much hard, thorny, and stony ground, with only one fourth becoming good,

---

[74] McRae, in *God Speed the Plough*, concludes that, with their use of agrarian language, "The Protestants forcefully declared a new vision for the 'fields' of the nation" (31).

receptive soil. Latimer interpreted the parable as a depiction of his preaching and its rejection.[75] He considered his work of sowing the Word in Lincolnshire as an act of obedience to Christ—the chief preacher—and as a form of *imitatio Christi*, a commitment transcending but touching upon all other considerations.[76]

Latimer's robust confidence in the preaching of the word as the primary means of religious and social reform was a source of encouragement for an evangelical minority longing for visible signs of fruit to appear (Works, II.210).[77] While only a small portion of the polity responded to the message of the evangelicals during the Edwardian period, a "catholic" vision informed their popular use of scripture as a means of reconstituting the Church in England. As Steinmetz asserts, "Preaching became for the reformers a third sacrament, coordinate with baptism and the eucharist, and largely replacing the sacrament of penance. The power of the keys, the power to bind and loose from sin, was exercised through the preaching of the gospel."[78] Laboring as God's ploughman, Latimer sowed the Word among the common folk of Lincolnshire, extending the invitation for all to become glad participants in the Christian commonwealth God was providentially bringing under the rule of Edward VI.[79] T.H.L. Parker writes,

> His feet are planted firmly on the ground, his language is simple and direct, his thought concrete. He is concerned about such things as peace being better than war, family life better than monasteries, about servants and masters, distribution of wealth, cheating in business, and so on. But none of these is treated secularly; always it is the activity of God in the world, the relationship of God to humanity, of humanity to God.[80]

---

[75] Haigh, *English Reformations*, 193-201; Whiting, *Local Responses to the English Reformation*, 171-82; idem, *The Blind Devotion of the People*, 223-40.

[76] Christ as teacher and model is emphasized by Erasmus. See the *Paraclesis*, 99-107. "If we desire to learn, why is another author more pleasing than Christ himself? If we seek a model for life, why does another example take precedence for us over that of Christ himself?"

[77] On the minority status of the Edwardians at the end of Edward's reign, see MacCulloch, *Tudor Church Militant*, 114-16; Haigh, *English Reformations*, 168-203; A.G. Dickens, "The early expansion of Protestantism in England, 1520-1558" in ed. Peter Marshall *The Impact of the English Reformation 1500-1640* (London, 1999), 85-116; Davies, *A Religion of the Word*, 232-33; Ryrie, "The problem of allegiance" 98-110.

[78] Steinmetz, "The Intellectual Appeal of the Reformation," 468.

[79] Marshall, *The Catholic Priesthood*, 61-62, 112. "While the reformed view of pastoral vocation rejected the view that there was an ontological difference between the priest and laity, it retained high expectations for godly character, although this was to be expressed in a new form of life." See Davies, *A Religion of the Word*, 94-108.

[80] *The English Reformers*, ed. T.H.L. Parker, Library of Christian Classics, Vol. XXVI. (Philadelphia, 1966), 328.

Conclusion

> But happy is the man whom death takes as he meditates upon this literature [of Christ]. Let us all, therefore, with our whole heart covet this literature, let us embrace it, let us continually occupy ourselves with it, let us fondly kiss it, at length let us die in its embrace, let us be transformed in it, since indeed studies are transmuted into morals (Erasmus, *the Paraclesis*).

This study has illumined vital aspects of Hugh Latimer's homiletic activity in the context of late medieval England. Laboring as God's ploughman for over two decades, Latimer arguably was England's most significant preacher and advocate for preaching as the primary instrument of personal regeneration and social reform. The character of the ploughman, the humble preacher of God's word, was modeled after the figure of Christ. The activity of the plough, a familiar figure of the cross, depicted the power of the gospel, which works through preaching to root up sin in the soul and plant seeds of godliness for salvation. This vision was grounded in the conviction that the future of the commonwealth was dependent upon the renovation of the church on a foundation built by priests committed to speaking God's word by means of vernacular scripture. As Richard Rex concludes, "Latimer was a towering figure among the early Reformers, exercising a preaching ministry whose contributions to the English Reformation are incalculable."

This construction of a "preaching life" has situated Latimer within the larger religious, political, and intellectual world of late medieval England. This approach differs from previous works on Latimer; since it is neither a biography, a work of intellectual or confessional history, or a literary analysis of discrete sermon texts. As a work in homiletic history it has drawn from the details of Latimer's milieu to construct an interpretive framework for his sermons but without allowing these details to overshadow the preaching performances that formed the core of his identity as a religious reformer who successfully mediated between the Crown and people. Its goal, therefore, has been to illumine the practical wisdom embodied in the content, form, and style of Latimer's sermons and to recapture a sense of their over-arching purpose, movement, and force.

Latimer's sermons have been discussed as pastoral discourse spoken to and for particular times, places, and people, and to accomplish particular purposes and effects. Sermons have been treated as both text and context to illumine their respective themes, forms, and rhetorical strategies in relation to their final shape and physical, ceremonial, and liturgical circumstances. Latimer's preaching, therefore, has been construed as a series of improvisations that enact the central theme which predominates throughout his career: the urgent need for religious and practical reform of church and society by means of the spoken word.

By integrating both historical and homiletic interpretation this "preaching life" has provided an appropriate medium for displaying the significance of Latimer's accomplishments by means of "reformation through practice." It has shown that Latimer made an immense contribution to the elevation of preaching from its late medieval status to a primary instrument of reform which enabled listeners to overcome past sins and habits and to take up new forms of faith and obedience. According to Latimer, a preaching clergy was equivalent to a sacerdotal priesthood, ". . . we cannot be saved without hearing the word, it is a necessary way of salvation . . . there must be preachers, if we look to be saved." The preaching office, therefore, was of necessity the office of salvation, and the only means that God had appointed to salvation. Through his preaching and his life, Latimer embodied a radical redefinition of priestly status and function, predicated not upon a sacerdotal character conferred at ordination, but rather on standards of personal godliness, and above all on the willingness and ability to preach the word of God.

Latimer's contribution to "reformation through practice" was instrumental in promoting a process of change that led to the official adoption of a new vision of preaching in the Church of England. From 1534 clergy were required to preach regularly in support of the royal supremacy and against the papal authority. The royal injunctions of 1536 obliged priests to declare the *Ten Articles*, to announce the abrogation of superfluous holidays, and to teach congregations the *Pater Noster*, the Ten Commandments, and the *Articles of Faith*. In 1538, priests were to ensure that at least once a quarter they would "purely and sincerely declare the Gospel of Christ." In 1547, the Edwardian *Injunctions* stipulated the reading of homilies every Sunday, while the 1550 *Ordinal* declared the clergy to be primarily a Ministry of the Word, set apart for the tasks of common prayer and preaching. A theology of the Word became the defining characteristic of the Church of England and its primary instrument of salvation.

At the heart of the struggle for reform was the definition and control of public discourse, the dissemination of knowledge, and the verbal articulation of faith. Accordingly, this study began by exploring the religious and intellectual setting in which Latimer was trained for pastoral ministry. It argued that educational improvements and innovations at Cambridge, most notable those introduced by John Fisher and Erasmus, stimulated a quantum leap in the importance of preaching for the renovation of English religious life. Intellectual foundations laid by evangelical humanism, especially the biblical scholarship of Erasmus, provided Latimer with the necessary tools for constructing a reformist vision of preaching that emphasized the power of scripture to render the living image of Christ, the defeat of superstition, the removal of religious abuses, the regeneration of faith, and the inspiration of devotion to God and charity toward neighbor. Informed by the wisdom of humanist rhetoric,

Latimer's practice of *decorum* enabled him to identify with changing audiences and to accommodate his speech for a variety of conditions. His preaching discourse, therefore, was simple, concrete, and enlivened by personal appropriation; it called for the revival and conversion of listeners by means of a "vernacular" theology which was capable of crossing the barriers which had divided the English realm.

During the reign of Henry VIII, Latimer moved from the role of academic evangelist to parish priest to emerge as a leading evangelical voice in support of the "King's Great Matter" and royal supremacy. Latimer was one of a generation of university-trained clergy and scholars that hoped to turn England towards a national church. Many of these viewed the realm as fallow ground for spiritual revitalization and moral reform, sharing a common desire to unite England around the word of God, to defeat superstition, to educate the laity, to improve priestly performance, and for a godly commonwealth free from papal authority. However, a key factor in Latimer's promotion and rise to national prominence was the Crown's recognition of the communicative power of speech as an instrument of reform.

During the 1530s Latimer capitalized on opportunities provided by his new role in local parishes, at Paul's Cross, before the Convocation of clergy, and from the cathedral of Worcester. His reformist speech and activity contributed to an explosion of preaching which utilized existing structures and provisions for new religious and political purposes. Due to the ambiguous nature of Henrician reform, Latimer's sermons were about neither doctrine nor structures in the church, but rather aimed to stir the imagination to promote elemental changes in worship, devotional practices, and personal piety. Latimer's protest, therefore, was aimed primarily against the church and its clergy for losing much of the fire, zeal, and passion for evangelism and pastoral work that would have guarded it from misapplied affections and abuses, failures that hindered an emphasis on inner grace, personal knowledge of God, salvation by faith, and growth in holiness.

After the death of Henry, Latimer played a major role during the early years of the Edwardian period. From 1548-1550 he was appointed to preach at strategic locations in London, most notably Paul's Cross and the royal court, where he vehemently attacked traditional religion and aggressively promoted a Protestant vision of a Christian commonwealth that radically redefined the role of church, priesthood, and people. Latimer's *Sermon of the Plough* highlights his use of biblical farming metaphors such as plowing, sowing, and harvesting to introduce an interpretation of the gospel prescribed by Edward's *Injunctions* and the official *Book of Homilies*. This timely performance, moreover, introduced Latimer as England's model ploughman; it established him as a prophet who spoke by means of scripture to inspire action towards the future, for the renewal of the church and Christianizing of the social order.

Latimer's dramatic Lenten sermons at the court of Edward VI in 1549-55 are exemplary of Latimer's authoritative use of biblical rhetoric, both prophetic and pastoral discourse within the context of royal pageantry. Conspicuous throughout Latimer's court preaching was a fear of God's wrath should England not heed the call to repentance, and a conviction that the resolution of the nation's troubles must be accomplished throughout the preaching of God's word and the obedience of God's people. This message inevitably lent a polemical edge to Latimer's sermons, since on the one hand his speech was directed against idolatry, and on the other, against social injustice. Latimer therefore viewed his primary task as bringing the Bible to life to overcome sin and create social righteousness; from first to last, his goal was to promote a Christian commonwealth through the power of the spoken word.

Latimer was deployed by Cranmer to the diocese of Lincolnshire where he preached among the commons from 1550-53. His plain, vernacular sermons embodied the homiletic wisdom required to implement the commonwealth vision articulated in the *Sermon of the Plough*. Latimer's popular preaching in Lincolnshire took place against the background created by Cranmer's more "gradualist" pastoral and liturgical program to convert England from traditional religion to evangelical faith and devotion. Latimer's Lincolnshire sermons demonstrate the manner in which he adopted a strategy of "evangelism through persuasion" for that contested region. Bridging the gap between "high and low," Latimer accommodated his discourse to listeners' capacities through the use of plain, biblical speech, thus opening lines of communication to cultivate new habits of faith and devotion embodied in the *Homilies* and *Book of Common Prayer*. This rhetorical strategy thus increased the potential for receptivity and softened the impact of the Edwardian reforms. Finally, Latimer utilized the popular sermons as a form of polemic to defend the new church and its faith against critics and opponents. On the one hand, he attacked traditionalists who remained loyal to the Church of Rome; on the other, he attacked the perceived threat of radicals, particularly Anabaptists, who desired faster and more far-reaching changes. The overall purpose of Latimer's moderate discourse to the commons was to break ground for a "middle way" and to plant new habits of faith and life for the creation of a Protestant nation.

By examining Latimer's preaching in the context of late medieval England, it has been possible to discern the dialectic of continuity and change throughout his career as a religious leader whose discourse effectively mediated between crown, church, and people. Because the English Reformation began as an argument among Catholic insiders, its early period was a time when what eventually became Protestantism developed alongside reformist Catholicism. Despite contrasting claims, the common roots of both sides within humanist soil meant that in practice there was more similarity in approach than either side was willing to admit. This study has shown that while Latimer attacked the failures of the pre-Reformation church, his discourse displayed continuity with important patterns of late medieval reformist thought and practice derived from Cambrian influence. It has also demonstrated that during both the Henrician and Edwardian periods, Latimer's polemical discourse highlighted differences between himself and more conservative, traditionalist opponents as a means of adjusting his listeners to England's changing religious and political situation. This dialectic of continuity and change enabled Latimer to both justify and realign Christian discourse and practice with the authority of scripture and the royal supremacy. Arguably the most influential contributor to England's reformation *through* preaching, Latimer ploughed new ground and sowed new seed for a reformation *of* preaching.

The story of Latimer's "preaching life" constitutes a major sub-plot within the drama of English Reformation history. A conclusion of this story would be remiss without an account of Latimer's final and most memorable sermon. In July 1553, soon after the death of Edward VI and the accession of Mary, Latimer was summoned from Warwickshire to appear before the Privy Council in London; in September he was committed to the Tower. According to Foxe, Latimer had advance warning of the pursuivant sent into the country to serve the summons. To the officer's surprise, Latimer is purported to have answered,

> My friend, you be a welcome messenger to me. And be it known unto you, and to all the world, that I go as willingly to London at this present, being called by my prince to render a reckoning of my doctrine, as ever I was at any place in the world. I doubt not that God, as He hath made me worthy to preach His word before two excellent princes, so will He able me to witness the same unto the third, either to her comfort or discomfort eternally (Works, I.321).

Latimer's journey to London took him through Smithfield, where, in 1539, he had preached for the execution of Friar Forest. In April 1554, along with Ridley and Cranmer, Latimer was transferred to Oxford for disputations on transubstantiation and the sacrifice of the Mass. The three evangelical leaders were adjudged to be heretics, excommunicated, and handed over to secular power. All three reformers were committed to Bocardo, the common gaol of Oxford, where they remained until September 1555. At this time, Latimer and Ridley were subjected to another trial under the sanction of papal commission, were condemned and sentenced to be executed on October 16, 1555 (Foxe, VII.464).

Two letters that were presumably written by Latimer from Bocardo are included among his extant correspondence. The first letter is addressed, "One in prison for the Profession of the Gospel." Its message is constructed by means of numerous biblical texts that tell a story of faith, suffering, and hope in following Christ and taking up his cross. Latimer concludes: "Let us that be of lively faith follow the Lamb wheresoever he goeth . . . Embrace Christ's cross, and Christ shall embrace you. The peace of God be with you for ever, and with all them that live in captivity with you in Christ!" (Works, II.434). The second letter is attributed to Latimer during the last months of his incarceration at Bocardo, "Mr Latimer to all the unfeigned lovers of God's truth." Its message is similar to the previous letter. In it Latimer rehearses and situates himself and his readers within the familiar narrative of Old and New Testament saints—

from the first of Genesis to the Apocalypse—whose suffering witnesses to Christ.

> But if ye had none of the fathers, patriarchs, good kings, prophets, apostles, evangelists, martyrs, holy saints, and children of God, (if you go forwards, as I trust you will) yet you have your general captain and master, Jesus Christ, the dear darling and only-begotten Son of God, in whom was all the Father's joy and delectation; ye have him to go before you: no fairer was his way than ours, but much worse and fouler, towards his city of the heavenly Jerusalem. Let us remember what manner of the way Christ found: begin at his birth, and go forth until ye come at his burial; and you shall find that every step of his journey was a thousand times worse than yours is. For he had laid upon him at one time the devil, death, and sin: and with one sacrifice, never again to be done, he overcame them all (Works, II.438).

As Brad Gregory has persuasively argued, martyrdom in early modern Europe was an interpretive category and inextricable from one's religious commitments; it helped to solidify group identities and altered the beliefs, theology, and spirituality of others.[1] Foxe therefore presents his account of Latimer's execution to accomplish both aims; on the one hand, to show the living content of Protestant belief, and on the other, to let actions speak even more loudly than words to evangelize and edify his readers.

> When Master Latimer stood at the stake, and the tormentors were about to set the fire upon him and that most reverend father Doctor Ridley, he lifted up his eyes towards heaven, with a most amiable and comfortable countenance, saying these words, 'God is faithful, which does not suffer us to be tempted above our strength.' Addressing himself also to Bishop Ridley, he said, 'Be of good comfort, Master Ridley, and play the man: we shall this day light such a candle, by God's grace, in England, as I trust shall never be put out'. Then, soon after the fire had been kindled, and the flames had begun to envelope the sufferers, Master Latimer soon passed into a better life, whilst earnestly calling upon God to receive his soul.

Foxe's account renders Latimer's death as an eloquent and persuasive sermon.[2] It communicates a central conviction articulated by Latimer throughout his career: that preaching God's word and following Christ will provoke persecution, but the power of faith and the grace of God maintain the oppressed and bestow ultimate victory. Moreover, Foxe demonstrates that Latimer's willingness to witness unto death embodied his rejection of soteriological self-

---

[1] Brad S. Gregory, *Salvation at Stake: Christian Martyrdom in Early Modern Europe* (Cambridge, 1999), 5-15.

[2] See my brief excursus and footnotes on Foxe in chapter 1. See Freeman's discussion of Foxe's account of the execution at Oxford in "Reading and Misreading Foxe's 'Book of Martyrs,'" 42-47.

reliance and expressed emphatically his absolute trust in God's providence. As Gregory observes, "A shared faith and its practice in communities of belief, the answers that a particular commitment to Christ provided, the experiential fit between scripture and life, and the sacrifice of one's fellow believers in martyrdom, all these reinforced each other."[3] A comment made by Latimer during a Lincolnshire sermon illumines his conviction that preaching must be modeled on the Incarnation: the imitation of Christ in life and death.

> The highest promotion that God can bring his unto in this life is, to suffer for truth. And it is the greatest setting forth of his word; it is God's seed. And one suffering for the truth turneth more than a thousand sermons (Works, I.294).

In addition to the popular dissemination of Foxe's martyrology, Latimer's status as an exemplar of "reformation through practice" endured through his written legacy of 27 collected sermons which were reprinted at regular intervals throughout the sixty years following their first issue under Edward VI. Individual sermons were printed as early as 1537, during the Henrician reign, but the eventual presentation in a collection volume transformed the sermons into a "classic text" of the English Reformation. The chronological ordering, which is standard from 1571, suggest a corpus of works and practical thought, while Latimer's status in the Church of England as a Protestant martyr covered his words and life posthumously with a pall of orthodoxy. This enabled the identity and language of Latimer as England's Protestant ploughman-preacher to survive in the vocabulary of succeeding generations, as the complete canon of his works was reissued at critical periods in the life of the English Church to serve as a classic memory of reform embodied in his preaching.[4]

This "preaching life" of Hugh Latimer has aimed to demonstrate that the study of homiletic history may illumine the key role played by preachers and preaching in advancing and shaping the English Reformation. A court sermon preached by John Jewel before Elizabeth I, illustrates the continuing influence of Henrician and Edwardian transformations of the pastoral office which increasingly focused on the centrality of preaching as a means of religious renewal and reform.[5] Speaking to Elizabeth I within a decade of Latimer's death at Oxford, Jewel, Bishop of Salisbury, repeated the latter's passionate appeal to Edward VI for an increase of preaching to spread salvation across the realm. Jewel derive his appeal from the words of Christ in Matthew 9:37-38, "Wherefore pray the Lord of the harvest, the he would send labourers forth into his harvest," Jewel likened Elizabethan England to a great harvest field where

---

[3] Gregory, *Salvation at Stake*, 341.
[4] For a discussion of Latimer's literary legacy see Chester, *Hugh Latimer*, 187-89, 246-48.
[5] *The Works of John Jewel, Bishop of Salisbury: Certaine Sermons Preached Before the Queen's Majestie, at Paul's Cross, and elsewhere*. The Parker Society, ed. John Ayre (Cambridge, 1867), 1021-23.

many hungered and thirsted after the kingdom of God, the knowledge of the gospel, because, "The labourers are few." In a manner reminiscent of Latimer, Jewel lamented of bishops, prelates, priests and pastors who were "destroyers and wasters of the harvest," but not prophets and preachers, and who thereby deprived their people of the greatest blessing that could be received at God's hands.

Echoing themes from both the *Sermon of the Plough* and Latimer's court sermons, Jewel declared that when preaching is absent the flock is without a shepherd, the ship is without a pilot, and the child is without a nursemaid: "Labourers they must be, not loiterers!" Viewing the laws and policies of the realm as only a handmaid, Jewel declared that preaching must come first, since the church was built on the foundation of scripture, the prophets and apostles. Voicing a conviction which was central to the work of Erasmus, Jewel went on to state that although the people had been commanded to change their religion under Elizabeth, faith which was forced was no faith; the people must be healed of their errors, "gently brought in by persuasion."

The significance of Jewel's appeal to the Crown for an increase of preaching is indicative of the reformist work of England's bishops from 1520-79. From 1520-59 preaching became increasingly important for the office of bishop until the accession of Elizabeth, when the way was cleared for the establishment of a new episcopate where the role of bishop as preacher could take its place as the prime function of the holder of that office.[6] In addition, the ecclesial vision and pastoral achievements of Elizabeth's progressive bishops from 1559-79 has been described in the following manner, "As a prominent means by which the walls of papacy could be knocked down and new Protestant structures built in their place, preaching was preeminent in their minds."[7]

The legacy of Hugh Latimer provided what was arguably the most significant pastoral example of initiating and advancing reform during a period when preachers became "indescribable agents of salvation" and preaching the Word occupied a more central place in pastoral life than it had before.

---

[6] Kenneth Carleton, *Bishops and Reform in the English Church, 1520-59* (Woodbridge, 2001); Kenneth Fincham and Nicholas Tyacke, *Altars Restored: The Changing Face of English Religious Worship, 1547 – c. 1700* (Oxford, 2007), 50-72.

[7] Scott A. Wenig, *Straightening the Altars: The Ecclesiastical Vision and Pastoral Achievements of the Progressive Bishops under Elizabeth I, 1559-79* (New York, 2000), 47.

Bibliography

Aers, David. *Chaucer, Langland, and the Creative Imagination*. London: Routledge & Kegan Paul, 1980.

Anglo, Sidney. *Spectacle, Pageantry, and Early Tudor Policy*. Oxford: Oxford University Press, 1969.

Arnold, Duane and Pamela Bright, eds. *De doctrina christiana: A Classic of Western Culture*. Notre Dame: University of Notre Dame Press, 1995.

Aston, Margaret. *England's Iconoclasts*. 2 Volumes. Oxford: Oxford University Press, 1988.

— *Faith and Fire: Popular and Unpopular Religion, 1350-1600*. London: Hambledon, 1993.

— *Lollards and Reformers: Images and Literacy in Late Medieval Religion*. London: Hambledon, 1984.

Aston, Nigel and Matthew Cragoe, eds. *Anticlericalism in Britain: c. 1500-1914*. Thrupp: Sutton, 2000.

Auerbach, Erich. *Literary Language and Its Public in Late Antiquity and in the Middle Ages*. Ralph Manheim, trans. New York: Princeton University Press, 1965.

— *Mimesis: The Representation of Reality in Western Literature*. Willard Trask, trans. Princeton: Princeton University Press, 1953.

Augustijn, Cornelius. *Erasmus: His Life, Works, and Influence*. Toronto: University of Toronto Press, 1991.

Augustine, Aurelius. *Teaching Christianity: De doctrina christiana*. John E. Rotelle, ed. New York: New City Press, 1996.

Auksi, Peter. *Christian Plain Style: The Evolution of a Spiritual Ideal*. Montreal: McGill-Queen's University Press, 1995.

Ayris, Paul and David Selwyn, eds. *Thomas Cranmer: Churchman and Scholar*. Suffolk: Boydell, 1993.

Baker, Derek. ed. *Reform and Reformation: England and the Continent*. Oxford: Oxford University Press, 1979.

Bauckham, Richard. *Tudor Apocalypse: Sixteenth century apocalypticism, millenarianism and the English Reformation from John Bale to John Foxe and Thomas Brightman*. Oxford: Oxford University Press, 1978.

Becon, Thomas. *Works*. 2 Volumes. The Parker Society. Cambridge: Cambridge University Press, 1844.

Beilin, Elaine V. ed. *The Examinations of Anne Askew*. Oxford: Oxford University Press, 1996.

Bejczy, Istvan. *Erasmus and the Middle Ages: The Historical Consciousness of a Christian Humanist*. Leiden: Brill, 2001.

Bernard, G.W. 'The Piety of Henry III', in N. Scott Amos, Andrew Pettigree, and

H. van Nierop, eds. *The Education of a Christian Society*. Aldershot: Ashgate, 1999.

Bernard, G.W. *The King's Reformation: Henry VIII and the Remaking of The English Church*. New Haven and London: Yale University Press, 2005.

Birch, David. 'Early Reformation Polemics', in James Hogg, ed., *Elizabethan and Renaissance Studies* 92.7 (1983).

Blench, J.W. *Preaching in England: in the late Fifteenth and Sixteenth Centuries*. Oxford: Oxford University Press, 1964.

Block, P.M. *Factional Politics and the English Reformation: 1520-1540*. London: Methuen, 1993.

— 'Thomas Cromwell's Patronage of Preaching', *Sixteenth Century Journal* VIII (1997).

Bond, Ronald B. ed. *Certain Sermons or Homilies (1547) and A Homily against Disobedience and Wilful Rebellion (1570)*. Toronto: University of Toronto Press, 1987.

Bostick, Curtis V. *The Anti-Christ and the Lollards: Apocalypticism in Late Medieval and Reformation England*. Leiden: Brill, 1998.

Bossy, John. *Christianity in the West: 1400-1700*. Oxford: Oxford University Press, 1985.

Bouwsma, William. *A Usable Past: Essays in Cultural History*. Berkeley: University of California Press, 1990.

Bowker, Margaret. *The Herician Reformation: the Diocese of Lincoln under John Longland 1521-1547*. Cambridge: Cambridge University Press, 1981.

Boyle, Majorie O' Rourke. *Erasmus on Language and Method in Theology*. Toronto: University of Toronto Press, 1977.

— 'Rhetorical Theology: Charity Seeking Charity', in Walter Jost and Wendy Olmstead, eds. *Rhetorical Invention and Religious Inquiry: New Perspectives*. New Haven: Yale University Press, 1999.

Bradshaw, Brendan and Eamon Duffy, eds. *Humanism, Reform and the Reformation: the Career of Bishop John Fisher*. Cambridge: Cambridge University Press, 1989.

Brady, Thomas, Heiko Oberman, and James Tracy, eds. *Handbook of European History 1400-1600: Late Middle Ages, Renaissance, and Reformation*. 2 Volumes. Grand Rapids: Eerdmans, 1995.

Bray, Gerald. ed. *Documents of the English Reformation*. Minneapolis: Augsburg, 1994.

Breen, Quirinius. *Christianity and Humanism: Studies in the History of Ideas*. Grand Rapids: Eerdmans, 1968.

Brigden, Susan. *London and the Reformation*. Oxford: Clarendon, 1989.

Bucer, Martin. *De Regno Christi*. Wilhelm Pauck, trans. and ed., *Melanchthon and Bucer*, Library of Christian Classics, Vol. XIX. Philadelphia: Westminster, 1969.

Bush M.L. *The Government of Protector Somerset*. Oxford: Oxford University Press, 1975.

— 'Up the Commonweal: the significance of tax grievances in the English rebellions of 1536', *English Historical Review* 106 (1991).

Campbell, Charles L. *Preaching Jesus: New Directions for Homiletics in Hans Frei's Postliberal Theology*. Grand Rapids: Eerdmans, 1997.

Carlson, Eric Josef. ed. *Religion and the English People 1500-1640: New Voices, New Perspectives*. Kirksville: Thomas Jefferson University Press, 1998.

Carleton, Kenneth. *Bishops and Reform in the English Church, 1520-1559*. Woodbridge: Boydell, 2001.

Caspari, Fritz. *Humanism and the Social Order in Tudor England*. Chicago: University of Chicago Press, 1965.

Cessario, Romanus. O.P. *Christian Faith and the Theological Life*. Washington, D.C: Catholic University Press, 1996.

Charry, Ellen T. *By the Renewing of Your Minds: The Pastoral Function of Christian Doctrine*. Oxford: Oxford University Press, 1997.

Chester, Allan. *Hugh Latimer: Apostle to the English*. Philadelphia: University of Pennsylvania Press, 1954.

Clay, G.C. *Economic Expansion and Social Change: England 1500-1700*. 2 Volumes. Cambridge: Cambridge University Press, 1984.

Clebsch, William. *England's Earliest Protestants*. New London: Yale University Press, 1964.

Collinson, Patrick. *The Birthpangs of Protestant England: Religious and Cultural Change in the Sixteenth and Seventeeth Centuries*. New York: Barnes and Noble, 1988.

— 'Truth, lies, and fiction in Sixteenth-Century Protestant Historiography', in Donald R. Kelley and David H. Sacks, eds. *The Historical Imagination in Early Modern Britain: History, Rhetoric, and Fiction*. Cambridge: Cambridge University Press, 1998.

Cox, Leonard. *The Arte Or Craftye of Rhethoryke; With Introduction, Notes, and Glossiarial Index*. F.I. Carpenter, ed. Chicago: University of Chicago Press, 1899.

Crockett, Brian. *The Play of Paradox: Stage and Sermon in Renaissance England*. Philadelphia: University of Pennsylvania Press, 1995.

Cross, Claire. *Church and People 1540-1660: The Triumph of the Laity in the Church of England*. Trowbridge: Fontana, 1976.

Daniell, David. *William Tyndale: A Biography*. New London: Yale University Press, 1994.

Darby, Harold S. *Hugh Latimer*. London: Epworth, 1953.

Davies, Catherine,. *A Religion of the Word: The Defence of the Reformation in the Reign of Edward VI*. New York: Palgrave, 2002.

Davies, C.S.L. 'The Pilgrimage of Grace reconsidered', *Past & Present* 41 (1968).

Davies, Horton. *Worship and Theology in England: From Cranmer to Hooker*. 3 Volumes. Princeton: Princeton University Press, 1970.

Demaus, Robert. *Hugh Latimer: A Biography*. Nashville: Abingdon, 1869.

DeMolen, Richard. ed. *Essays on the Works of Erasmus*. New Haven: Yale

University Press, 1978.

Dickens, A.G. *The English Reformation*. 2nd. ed. University Park: Penn State University Press, 1989.

— and Whitney R.D. Jones. *Erasmus the Reformer.* London: Methuen, 1994.

Disson, Janett. *Language and Stage in Medieval and Renaissance England.* Cambridge: Cambridge University Press, 1998.

Gregory D. Dodds. *Exploiting Erasmus: The Erasmian Legacy and Religious Change in Early Modern England.* Toronto: University of Toronto Press, 2009.

Doran, Susan and Christopher Durston. *Princes, Pastors and People: The Church and Religion in England 1529-1689*. London: Routledge, 1991.

Dowling, Maria. 'John Fisher and the preaching ministry', *Archive for Reformation History* lxxxii (1991).

— *Fishers of Men: A Biography of John Fisher*. London: Methuen, 1999.

Duffy, Eamon. *The Stripping of the Altars: Traditional Religion in England 1400-1580*. Cambridge: Cambridge University Press, 1992.

Dunnan, D. Stuart. 'Hugh Latimer: A Reappraisal of his Preaching'. Oxford University Ph.D., 1991.

Eden, Kathy. *Hermeneutics and the Rhetorical Tradition: Chapters in the Ancient Legacy and Its Humanist Reception*. New Haven: Yale University Press, 1997.

Eire, Carlos M.N. *War Against the Idols: The Reformation of Worship from Erasmus to Calvin.* Cambridge: Cambridge University Press, 1996.

Elton, G.R. 'Reform and the Commonwealth Men of Edward's Reign', in P. Clark and others, eds. *The English Commonwealth, 1547-1640*. New York: Barnes and Noble, 1979.

— *Policy and Police: The Enforcement of the Reformation in the Age of Thomas Cromwell*. Cambridge: Cambridge University Press, 1972.

— *Reform and Reformation*. Edward Arnold, 1977.

English, Edward D., ed. *Reading and Wisdom: The De doctrina christiana of Augustine in the Middle Ages*. Notre Dame: University of Notre Dame Press, 1995.

Erasmus, Desiderius. *Opera Omni*. J. Le Clerc, ed. 11 Volumes. Leiden: Brill, 1703-1706., 1962 rpr.

— *In Praise of Folly*. Clarence H. Miller, trans. New Haven: Yale University Press, 1979.

— *Collected Works of Erasmus*. Toronto: University of Toronto Press, 1977-.

— *Erasmi Epistolae*. 12 Volumes. P.S. Allen, ed. Oxford: Oxford University Press, 1906-58.

Ferguson, Arthur B. 'By Little and Little: The Early Tudor Humanists on the Development of Man', in Rowe, J.R. and W.H. Stockdale, eds. *Florilegium Historiale: Essays Presented to Wallace K. Ferguson*. Toronto: University of Toronto Press, 1971.

Ferrell, Lorri Anne and Peter McCullough, eds. *The English Sermon Revised: Religion, Literature, and History, 1600-1750*. Manchester: Manchester University Press, 2000.

Fincham, Kenneth and Nicholas Tyacke. *Altars Restored: The Changing Face of English Religious Worship, 1547 – c. 1700*. Cambridge: Cambridge University Press, 2007.

Fowl, Stephen and Gregory Jones. *Reading in Communion: Scripture and Ethics in Christian Life*. Grand Rapids: Eerdmans, 1991.

Foxe, John. *Acts and Monuments of these latter and perilous days*....London: John Day, 1563.

— *The Acts and Monuments*. 7 Volumes. R.R. Medham and Joiah Pratt, eds. London: 1875.

Freeman, Thomas. 'Text, Lies, and Microfilm: Reading and Misreading Foxe's *Book of Martyrs*', *Sixteenth Century Journal* XXX 1 (1999).

Frei, Hans W. *The Eclipse of Biblical Narrative: A Study in Eighteenth and Nineteenth Century Hermeneutics*. New Haven: Yale University Press, 1974.

Frith, K.R. *The Apocalyptic Tradition in Reformation Britain 1530-1645*. Oxford: Oxford University Press, 1979.

Garver, Eugene. *Aristotle's Rhetoric: An Art of Character*. Chicago: University of Chicago Press, 1994.

Gray, Charles Montgomery. *Hugh Latimer and the Sixteenth Century*. Cambridge: Harvard University Press, 1950.

Gordon, Bruce. ed. *Protestant History and Identity in Sixteenth-Century Europe*. 2 Volumes. Aldershot: Ashgate, 1996.

Green, Ian. *The Christian's ABC: Catechisms and Cathechizing in England c. 1530-1740*. Oxford: Oxford University Press, 1996.

Gregory the Great. *Pastoral Care*. Henry Davis S.J., trans. and ed. Ancient Christian Writers. New York: Fordham University Press, 1950.

Ha, Polly and Patrick Collinson, *The Reception of Continental Reformation in Britain*. Oxford: Oxford University Press, 2010.

Hadgett, Gerald A.J. *History of Lincolnshire*. 7 Volumes. Lincolnshire: History of Lincolnshire Committee, 1975.

Hadot, Pierre. *Philosophy as a Way of Life: Spiritual Exercises from Socrates to Foucault*. Michael Chase, trans. Arnold I. Davidson, ed. Oxford: Oxford University Press, 1995.

Haigh, Christopher. *English Reformations: Religion, Politics, and Society under the Tudors*. Oxford, Oxford University Press, 1993.

— ed. *The English Reformation Revised*. Cambridge: Cambridge University Press, 1990.

— *Reformation and Resistance in Tudor Lancashire*. Cambridge: Cambridge University Press, 1975.

Hall, Basil. *Humanists and Protestants*. Edinburgh: Edinburgh University Press, 1991.

Hawkins, Peter. *Dante's Testaments: Essays in Scriptural Imagination*. Stanford: Stanford University Press, 1999.

Hayward, John. *The Life and Raigne of King Edward the Sixth*. Barret L. Beer, ed. Kent: Kent State University Press, 1993.

Heal, Felicity. *Of Princes and Prelates: A Study of the Economic and Social Position of the Tudor Episopate.* Cambridge: Cambridge University Press, 1980.

Helgerson, Richard. *Forms of Nationhood: The Elizabethan Writing of England.* Chicago: University of Chicago Press, 1992.

Hill, J.F.H. *Tudor and Stuart England.* Cambridge: Cambridge University Press, 1956.

Hill, Ordelle G. *The Manor, the Plowman, and the Shepherd.* Selinsgrove: Susquehanna University Press, 1993.

Hoak, D.E. *The King's Council in the Reign of Edward VI.* Cambridge: Cambridge University Press, 1976.

Holmer, Paul L. *The Grammar of Faith.* San Francisco: Harper and Row, 1978.

Hopf, Constantin. *Martin Bucer and the English Reformation.* Oxford: Oxford University Press, 1946.

Horst, I.B. *The Radical Brethren.* Nieuwkoop: 1972.

Howell, Wilbur S. *Logic and Rhetoric in England: 1500-1700.* Princeton: Princeton University Press, 1956.

Hutchinson, Roger. *Works.* The Parker Society. Cambridge: Cambridge University Press, 1968.

Hudson, Anne. *The Premature Reformation.* Oxford: Oxford University Press, 1988.

— 'The Legacy of Piers Plowman', in John A. Alford, ed., *A Companion to Piers Plowman.* Berkeley: University of California Press, 1988.

— *Lollards and their Books.* London: Hambledon, 1985.

Ives, E.W. *Anne Boleyn.* Oxford: Oxford University Press, 1986.

Janton, Pierre. *L'eloquence et la rhetorique dans les Sermons de Hugh Latimer: etude de l' art et la technique oratoire.* Paris: Presses Universitaires de France, 1968.

Jones, Norman. *The English Reformation: Religion and Cultural Adaptation.* Oxford and Malden: Blackwell, 2002.

Jones, Whitney R.D. *The Mid-Tudor Crisis 1539-1563.* London: Barnes and Noble Books, 1973.

— *The Tudor Commonwealth 1529-1559.* London: Barnes and Noble, 1970.

Kantorowizc, Ernst. *The King's Two Bodies: A Study in Medieval Political Theology.* Princeton: Princeton University Press, 1957.

Kaufman, Peter Iver. *Augustinian Piety and Catholic Reform: Augustine, Colet, and Erasmus.* Macon: Mercer University Press, 1982.

— *Church, Book, and Bishop: Conflict and Authority in Early Latin Christianity.* Boulder: Westview, 1996.

Kelly, J.N.D. *Early Christian Doctrines.* San Francisco: Harper and Row, 1978.

Kelly, Robert L. 'Hugh Latimer as Piers Plowman', *Studies in English Literature* 17 (1977).

King, John N. *English Reformation Literature: The Tudor Origins of the Protestant Tradition.* Princeton: Princeton University Press, 1982.

— *Tudor Royal Iconography: Literature and Art in an Age of Religious Crisis*. Princeton: Princeton University Press, 1989.

— 'Fiction and Fact in Foxe's Book of Martyrs', in David Loades, ed., *John Foxe and the English Reformation*. Aldershot: Ashgate, 1997.

— and Christopher Highley, eds. *John Foxe and his World*. Aldershot: Ashgate, 2002.

Kolb, Robert. *Luther and the Stories of God: Biblical Narratives as a Foundation for Christian Living*. Grand Rapids: Baker Academic, 2012.

Knowles, David. *The Religious Orders in England*. 3 Volumes. Cambridge: Cambridge University Press, 1959.

Kumin, Beat. *The Shaping of a Community: the rise and Reformation of the English Parish, c. 1400-1560*. Aldershot: Ashgate, 1996.

Lake, Peter and Maria Dowling, eds. *Protestanism and the National Church in Sixteenth Century England*. London: Croom and Helm, 1987.

Lamb, John. *A Collection of Letters, Statutes, and Other Documents from the MS. Library of Corpus Christi College, Illustrative of the History of the University of Cambridge during the period of the Reformation, from, A.D. M.D. to MDLXXII*. London: 1881.

Lambert, Malcolm. *Medieval Heresy: Popular Movements from the Gregorian Reform to the Reformation*. 2nd ed. London: Blackwell, 1992.

Lanham, Richard A. *A Handlist of Rhetorical Terms*. Berkeley: University of California Press, 1991.

Latimer, Hugh. *The Works*. 2 Volumes. The Parker Society. George Corrie, ed. Cambridge: Cambridge University Press, 1968.

Leader, Damien Riehl. *A History of the University of Cambridge*. 3 Volumes. Cambridge: Cambridge University Press, 1988.

Levy, Benard. ed. *The Bible in the Middle Ages*. Binghamton: SUNY Press, 1992.

Lindbeck, George. *The Nature of Doctrine: Religion in a Postliberal Age*. Philiadelphia: Westminster, 1984.

— 'Scripture. Consensus, and Community', in Richard J. Neuhaus, ed., *Biblical Interpretation in Crisis*. Grand Rapids: Eerdman, 1989.

— 'Atonement and the Hermeneutics of Social Embodiment', *Pro Ecclesia* Vol. V. no. 2 (1996).

Lischer, Richard. 'Luther and Contemporary Preaching: Narrative and Anthropology', *Scottish Journal of Theology* 36 (1988).

Loades, David. *The Oxford Martyrs*. London: Oxford University Press, 1970.

— 'The New Edition of the Acts and Monuments: A Progress Report', in David Loades, ed., *John Foxe: A Historical Perspective*. Aldershot: Ashgate, 1999.

— 'Anabaptism and English Sectarianism in the mid-sixteenth century', in Derek Baker ed. *Reform and Reformation: England and the Continent*. Oxford: Oxford University Press, 1979.

— *John Dudley, Duke of Northumberland*. Oxford: Clarendon, 1996.

Locher, Gottfried W. *Zwingli's Thought: New Perspectives*. Leiden: Brill, 1981.

MacCulloch, Diarmaid. *Thomas Cranmer: A Life*. London: Yale University Press,

1996.
— ed. *The Reign of Henry VIII: Politics, Policy, and Piety*. New York: St. Martin's, 1995.
— *The Later Reformation in England, 1547-1603*. 2nd. ed. London: Palgrave, 2001.
— *The Boy King: Edward VI and the English Reformation*. New York: Palgrave, 2001.
Macintyre, Alasdair. *After Virtue: A Study in Moral Theory*. Notre Dame: University of Notre Dame Press, 1984.
Mack, Peter. *Renaissance Argument: Valla and Agricola*. Leiden: Brill, 1993.
Maclure, Millard. *The Paul's Cross Sermons: 1534-1642*. Toronto: University of Toronto Press, 1958.
Maltby, Judith. *Prayer Book and People in Elizabethan and Early Stuart England*. Cambridge: Cambridge University Press, 1998.
Manning, Roger. *Village Revolts: Social Protest and Popular Disturbances in England, 1509-1640*. Oxford: Oxford University Press, 1988.
Marsh, Christopher. *Popular Religion in Sixteenth Century England*. New York: St. Martin's Press, 1999.
Marshall, Peter. ed. *The Impact of the English Reformation: 1500-1640*. London: Routledge, 1997.
— *The Catholic Priesthood and the English Reformation*. Oxford: Oxford University Press, 1994.
— Marshall and Ryrie. eds. *The Beginnings of English Protestantism*. Cambridge: Cambridge University Press, 2002.
__ *Beliefs and the Dead in Reformation England*. Oxford: Oxford University Press, 2002.
Martin, W.J. *Religious Radicals in Tudor England*. London: Methuen, 1989.
Matheson, Peter. *The Rhetoric of the Reformation*. Edinburgh: T & T Clark, 1998.
— *The Imagination of the Reformation*. Edinburgh: T & T Clark, 2000.
Mayor, John. ed. *The English Works of John Fisher: Bishop of Rochester*. 2 Volumes. London: Early English Text Society, 1876.
McConica, James. *English Humanists and Reformation Politics*. Oxford: Oxford University Press, 1965.
— *Erasmus*. Oxford: Oxford University Press, 1991.
McCullough, Peter E. *Sermons at Court: Politics and religion in Elizabethan and Jacobean preaching*. Cambridge: Cambridge University Press, 1998.
McEachern, C. and Debora Shuger, eds. *Religion and Culture in Renaissance England*. Cambridge: Cambridge University Press, 1997.
McGrath, Alister. *Reformation Thought*. Oxford: Blackwell, 1997.
McNeill, John T. *A History of the Cure of Souls*. New York: Harper and Row, 1951.
McRae, Andrew. *God Speed the Plough: The Representation of Agrarian England*. Cambridge: Cambridge University Press, 1996.
Meeks, Wayne. 'A Hermeneutics of Social Embodiment', *Harvard Theological*

God's Ploughman

Review 79 (1986).

Monfasani, John. 'Humanism and Rhetoric', in Albert Rabil Jr. ed. *Reniassance Humanism: Foundations, Forms and Legacy.* 3 Volumes. Philadelphia: University of Pennsyvania Press, 1988.

Moorhouse, Geoffrey. *The Pilgrimage of Grace.* London: Orion House, 2003.

Morrissey, Mary. 'Interdisciplinarity and the Study of Early Modern Sermons', *Historical Journal* 42 (1999).

Mueller, Janet L. *The Native Tongue and the Word: Developments in English Prose Style 1380-1580.* Chicago: University of Chicago Press, 1984.

Muller, Richard A. and John L. Thompson, eds. *Biblical Interpretation in the Era of the Reformation: Essays Presented to David C. Steinmetz in Honor of his Sixtieth Birthday.* Grand Rapids: Eerdmans, 1996.

Muller, J.A. ed. *The Letters of Stephen Gardiner.* Cambridge: University of Cambridge Press, 1933. rpt. 1970.

— *Stephen Gardiner and the Tudor Reaction.* New York: MacMillan, 1926.

Mullett, Michael. *The Catholic Reformation.* London: Routledge, 1999.

Murphy, James J. *Rhetoric in the Middle Ages: A History of Rhetorical Theory from Saint Augustine to the Renaissance.* Berkeley: University of California Press, 1974.

— ed. *Renaissance Eloquence.* Berkeley: University of California Press, 1983.

Nichols, Aidan. O.P. *The Panther and the Hind: A Theological History of Anglicanism.* Edinburgh: T&T Clark, 1993.

Nichols, J.G. ed. *The Literary Remains of Edward the Sixth.* 2 Volumes. Roxburghe Club: Ben Franklin, 1857.

Nussbaum, Martha C. *The Therapy of Desire: Theory and Practice in Hellenistic Ethics.* Princeton: Princeton University Press, 1994.

O'Carroll, Mary E. SND. *A Thirteenth-Century Preacher's Handbook: Studies in MS Laud Misc. 511.* Toronto: University of Toronto Press, 1997.

O'Day, Rosemary. *The Debate on The English Reformation.* London: 1986.

— 'Hugh Latimer, Prophet of the Kingdom', *Historical Research* LXV, 158 (1992).

O'Malley, John. 'Introduction: Medieval Preaching', in Thomas Amos, Eugene Green, and Beverly Mayne Kienzle, eds. *Ore Domini: Preacher and Word in the Middle Ages.* Kalamazo: Medieval Institute Publications, 1989.

Old, Hugh O. *The Reading and Preaching of the Scriptures in the Worship of the Christian Church.* 2 Volumes. Grand Rapids: Eerdmans, 1998.

Olin, John C. ed. *Christian Humanism and the Reformation.* New York: Fordham University Press, 1987.

Ong, Walter J., S.J. *Rhetoric, Romance, and Technology.* Ithaca: Cornell University Press, 1971.

Owst, G.R. *Literature and Pulpit in England.* Cambridge: Cambridge University Press, 1933.

— *Preaching in Medieval England.* Cambridge: Cambridge University Press, 1926.

Pabil, Hilmar M. 'Promoting the Business of the Gospel: Erasmus' Contribution to Pastoral Ministry'. In *Erasmus of Rotterdam Society Yearbook* 15 (1995).

— *Conversing With God: Prayer in Erasmus' Writings*. Toronto: University of Toronto Press, 1997.

— ed. *Erasmus' Vision of the Church*. Kirksville: Thomas Jefferson University Press, 1999.

Parker, Douglas H. ed. *An exhortation to the diligent studye of scripture and an exposition in to the seventh chaptre of the pistle to the Corinthians*. Toronto: University of Toronto Press, 2000.

— ed. *The praier and complyante of the ploweman unto Christe*. Toronto: University of Toronto Press, 1997.

Parker, T.H.L. ed. *The English Reformers*. Library of Christian Classics. Vol. XXVI. Philadelphia: Westminster, 1966.

Pelikan, Jaroslav. *The Christian Tradition*. 5 Volumes. Chicago: University of Chicago Press, 1978.

— *Christianity and Classical Culture: The Metamorphosis of Natural Theology in the Christian Encounter with Hellenism*. New Haven: Yale University Press, 1993.

Petegree, Andrew. *Foreign Protestant Communities in Sixteenth Century London*. Oxford: Oxford University Press, 1986.

__Reformation and the Culture of Persuasion*. Cambridge: Cambridge University Press, 2005.

Petty, Daniel. 'Anabaptism and the Edwardian Reformation'. Texas Christian University Ph.D., 1988.

Philips, Jane E. 'The Gospel, the Clergy, and the Laity in Erasmus' *Paraphrase on the Gospel of John, Erasmus of Rotterdam Society Yearbook* 10 (1985).

Phillips, Margaret Mann. *Erasmus and the Northern Renaissance*. Woodbridge: Hodder & Stoughton, 1981.

Pincaers, Servais. O.P. *The Sources of Christian Ethics*. Sr. Mary Thomas Noble, O.P. trans. Washington, D.C: Catholic University Press, 1995.

Pineas, Rainer. *Thomas More and Tudor Polemics*. Bloomington: Indiana University Press, 1968.

Pole, Reginald. *Defense of the Unity of the Church*. Joseph G. Dwyer ed., Westminster: Newman, 1965.

Porter, H.C. *Reformation and Reaction in Tudor Cambridge*. Cambridge: Cambridge University Press, 1958.

Radner, Ephraim. 'Doctrine, Destiny, and the Figure of History', in E. Radner and George Sumner, eds. *Reclaiming Faith: Essays on Orthodoxy in the Episcopal Church*. Grand Rapids: Eerdmans, 1993.

Reeves, Marjorie. *The Prophetic Sense of History in Medieval and Renaissance Europe*. Variorum Collected Series. Aldershot: Ashgate, 1999.

Resner, Andre. *Preacher and Cross: Person and Message in Theology and Rhetoric*. Grand Rapids: Eerdmans, 1999.

Rex, Richard. *The Theology of John Fisher*. Cambridge: Cambridge University

Press, 1991.
— *Henry VIII and the English Reformation*. New York: St. Martin's, 1993.
Ridley, Nicholas. *The Works of Bishop Ridley*. H. Christmas, ed. The Parker Society. Cambridge: Cambridge University Press, 1851.
Robinson, Hastings. ed. *Original Letters Relative to the English Reformation*. The Parker Society. Cambridge: Cambridge University Press, 1847.
Rupp, E.G. *Studies in the Making of the English Protestant Tradition: Mainly in the Reign of Henry VIII*. Cambridge: Cambridge University Press, 1949.
Rummel, Erika. *The Humanist-Scholastic Debate: In the Renaissance and Reformation*. Cambridge: Cambridge University Press, 1995.
Ryrie, Alec. 'The Strange Death of Lutheran England', *Journal of Ecclesiastical History* 53 (2002).
__*The Gospel and Henry VIII: Evangelicals in the Early English Reformation*. Cambridge: Cambridge University Press, 2003.
Scarisbrick, J.J. *The English Reformation and the English People*. Oxford: Oxford University Press, 1984.
Schoeck, Richard J. 'Humanism in England', in Albert Rabil Jr. ed. *Renaissance Humanism: Foundations, Forms, and Legacy*. 3 Volumes. Philadelphia: University of Pennsylvania Press, 1988.
— *Erasmus Grandescens: The Growth of a Humanist's Mind and Spirituality*. Nieuwkoop, 1988.
Senn, Frank. 'The Reform of the Mass', in Carl Bratten and Robert W. Jenson, eds. *The Catholicity of the Reformation*. Grand Rapids: Eerdmans, 1996.
Shuger, Debora K. *Sacred Rhetoric: The Christian Grand Style in the English Renaissance*. Princeton: Princeton University Press, 1988.
— *The Renaissance Bible: Scholarship, Sacrifice, and Subjectivity*. Berkeley: University of California Press, 1998.
Simpson, James. *English Fundamentalism and Its Reformation Opponents*. Cambridge and London: Belknap, 2007.
Skeeters, Martha C. *Community and Clergy: Bristol and the Reformation, c.1500-c.1570*. Oxford: Oxford University Press, 1993.
Spencer, H. Leith. *English Preaching in Late Medieval England*. Cambridge: Cambridge University Press, 1996.
Steinmetz, David C. 'The Intellectual Appeal of the Reformation', *Theology Today* Vol. 57 no. 4 (2001).
— *Luther in Context*. Bloomington: Indiana University Press, 1986.
— *Reformers in the Wings: from Geiler von Kaysersberg to Theodore Beza*. 2nd. ed. Oxford: Oxford University Press, 2001.
Targoff, Ramie. *Common Prayer: The Language of Public Devotion in Early Modern England*. Chicago: University of Chicago Press, 2001.
Taylor, H.O. *Thought and Expression in the Sixteenth Century*. New York, 1925.
Taylor, Larissa. ed. *Preachers and People in the Reformations and Early Modern Period*. Leiden: Brill, 2001.
Thirsk, Joan. *The Rural Economy of England: Collected Essays*. London:

Hambledon, 1984.

Thomson, D.F.S and H.C. Porter, trans. and eds. *Erasmus and Cambridge: The Cambridge Letters of Erasmus*. Toronto: University of Toronto Press, 1963.

Thomson, John A.F. *The Early Tudor Church and Society: 1485-1529*. London: Routledge, 1993.

Tjernagel, Neelak. *Henry VIII and the Lutherans*. Saint Louis: Concordia, 1965.

Trapp, J.B. *Background to the English Renaissance*. London: 1974.

Trinkaus, Charles. *In Our Image and Likeness*. 2 Volumes. Chicago: University of Chicago Press, 1970.

Trueman, Carl R. *Luther's Legacy: Salvation and the English Reformers*. Oxford: Clarendon, 1994.

Tugwell, Simon. O.P. ed. *Early Dominicans: Selected Writings*. New York: Paulist, 1982.

Tyacke, Nicholas. ed. *England's Long Reformation: 1500-1800*. London: Ashgate, 1998.

Van Ortroy, F. ed. 'Early Life of John Fisher', *Analecta Bollandiana*, Vol. X (1891).

Verkamp, Bernard J. *The Indifferent Mean: Adiaphorism in the English Reformation to 1554*. Columbus: Ohio University Press, 1979.

Vermigli, Peter Martyr. *Life, Letters, and Sermons*. John Patrick Donnelly. S.J., trans. and ed. The Peter Martyr Library. 5 Volumes. Kirksville: Truman State University Press, 1997.

Wabuda, Susan. 'The Provision of Preaching during the Early English Reformation: with Special Reference to Itineration, c. 1530-1547', Cambridge University Ph.D., 1992.

— 'Bishops and Homilies', *Sixteenth Century Journal* XXV/3 (1994).

— *Preaching During the English Reformation*. Cambridge: Cambridge University Press, 2002.

Wailes, Stephen L. *Medieval Allegories of Jesus' Parables*. Berkeley: University of California Press, 1987.

Walsham, Alexandra. *The Reformation of the Landscape: Religion, Identity, and Memory in Early Modern Britain and Ireland*. Oxford: Oxford University Press, 2011.

Wall, John N. 'The Vision of a Christian Commonwealth in the Book of Homilies of 1547' Harvard University Ph.D., 1979.

— 'Godly and Fruitful Lessons: The English Bible, Erasmus' Paraphrases and the Book of Homilies', in John E. Booty ed., *The Godly Kingdom of Tudor England: Great Books of the English Reformation*. Wilton: 1981.

— *Transformations of the Word: Spenser, Herbert, and Vaughn*. Athens: University of Georgia Press, 1988.

Weiss, Roberto. *Humanism in Fifteenth-Century England*. 3rd ed. Oxford: Oxford University Press, 1965.

Wenig, Scott A. *Straightening the Altars: The Ecclesiastical Vision and Pastoral Achievements of the Progressive Bishops under Elizabeth I, 1559-1579*. New

York: Peter Lang, 2000.

White, Helen C. *Social Criticism in Popular Religious Literature of the Sixteenth Century*. New York: Harper and Row, 1944.

White, Paul Whitfield. *Protestantism, Patronage, and Playing in Tudor England*. Cambridge: Cambridge University Press, 1993.

Whiting, Robert. *Local Responses to the English Reformation*. New York: St. Martin's, 2000.

Wickham, Glynee. *Early English Stages: Their Plays and Their Makers 1300-1660*. 2 Volumes. London: Methuen, 1991.

Wilkins, David. ed. *Concilia Magna Britanniae et Hiberniae*. 4 Volumes. Oxford: Clarendon, 1965.

Williams, C.H. ed. *English Historical Documents*. London: 1967.

Williams George. *The Radical Reformation*. 3rd. ed. Kirksville: Truman State Press, 1992.

Witt, Ronald G. 'The Humanist Movement', in Thomas A. Brady Jr., Heiko A. Oberman, and James D. Tracy, eds. *Handbook of European History, 1400-1600: Late Middle Ages, Renaissance, and Reformation*. 3 Volumes. Grand Rapids: Eerdmans, 1995.

Wooding, Lucy E.C. *Rethinking Catholicism in Reformation England*. Oxford: Clarendon, 2000.

Wuthnow, Robert. *Communities of Discourse: Ideology and Social Structure in the Reformation, Enlightenment, and European Socialism*. Cambridge: Cambridge University Press, 1989.

Yoder, John H. *The Priestly Kingdom: Social Ethics as Gospel*. Notre Dame: University of Notre Dame Press, 1984.

Yost, J.K. 'The Christian Humanism of the English Reformers'. Duke University Ph.D., 1965.

Youings, Joyce. *The Dissolution of the Monasteries*. London: Hambledon, 1971.

Author index

Elton, G.R., 32, 40, 53, 56, 59, 60, 61, 68, 102, 110, 123, 135, 136
Euler, C., 88

Ferguson, A.B., 110
Fincham, K., 83
Fowl, S., 177
Freeman, T., 33-34
Frei, H., 116, 191
Frith, K.R., 92

Gregory, B., 200
Gregory, J., 139
Guy, J., 31, 43, 60, 135

Hadgett, G.A.J., 151, 152, 166
Hadot, P., 19, 92, 137
Haigh, C., 31, 32, 36, 70, 76, 103, 110, 139, 169, 185, 193
Halkin, L.-E., 12
Hall, B., 164
Harper-Bill, C., 67
Hawkins, P., 149
Hayward, J., 141
Heal, F., 81, 95, 98
Heath, P., 147
Helgerson, R., 116
Hill, J.F.H., 151
Hill, J.W.F., 152
Hill, O.G., 86
Hoak, D.E., 101, 135
Hoffman, M., 12, 13, 15, 18, 20, 21, 22, 28
Holmer, P.L., 159
Hopf, C., 111, 140
Horst, I.B., 127, 151-52, 171, 183
House, S.B., 42, 67
Hoyle, R.W., 70
Hudson, A., 38, 87, 88, 94
Hutton, R., 70

Ives, E.W., 58

Jones, L.G., 177

Jones, N., 71, 76, 80, 103
Jones, W.R.D., 97
Jordan, W.K., 111, 121

Kahn, V., 15, 94
Kantorowizc, E., 108
Kaufman, P.I., 29, 67
Kelly, J.N.D., 184
Kelly, R.L., 87
King, J.N., 33, 46, 54, 76, 82, 84, 85, 87, 103, 104, 107, 108, 109, 111, 114, 115, 118, 121, 124, 132, 135, 145, 148, 149, 169, 170
Knowles, D., 147, 153
Kolb, R., 120, 179

Lambert, M., 94
Lanham, R.A., 120
Leader, D.R., 11
Lindbeck, G., 83, 116, 117, 118, 180
Lischer, R., 179, 180, 185
Little, A.G., 147, 153, 190
Loades, D.M., 32, 33, 41, 127, 141, 171
Locher, G.W., 106
Lucy, E.C., 6

Maclure, M., 62, 71, 89, 90
MacCulloch, D., 38, 39, 40, 44, 57, 58, 61, 62, 70, 72, 76, 79, 81, 84, 86, 90, 91, 98, 100, 101, 103, 104, 106, 018, 110, 111, 113, 116, 119, 121, 122, 125, 127, 128, 131, 135, 139, 141, 143, 144, 156, 169, 170, 171, 173, 183, 185, 186, 193
MacIntyre, A., 177
Maltby, J., 142
Manning, R., 97
Marsh, C., 139, 182
Marshall, P., 38, 41, 44, 63, 66, 67, 68, 86, 92, 100, 134, 147,

Scripture index

Subject index

accommodation, 23, 25, 105, 119, 149, 150, 168, 180
Act for Punishment of Heresy, 57
Act for the Submission of the Clergy, 57
Act in Restraint of Annates, 43
Act in Restraint of Appeals, 43
Act of Abolishing Diversity of Opinions, 77
Act of Dissolution, 70
Adam, 45, 50, 87, 130n.88
a Lasco, John, 172-73, 174
Anabaptists, 4, 76, 127, 128, 129, 143n.16, 151, 170, 171, 171n.9, 172, 174, 175, 176, 184, 185, 197
Articles of Faith, the, 2, 147, 195
Aske, Robert, 70
Augustine, 29, 46, 47, 51, 86, 92, 113, 148, 149, 161

Barnes, Robert, 8
Baynton, Edward, 48, 50, 51
Becon, Thomas, 7, 30
Bernher, Augustine, 81
Bidding Prayer, the (1534), 56
Bilney, Thomas, 7, 27, 48, 134
Bishop's Book, the, 60-61, 73-74, 82
Boleyn, Anne, 38, 43, 56, 58, 62
Bonner, 123, 124-25
Book of Common Prayer, the, 4, 82, 84, 100, 111, 143, 144, 145, 165, 172, 173, 186, 189, 190, 197
Book of Homilies, the, 4, 79, 80, 81, 82, 85, 94, 95, 103, 106, 117, 118, 122, 123, 130n.89, 132n.94, 136, 137, 140, 149, 152, 154, 168, 185, 190, 196, 197

Bradford, John, 107
Brandon, Katherine, 152
break with Rome, 43
Brown, Richard, 53-54
Bucer, Martin, 89n.43, 111-12, 115-16, 115n.39, 123, 140
De Regno Christi, 140
Bullinger, 170, 171, 172, 173, 174, 184
Bullock, Thomas, 27
Burcher, John, 172

Calvin, John, 140
celestial flesh, 184
Chantries Act, the, 79
Christ, 1, 3, 9, 10, 13, 17, 18, 19, 20, 21, 22, 23, 24, 25, 27, 28, 29, 35, 42, 44, 45, 46, 48, 51, 52, 52n.40, 54, 55, 59, 63, 65, 67, 71, 75, 86, 87, 93, 94, 97, 100, 103, 105, 106, 117, 120, 126, 128, 129, 130, 130n.90, 131, 131n.92, 133, 134, 136, 140, 149, 153, 154, 156, 159, 169, 180, 181, 182, 186-87, 188n.61, 189, 190, 191, 192, 194, 195, 198, 199
and eschatological pilgrimage, 167
as divine *sermo*, 19-20
as school master, 159, 159n.66, 164
glory of, 25
humility of, 149
preaching, 188, 192-93, 193n.76
redeemer, 13
saviour, 13
Chrysostom, John, 95, 109, 131
clergy corruption, 42
clerical marriage, 185-87

preaching mission, 152
prominence, 31, 42, 78, 90, 139
prophet, 41, 80, 89, 97, 137
prophetic tone, 105, 196
reformed Catholic, 143n.16
reformist preaching, 31, 32
royal protection, 43
sermon on the leper, 188-89
sermon on the Parable of the
Sower, 192-93
sermon on the wedding at Cana,
186-87
sermons, 142n.12, 148
silent years, 77
social gospel, 152
university preacher, 6
use of language, 145-46
willingness to suffer, 155
Latimer's works:
*A Fruitful Exhortation to the
Readying*, etc, 181
*Against Whoredom and
Adultery*, 185
*An Exhortacion concernying
Good Odre*, etc, 179
An Exhortacion to Obedience,
176
*An Homelie against Contencion
and Brawlynge*, 106
Sermons on the Cards, 32, 34-
37, 52
The Sermon of the Plough, 3, 4,
78, 85-87, 89, 90-98, 102, 104,
105, 122, 142, 146, 153, 192,
196, 197, 201
Lever, Thomas, 171-72
Longland, John, 150-51, 166
Luther, Martin, 8, 30, 31, 88,
89n.43, 120n.50, 171

martyrdom, 199
Melanchthon, Philip, 6
More, Thomas, 32, 39n.6, 43
Morice, Ralph, 31, 54, 66n.87

Muntzer, Thomas, 89n.43

New Jerusalem, the, 87, 98, 107

obedience, 2, 4, 9, 12, 51, 55, 72,
73, 80, 107, 111, 117, 118, 129,
136, 150, 163, 175, 179, 180,
181-82, 183, 187, 189
Ochino, Bernadino, 112, 113, 115,
115n.39, 173

pastoral ministry, 2, 13, 27
Pater Noster, the, 2, 54, 73
persecution, 45, 65, 116, 199
piety, 3, 9, 10, 12, 13, 14, 17, 19,
22, 27, 28, 36
Pilgrimage of Grace, the, 166, 177
Pole, Reginald, 130
Powell, Edward, 53
prayer, 2, 128, 134, 139, 156, 168
preacher(s), 1, 2, 9, 10, 15, 16, 18,
22, 25, 26, 29, 40, 45, 48, 50,
56, 58, 68, 88, 91, 94, 114, 115,
126, 128-131, 136, 139, 141,
164, 176, 178, 182, 190, 201
preaching, 1, 2, 3, 4, 5, 8, 11, 13,
14, 17, 22, 29, 31, 40, 42, 43,
44, 48, 49, 50, 52, 58, 59, 63,
67, 68n.95, 78, 80, 81, 86, 93-
94, 95, 96, 100, 101, 104, 107,
108, 109, 111, 115, 122, 125,
126, 128-132, 135, 137n.105,
139-68, 157, 160, 163, 168, 177,
192, 193, 195
preaching office, the, 2, 140, 154
purgatory, 54-55, 64, 66, 69, 99,
129, 151

Reformation, the, 39, 39n.6, 40,
90n.48, 104, 139
reformers, 1, 40, 59, 79, 87, 88,
89, 91-92, 97, 126n.77, 142,
158, 169, 190n.66

ND - #0089 - 090625 - C0 - 229/152/13 - PB - 9781842277973 - Gloss Lamination